Transforming Cape Town

CALIFORNIA SERIES IN PUBLIC ANTHROPOLOGY

The California Series in Public Anthropology emphasizes the anthropologist's role as an engaged intellectual. It continues anthropology's commitment to being an ethnographic witness, to describing, in human terms, how life is lived beyond the borders of many readers' experiences. But it also adds a commitment, through ethnography, to reframing the terms of public debate—transforming received, accepted understandings of social issues with new insights, new framings.

Series Editor: Robert Borofsky (Hawaii Pacific University)

Contributing Editors: Philippe Bourgois (University of Pennsylvania), Paul Farmer (Partners in Health), Alex Hinton (Rutgers University), Carolyn Nordstrom (University of Notre Dame), and Nancy Scheper-Hughes (UC Berkeley)

University of California Press Editor: Naomi Schneider

Transforming Cape Town

Catherine Besteman

UNIVERSITY OF CALIFORNIA PRESS
Berkeley · Los Angeles · London

University of California Press, one of the most distinguished university presses in the United States, enriches
lives around the world by advancing scholarship in the
humanities, social sciences, and natural sciences. Its
activities are supported by the UC Press Foundation
and by philanthropic contributions from individuals
and institutions. For more information, visit
www.ucpress.edu.

University of California Press
Berkeley and Los Angeles, California

University of California Press, Ltd.
London, England

Library of Congress Cataloging-in-Publication Data

Besteman, Catherine Lowe.
    Transforming Cape Town / Catherine Besteman.
        p.   cm. — (California series in public anthro-
pology ; 19)
    Includes bibliographical references and index.
    ISBN 978-0-520-25670-5 (cloth : alk. paper) —
ISBN 978-0-520-25671-2 (pbk. : alk. paper)
    1. Cape Town (South Africa)—Social conditions.
2. Sociology, Urban—South Africa.   3. Cape Town
(South Africa)—Race relations.   4. Group identity—
South Africa—Cape Town.   I. Title.

    HN801.C36B47   2008
    307.76096873'55—dc22   2007050928

Manufactured in the United States of America

17 16 15 14 13 12 11 10 09 08
10 9 8 7 6 5 4 3 2 1

This book is printed on Cascades Enviro 100, a 100%
post consumer waste, recycled, de-inked fiber. FSC
recycled certified and processed chlorine free. It is acid
free, Ecologo certified, and manufactured by BioGas
energy.

For Jorge, Gabriela, and Darien

Contents

Illustrations

Acknowledgments

My debts are many to the Capetonians who opened their homes and shared their lives with me. Eth Witten, Bev and Allistair Witten, Heléne Schoeman, and Anton Schoeman gave me a lifetime of lessons about generosity and friendship. I hope this book is a small token of gratitude.

For teaching me so much about Cape Town I am grateful to Terry and Barbara Bell, Andy and Marinella Dawes, Whitey Dilima, Bernard and Ruth Dudley, Raymond and Pat Engelbrecht, Lorna Engledoe, John and Pam Gilmour, Zelda and Alan Jansen, Stephanie Kilroe, Susan Levine, Michael Masibulele Matshaba, Frank Ndzaba, Khanyisa Ntebe, Bonisile Ntlemeza, Evaron and Nadine Orange, William Page, Dizu Plaatjies, Pat Qokweni, Fiona Ross, Anne Roux, Maggie Sauls, Siyabonga Shwala, Anele Silekwe, Ayanda Tsoanyane, Vunqi Tunke, Warra, and Emile YX?. I also thank those who requested anonymity for their honesty in talking with me about difficult issues.

I am grateful to those who read parts or all of the manuscript and offered insightful and critical comments: an anonymous reviewer, Lindsay Braun, John Gilmour, Donna Goldstein, Angelique Haugerud, Stephanie Kilroe, Fiona Ross, Heléne Schoeman, and Bev Witten. I have not been able to incorporate all their comments, and of course remaining errors and oversights are my responsibility. With gifts of books, Bill Finnegan provided direction at critical junctures. Thanks as well to my wonderful colleagues Jeff Anderson and Mary Beth Mills, who graciously accepted my leaves to do this research, and to Colby College for grant support.

I hope my study abroad students will continue to fashion lives that embrace the lessons we learned in Cape Town, and I thank them for their thoughtfulness and curiosity. A special acknowledgment goes to the Colby-Bates-Bowdoin study abroad program staff in Cape Town, whose love for their city was obvious and stimulated my own.

I am grateful to John and Kay Besteman for their encouragement. Laurie Besteman and Jack Lauderbaugh offered welcome support and introductions in Cape Town. My debt is great.

My family moved back and forth across the Atlantic many times to support this research. They allowed me long stints away from home and cheerfully tolerated my obsession with this project. My love and gratitude are more than I can express in words.

Introduction

Transformation Stories

And there we are, celebrating democracy as the only answer
to any political question, when a young man gets up. He is
eighteen years old. He is going to vote for the first time. He
is so excited and proud. And so angry! And he says to Evita
Bezuidenhout, this woman on stage who doesn't even exist:
"Madam, we fought for freedom! All we got was democracy!"

Pieter-Dirk Uys, Elections and Erections

Over a decade after the end of apartheid, South Africans daily confront
the contradictions of living through one of the most remarkable political
and social transformations of our era. In 1994, as horrific genocide tore
apart Rwanda, as child soldiers in Liberia wreaked havoc, as Somalis
massacred one another, as refugees poured across African borders in all
directions, South Africa held its very first democratic elections, peacefully
bringing to power the former convicted terrorist and world icon Nelson
Mandela and his political party, the African National Congress (ANC).
The end of apartheid in South Africa offered a hugely optimistic note in
the otherwise dreadful events plaguing the African continent.

Until the 1990s, South Africa was ruled by a white supremacist government that brutally enforced a system of racial hierarchy known as
apartheid. Black people were denied citizenship rights, could not own
property, and were subject to a complicated and demeaning barrage of
laws governing their movements and their bodies. Anti-apartheid groups
seeking to overthrow the apartheid regime had been battling South
Africa's notorious security forces in a low-grade war for decades. By the
late 1980s, South Africa's National Party government, acknowledging
post–cold war national and global currents, began brokering a power-
sharing agreement with the anti-apartheid movement, whose leaders

were incarcerated as terrorists. By 1994, in a transition heralded around the world as a miracle, a political revolution had dismantled the legal structures of apartheid and inaugurated a new democratic government committed to nonracialism. In the decade that followed, South Africans set about the process of transforming their society from one based on state-enforced racial inequality and infused with racially based hatred and ignorance to one of multiculturalism, tolerance, and equal citizenship and opportunity. This remarkable vision of hope, mutual humanity, and a belief in the possibility of a better world is one of the twentieth century's most important stories.

Today, South Africans are deeply involved in the struggle to bring the promise of South Africa's miracle to fruition. It is an uphill battle. Many recall the sense of hopefulness and euphoria they felt after the first national democratic election in 1994, when Mandela's insistence on reconciliation rather than revenge and his party's promise of a better life for all gave comfort and hope to people battered by the violence and trauma of apartheid. White South Africans hoped that the peaceful transition and the language of reconciliation meant they could put the past behind them and move on. South Africans of color believed they could finally improve their material circumstances and opportunities. Standing between these two dreams, however, was the awkward truth that "reconciliation" did not include a redistribution of resources, which had been unfairly apportioned to white people under apartheid. White South Africans were allowed to retain their wealth, and the African National Congress, overlooking its historic ties to the trade unions and the Communist Party, pursued neoliberal policies that economists promised would nurture economic growth through domestic fiscal constraint and foreign investment.

In macroeconomic terms, the government's strategy has successfully produced, according to a 2006 survey published in the *Economist,* "an impressive 87 straight months of growth (currently running at about 5% a year), low budget deficits and low inflation." But "little of this growth has benefited [the government's] own core supporters, who are overwhelmingly poor and black."[1] As the economy has grown, so have unemployment, poverty, and inequality. The wealth gap that previously separated white and black people now divides the black population as well. Transformation has brought unprecedented economic opportunities to the wealthiest and most educated black South Africans, but the bottom 40 percent have experienced deepening poverty. Adam Ashforth reports figures based on the 1991 and 1996 censuses:

In 1991, the richest 20 percent of African households earned nineteen times
more than the poorest 40 percent; by 1996, the top group was earning
thirty-one times more. . . . By the turn of the century, [the economist
Sampie] Terreblanche estimates, the top group of African households en-
joyed more than forty times the income of the poorest 40 percent of families. . . . A quarter century earlier, the difference had been a factor of 8, and
while the richest 20 percent of African households improved their circumstances enormously within that time, the rest had become significantly
poorer. . . . The rapidity of these developments can hardly be overempha-
sized. Within the space of one generation, the social landscape of black
South Africans changed dramatically.[2]

In the decade after Mandela's victory, the euphoria of liberation,
democracy, and peace has thus been confounded by an entrenchment of
poverty for a significant number of black South Africans, and by growing wealth disparities that are no longer solely defined by race. Government promises for better housing, services, schools, and jobs for the poor
have not been kept, the economy has lost jobs, crime has increased, and
black people have realized that the concept of reconciliation does not
offer equal opportunity for the previously subjugated and does not, for
most whites, imply a sharing or redistribution of wealth and property.
South Africa's Gini coefficient, which is used as an indicator of inequality, is currently among the highest in the world.[3]

This book tells stories about how South Africans are making sense of
these contradictions as they grapple with the inadequacies of reconciliation and democracy as the means to overcoming deeply rooted inequality and profound racial mistrust. These stories communicate what South
Africans living through this tumultuous time think about democracy,
race, trust, community, and transformation. How do ordinary people
whose entire lives had been defined by legally enforced white supremacy
and black subjugation imagine nonracialism? How does one learn to
trust people whom one was taught to fear and loathe? How does one understand the responsibilities of citizenship in a new democracy characterized by uncertainty, ignorance about one's fellow citizens, and a gap-
ing wealth gap?

To address these questions, I turn to Cape Town, a city of remarkable
beauty and fearsome poverty, gloriously situated at the southern tip of
Africa. Cape Town is a thriving multiracial city with strong ties to rural
South Africa and to the international arena. Cities offer thrilling opportunities for crossing cultural borders and fashioning new identities. But
cities can also be sites of profoundly parochial neighborhoods, where

fear of the "other" is more intense because the other is just a few blocks away. In Cape Town, fabulous wealth rubs shoulders with devastating poverty. This book explores how Capetonians make sense of these connections and disparities.

I began spending time in Cape Town in 1999, staying two to six months every year until 2004. Working as an anthropologist, I listened to and interviewed people about their experiences of post-apartheid transformation. Other researchers studying transformation have investigated how political institutions, government structures (such as the police, the judiciary, the civil service), and corporations are changing, and the celebrated Truth and Reconciliation Commission has attracted a large share of this research. My interest is ordinary people who grapple with intimate questions about love, family, and community.

In this book, I use the basic racial terminology common in South Africa: Indian, white, African (to indicate black African-language speakers such as Zulu and Xhosa), coloured (using the South African spelling, from the Apartheid category that included those of mixed race, Khoisan, and South and Southeast Asian ancestry), and black (following the anti-apartheid political usage of the term to encompass everyone excluded from the privileged white category under apartheid, a category I also identify as people of color). These terms reflect South African usage, and they appear here without quotation marks or "so-called." Readers are reminded that all racial monikers are cultural constructs, created out of particular historical moments to serve particular political, economic, and social agendas.

A BRIEF HISTORICAL OVERVIEW

South Africa's complexities of race and class began when the Dutch East India Company (*Verenigde Oostindische Compagnie* in Dutch, or the VOC) established a small settlement at the cape in 1652 to support its shipping trade between Europe and Asia.[4] Over the next century, the Dutch-speaking settlers conquered or absorbed the indigenous Khoisan foragers and herders, whom they called Bushmen and Hottentots, and imported slaves from Madagascar, elsewhere in Africa, and especially Indonesia, India, and Ceylon (now Sri Lanka) to build port infrastructure and agriculture. The British took over the cape in 1795 and abolished the external slave trade in 1807, after which colonial cape society grew and striated significantly. By 1820 it included at least three major groups: newer English immigrants, who retained their cultural and linguistic distinction from the Dutch settlers; the earlier Dutch-speaking settlers and their descendants, who now called themselves Afrikaners; and former slaves, who together with surviving Khoi were officially known as the Cape Coloureds and constituted the largest and most diverse segment of the population. The Dutch language of the early settlers had evolved into Afrikaans through the creative process of linguistic accommodation between masters and slaves, whose descendents shared the Dutch-based patois that became Afrikaans as a common first language.

Colonial anti-slavery policies and linguistic convergence did not, however, signify integrationist desires. Within another hundred years, land-hungry white settlers, speculators, and prospectors had spread to the east and into the interior highveld and northeastern lowveld. There, they formed a series of republics and colonies where small white minorities extended their rule by threat and force over established African states. By 1870, four white-dominated states controlled almost the entire area of modern South Africa and ruled over much larger African, coloured, and Indian populations (the latter having arrived on the coast as indentured laborers).[5] With the massive development of diamond and gold mining in the interior after 1870, white political authorities worked together with the oligopoly of white-owned mining companies to create and enforce "native" policies that ensured a large pool of highly controlled, segregated, exploitable black migrant workers.

The British defeated the Afrikaners in the South African War of 1899–1902 (during which the British created concentration camps to incarcerate Afrikaners and Africans), and in 1910 the four South African colonies together became the Union of South Africa, a self-governing British dominion. The union government, under the political sway of the mining and rural farming interests, continued to expand the policies of racial segregation and hierarchy. African people were denied political rights; they remained subject to pass laws and job color bars, restricting their movement and barring them from certain jobs; and they were forbidden to form workers' unions. African access to land was severely curtailed by the 1913 Native Land Act. Although Africans constituted more than two-thirds of the population, the areas delineated for African landownership under the act totaled just 7 percent of the country's land base, and the burdens of taxation, population growth, and exhausted land made African peasant farming unsustainable, forcing Africans to leave the reserves to seek wage employment. The reserves became, in the words of the historian Leonard Thompson, "reservoirs of cheap, unskilled labor for white farmers and industrialists."[6]

Missions initially ran the only schools open to black people, some of whom attained high levels of education and began forming political organizations to advocate for political rights through negotiation and dialogue. One such group was the South African National Congress, which formed in 1912 and later became the African National Congress. Despite these efforts, white South Africans continued to support restrictions on Africans, and in 1948 they voted the National Party into power, with its specific political platform of apartheid. Just as most other African countries were gaining independence from colonial white rule and establishing democratically elected black governments, South Africa expanded its policies of racist segregation and white supremacy.

Over the next two decades, the South African government destroyed all remnants of black participation in the political system, passed a barrage of repressive and restrictive laws controlling black people and oppositional political activities, and provided massive state assistance to white people that ended white poverty, guaranteed white employment, and ensured sustained white success through education. The state assigned everyone a racial classification (African, Coloured, White, or Asian/Indian), which determined where one could live, travel, and work, how much one could earn, the subjects one could study, and whom one could marry. After 1951, the African reserves were restructured into "Homelands," dubbed "Bantustans," as a convenient way to officially strip Africans of South African citizenship. The Homelands, such as Transkei, Ciskei, Venda, and Bophuthatswana, were small and fragmented, overcrowded, administered by corrupt leaders who were manipulated by the South African government, and dependent on wages earned by African migrant workers in South Africa. African workers who were allowed to live outside the Homelands because they had legitimate jobs in South Africa were required to carry passes, and millions were arrested for violating the pass laws.

In cities, the Group Areas Act of 1950 enabled municipal authorities to forcibly relocate millions of African, coloured, and Indian people to separate townships. Inadequate housing in the townships and impoverished land and few opportunities in the Homelands meant the development of sizable illegal squatter settlements around cities and towns throughout South Africa. Public interracial interaction was tightly controlled by "petty apartheid" laws mandating separate public amenities, transport, sports, and education. The Bantu Education Act of 1953 brought education for Africans under state sponsorship, but attendance was not compulsory and few benefited from the vastly inferior, understaffed, and poorly supplied schools. The laws controlling political organization allowed the government to ban political meetings and organizations and to incarcerate people secretly. A vast, expensive bureaucracy enforced these laws, ensuring full employment for white people, although some black people found employment in the apartheid bureaucracy as well.

Government control of the media and church complicity in apartheid meant that many white people lived insular, protected lives of material comfort, unaware of black peoples' grievances. The vast majority of Africans lived in precarious economic circumstances with enormous strains on their families, high levels of violence, and anger over the massive racial inequalities in income, health, education, living standards, resources, and opportunity.

The system, of course, did not go unchallenged. Black political organizations, women, workers, and students organized a potent anti-apartheid movement supported by an active international component with branches throughout the world. The ANC adopted the famous Freedom Charter as a doctrine of equal rights in 1955, which became a powerful symbol in the struggle. In the early 1960s, a wave of mass protests, sparked by a police massacre of anti–pass law demonstrators in the township of Sharpeville, swept the country. The government declared a state of emergency and outlawed both the ANC and the Pan-Africanist Congress (PAC), another black political organization that had formed in the mid-twentieth century, forcing them underground and into exile. Believing that attempts at solely peaceful resistance would fail, both the ANC and the PAC created military branches to launch violent attacks against symbols of government authority and wealth. The government fought against the armed resistance movements by banning and incarcerating their leaders, including Nelson Mandela, for life.

By the mid-1970s, workers and students had reinvigorated the protest movement. A police attack in 1976 on students demonstrating in Soweto against mandatory Afrikaans instruction in the school curriculum sparked further demonstrations. As strikes and protests grew, so did repression; student leaders were jailed, and Steve Biko, the charismatic student activist and Black Consciousness leader, was arrested and beaten to death by police. His death and the images of Soweto and other protests provoked international condemnation of the South African government—the United Nations General Assembly called apartheid "a crime against humanity"[7]—but the international community's criticisms had limited effect. A formidable military and economic power, South Africa dominated southern Africa, benefited from eager international investors, and manipulated cold war fears by claiming that the anti-apartheid movement consisted of communist terrorists supported by the Soviet Union and Cuba.

In an effort to deflect criticism and appease some constituents, Prime Minister P. W. Botha introduced a few reforms in the 1980s that scaled back pass laws, repealed some "petty apartheid" laws, and legalized black trade unions. A new parliamentary structure was designed to give coloured and Indian people some political representation, although still under white rule. A black trade union movement exploded, and a new political umbrella organization, the United Democratic Front (UDF), was formed in 1983. Representing hundreds of community-based and activist groups and drawing on the ANC's Freedom Charter, the UDF challenged the undemocratic new parliamentary and local African government structures, worked with labor activists to launch strikes, boycotts, and work stay-aways, and protested the ongoing inequalities of Bantu education, pass laws, residential segregation, Homelands policies, and other dimensions of apartheid inequality.[8]

The mid-1980s were years of mass protest, violence, uprisings, and state brutality. Encouraged by anti-apartheid leaders, township youth revolted and closed schools for months at a time. The government repeatedly declared states of emergency between 1984 and 1986, outlawed the UDF in 1988, created secret death squads that murdered activist leaders, and utilized a range of tyrannical laws and practices to arrest, detain, interrogate, and torture thousands of people. Despite the unwillingness of world leaders Ronald Reagan and Margaret Thatcher to publicly condemn the South African government, the international anti-apartheid movement gained momentum with student protests and investor alarm. The international divestment movement significantly impacted the South African economy and made clear South Africa's status as a global pariah.

When F. W. de Klerk replaced P. W. Botha following the latter's stroke in 1989, he inherited a disastrous and unsustainable political situation: a struggling economy straining to support an exorbitant bureaucracy and security apparatus, an increasingly polarized and anxious white electorate, an enraged disenfranchised black majority, and international disgust. The collapse of the Soviet Union had diminished the specter of a black communist takeover, making cold war rhetoric seem irrelevant. White civic and business leaders had already opened dialogues with ANC leaders in exile, and government officials during Botha's reign had begun secret negotiations with the imprisoned Nelson Mandela. De

Klerk and Mandela continued these discussions and agreed on a set of terms to begin a transition to democracy. In 1990, de Klerk lifted the ban against outlawed political parties, and Nelson Mandela, after twenty-seven years in prison, gained his freedom.

In preparation for democracy, the government dissolved remaining apartheid laws, allowed exiles to return, and released its political prisoners. As negotiations about a transition to democracy got under way, South Africa unfortunately experienced an upward spiral of violence. In a strange and contradictory undercurrent, the government secretly supported the Zulu-based Inkatha Freedom Party in violent struggles with the ANC, and the South African police and security forces continued to assassinate and terrorize activists. Over sixteen thousand people were killed in political violence from 1990 to 1994. Despite this instability and tension, the difficult, fraught negotiations among political leaders concluded with an interim constitution in 1993, and in 1994, the first national democratic election. The ANC won 63 percent of the national vote but lost to the Inkatha Freedom Party in Kwazulu-Natal and to the National Party in the Western Cape.

South Africa's new president, Nelson Mandela, and his government faced astoundingly difficult challenges. Reconciling past enemies and addressing the effects of violence, rage, and grief from decades of struggle were important first steps for integrating a fragmented nation. The majority of newly enfranchised Africans—the ANC's primary support base—expected a dramatic improvement in their impoverished living conditions. Instilling a culture of democracy and overcoming racism and inequality would be critical to the success of a new South Africa.

As part of the negotiations for democratization, the National Party leadership had demanded that South Africa's democratic government find a way to protect people who had committed human rights abuses as part of their service to their country. Anti-apartheid fighters as well had committed atrocities during the struggle years. In a thoughtful attempt to link amnesty with reconciliation, Parliament created the Truth and Reconciliation Commission (TRC) in 1996 as a vehicle to acknowledge gross human rights violations carried out since 1960. The TRC held public hearings all over South Africa and invited victims and perpetrators to testify about their experiences and actions. Victims who testified might receive compensation from the government, families who lost loved ones during the struggle might finally learn their fate, and perpetrators who told the full truth and who could prove their actions were politically motivated could be granted amnesty. For over two years, South Africans listened to stories of kidnapping, murder, assassination, torture, and rape, and learned the extent of the apartheid government's secret and horrible tactics to quash protest and rebellion.

Assessments of the successes and failures of the TRC are a small growth industry. Many agree that while the TRC offered a remarkable and dramatic vision of the possibilities of reconciliation, its accomplishments were rather more limited. The tens of thousands of testimonies collected by the TRC established an official, undeniable history of apartheid's violent excesses, and thus critics agree that the TRC achieved some success in uncovering the truth. The verdict on reconciliation is more difficult to assess. Most of the perpetrators who filed for amnesty were black, and none of the highest-ranking white officials in the apartheid state and security apparatus agreed to testify openly and honestly. Critics argue that the TRC sacrificed justice for truth and that reconciliation will come only with economic development. The TRC's orientation toward restorative justice rather than punishment may have benefited some victims for whom speaking about their pain began a healing process, and some perpetrators showed genuine remorse and sought forgiveness for their actions. But many South Africans seem less enthralled with the idea that truth will produce reconciliation, favoring instead a model of retributive justice.[9]

In a disappointing conclusion to the TRC process, the government did not offer victims who testified compensation for their suffering and loss at the level many expected, leading critics to complain that perpetrators got amnesty while victims got nothing. Since only the most egregious human rights violations were considered by the TRC, the structural inequalities of apartheid were left unaddressed. The TRC mandate was not extended to exposing the experiences of millions of black South Africans rendered homeless by discriminatory laws on property ownership and residential segregation, living with compromised health and in poverty because they lacked access to health care, education, and job opportunities, and suffering from the ravages of domestic abuse and criminal violence in their homes and communities. As anthropologist Stuart Douglas told me in 2000 about all the foreigners arriving to study the internationally celebrated TRC, the real post-apartheid issue is not reconciliation at all. It is poverty.

The government justified its reluctance to offer higher levels of compensation to victims who testified before the TRC by arguing that although the TRC's mandate extended only to specific kinds of gross human rights violations, the majority of black South Africans suffered from economic exploitation and poverty under apartheid. Rather than offer substantial compensation to only a few, the government reasoned it was more democratic to invest in broader reforms that would benefit everyone who suffered under apartheid. Unfortunately, South Africa's transition to democracy and readmission to the global community occurred at an inopportune time for combating poverty.

South Africa's transition coincided with the conversion of most formerly communist countries to neoliberal capitalism following the collapse of the Soviet Union. The ANC's promise to use the state as an engine of redistribution and equitable economic management was woefully out of step with the winner-take-all attitude fostered virtually everywhere else in the world. The model of neoliberal globalization promoted by leading global financial institutions and world powers emphasized scaling back government services and redistribution, dismantling state management of the economy and economic resources, and prioritizing privatization—exactly the opposite approach than that promised by the ANC to its poorest constituents. The 1995 unemployment rate in South Africa for Africans was somewhere around 40 percent, and close to 20 percent of adult Africans had never even attended school. Economist Francis Wilson says that 45 percent of the population earned less than the "widely agreed minimum living level."[10] Because the poverty of Africans had become entrenched by class rather than simply by race and was sustained by huge gaps in skills, training, and education, simply deracializing the system would have limited effect in the absence of state-directed economic restructuring that targeted class divides rather than only racial segregation.[11] Analysts argue that the ANC's decision to adopt, in the words of journalist Allister Sparks, "an unvarnished free market program, directly in line with the neo-liberal agenda" perpetuated and widened rather than narrowed inequality during democracy's first decade.[12]

Furthermore, a key concession demanded by the National Party leadership during the negotiations was a promise to protect white wealth. While the ANC embarked on an ambitious program to build homes and deliver services to the country's poorest citizens, white people were allowed to retain their wealth, property, and jobs. White civil servants, including the military, retained their positions with full benefits. Affirmative action and black empowerment programs benefited black people with education and skills but did nothing for the undereducated, unskilled impoverished masses; educational reforms have not yet demonstrated success. The assumption that segregation and inequality could be solved through neoliberal economic policies, educational reform, and the upward mobility of black South Africans failed to recognize the brutal, enduring legacy of apartheid for the African majority, many of whom utterly lack the skills to compete for jobs in a market economy.

This profound contradiction in South Africa's first decade of democracy has yet to be resolved. What does it mean to be liberated politically if one is destitute? If one can't feed, clothe, protect, or properly school one's family? The question Michael Brown and his colleagues pose about the post–civil rights era in the United States resonates in post-1994 South Africa: "What good were civil rights if one was too poor to use them?"[13]

CAPE TOWN

The particular story of Cape Town is, of course, bound up with these themes of segregation and racism, reconciliation, and poverty. Under apartheid, Cape Town was known for its relatively relaxed approach to enforcing apartheid segregation laws and for its white opposition to the National Party. Since the end of apartheid, Cape Town has been known as the least integrated city in South Africa and the base of white and coloured opposition to the ANC. Unlike Johannesburg, which has rapidly been transformed as a base of the growing black middle class, and unlike rural South Africa, which has remained largely impoverished, Cape Town's first decade of transformation offers a more complicated story because of its racial history. In what follows, I turn to Cape Town to introduce the central questions of this ethnography.

Racial Categories

> "Some things are better now. I can sit at the waterfront in a café and be served by a white girl," comments Bonisile, with a humorous grin as he is served his soft drink.

Racial categories, as social constructions, are terribly malleable, shamelessly deployed in politics, brazenly filled with stereotypes and assumptions, profoundly political and personal. Apartheid-era racial categories in all of their absurdity continue to be utilized, but their meanings are shifting. Part of the process of transforming society and embracing non-racialism is a deconstruction of these socially constructed categories. The hard personal work of transformation is figuring out how to make sense of the significance and relevance of these old categories by asking questions like "Who am I in a democratic South Africa?" "Who is my community, now that the world of possibility is much broader?" "How do I go about creating a new identity, unburdening myself of the baggage of the past?" "How do I go about forging new social relationships and building trust across old racial divides?" As Father Peter John Pearson of Cape Town's Catholic diocese explained: "Because of deep divisions, we were never able to determine a common humanity or give shape to a common humanity. We must do this." But how?

Does speaking of race continue to keep discredited categories alive, or does it provide a way to acknowledge how the injustices of the past continue to structure the present? One newspaper columnist complains that white South Africans are still in denial that they benefited from apartheid and argue that "confronting the past is no longer necessary and is some way anti-progressive. The argument that we must stop "reliving the past" is an effective way of cutting off debate around our integration problems in the present."[14] Integration is certainly a problem in the new South Africa. Political commentator Thabisi Hoeane writes: "The most serious problem facing post-apartheid South Africa is the persistent failure to forge cross-cutting relationships between races." Citing the 2004 Reconciliation Barometer Survey—in which over a third of South Africans interviewed reported having no daily contact with people of other races, almost 60 percent of respondents reported never socializing with people from races other than their own, and 40 percent reported that they do not trust those of other racial backgrounds—Hoeane asks what happened to the rainbow image so heralded in the early 1990s? Race became a taboo subject, Hoeane suggests, and people are afraid of being accused of "re-racializing society." But not talking about race ignores the tensions around race that are South Africa's present reality.[15]

In Cape Town, it seems that nothing has changed and everything has changed. The city's urban geography, its apartheid-era separations and segregations, its racial terrors, and its ignorances remain; but at the same time newly imagined identities and selves, border crossings, and cultural creolizations are happening all over the place. Racial politics are particularly complex in Cape Town because of the majority coloured population, officially defined as a racial group under apartheid and used as a buffer between African and white people. Cape Town's 2001 census suggests the city's population is 48 percent coloured, 32 percent African, 19 percent white, and 1 percent Indian.[16] Some Capetonians suggest that rather than standing as a buffer category, coloured identity can offer a path toward a nonracialist future by deconstructing and blurring racial boundaries.

Perhaps because of this possibility, Cape Town seems to offer more opportunities for imagining border crossings.[17] Urban living, in particular, offers opportunities for coming together with those of different backgrounds, because of the cosmopolitanism that characterizes urban environments such as Cape Town. "What do the spaces of change and dynamism look like?" asks the geographer Jennifer Robinson.[18] Cultural Studies scholar Sarah Nuttall suggests that "investigating the now" in South Africa requires a shift of focus from apartheid-era categories to study "movement rather than boundaries; spaces and relations of transformation rather than ongoing divisions and inequalities."[19] While this is a good point, and much of this ethnography will be about spaces of fluidity and mobility, we will also catalog some of the many ways in which such movements are hindered and attacked. The racial/cultural dividing lines laid down by apartheid are real and were really felt and imagined; moving across them was and remains a conscious choice. The pull inward, away from the boundaries, is still forceful, and it is important to remind ourselves why, a decade after the end of apartheid. Why is it challenging to cross these old dividing lines? Why isn't everyone doing it?

Since the end of apartheid, the terms on which people are mixing and the urban arena where people come together have changed in fundamental ways. The cultural and personal spaces of intimacy that people in Cape Town create when forging new groups and new relationships are, in fact, really new. It is interesting to trace what ideas and behaviors from the bad old days remain and how people deal with those remnants, and what is newly imagined. Although some Capetonians experienced flexibility in their racial status under apartheid (passing for white, for example), contemporary Cape Town allows for race to be deconstructed, reconstructed, and imagined in novel ways. Experimental identities allow creative Capetonians to redefine themselves and to transcend race. Having said this, understanding the baggage of race has become, according to some boundary crossers, more important than ever.

Democracy

"The most amazing thing about the end of apartheid," Anne says as we cook dinner one evening in Cape Town, "was seeing pornography for the first time. We'd never seen anything like it before, and it was so shocking! People didn't know what to think."

"People began swearing, using words that no one would have *dared* use before!" recalls Johanna about the advent of democracy. "Saying those forbidden words out loud was so thrilling, so *delicious.*"

> Democracy means "we are human beings, with rights," says high school student Babalwa. Her comment echoes comedian Pieter-Dirk Uys's quip, during one of his signature drag performances as fictional National Party politician Evita Bezuidenhout, that her African maid "has only been a human being for 9 years [since 1994]."[20]

Western leaders champion democracy as the defining basis of freedom, but the fact is that for people in newly democratic countries, democratization brings feelings of liberation *and* uncertainty. A transition to democracy means broader freedom to choose politicians, but it also means that old lines of authority and hierarchy are up for grabs and the legitimacy of authority is less assured. Whose opinions are more valid in a democracy? It is not uncommon in Cape Town to hear people question whether the majority of their fellow citizens really are capable of making good decisions. After Capetonians voted the National Party back into power in local elections, activists, intellectuals, and ANC politicians suggested that an uneducated, uninformed electorate did not understand the significance of their vote. Racism and racial politics contribute to such views.

Such doubts plague not only voters but politicians as well. One afternoon, I listened in astonishment to a member of Parliament (MP) with unimpeachable "struggle credentials" (imprisonment, torture, and exile for his anti-apartheid activities) talk about his frustrations with democracy. His political party's insistence on 30 percent female representation in Parliament has meant, he complained, that "overweight, older, rural women who don't read well" get to serve as MPs. Blurting out, rather shockingly, "They are dodos!" he argued that these women "would not make it outside of Parliament" because their childbearing years are over and they have no skills and are not employable. Of course, he quickly acknowledged, they were the backbone of the anti-apartheid struggle, but nevertheless they are totally unfit for an official role in South Africa's democratic government.

The uncertainties of transformation are thus partly tied up with questions about the processes of democracy. In addition to uncertainty about the political intelligence of their fellow citizens, people wonder to what extent democratic decision-making processes should pervade other realms of life. Does living in a democracy mean that democratic approaches must be nurtured within old structures of authority, such as the media, schools, the family, or the church? A famous Cape Town hip-hop artist argues that democracy cannot extend, for example, to music competitions, because corporate interests are now too involved in shaping public opinion. "You can't be democratic, because the wrong kind of hip-hop—Eminem—will win," he says. "There are some places where democracy doesn't work." A township school principal struggling with an argumentative staff laments, "This democracy thing has caused us so many problems! Now everyone thinks they have a say or their rights are being violated!" A coloured socialist union organizer who was repeatedly jailed in the 1980s for fighting for workers' rights tells me that the freedom and liberalization brought by democracy also brought gangs and criminality. "Wait," I interject. "Are you saying democracy promotes gangsterism?" "Yes!" he nods emphatically. "Yes!" He believes gangsters and criminals take advantage of the human rights laws that came with democracy. The extent to which democratic approaches should reconfigure gender relations and patriarchal family structures is hotly contested.

In the current global environment, a post–cold war transition to democracy also means embracing globalization. Becoming an open, democratic society in a global world of media and consumption, after decades of state censorship and state-controlled media, means seeing pornography for the first time. It means a panoply of images of alternative lifestyles and identity possibilities, and it offers the consumer goods needed to claim those identities as one's own. The race to adopt consumerism has struck some Capetonians as detrimental to community: individualism is promoted over the collective, material goods are valued more than friends and kin, social status is tied more to consumption than to wealth in people or wisdom. Many lament that status, measured by consumption, has altered friendships and infected extended families. A coloured woman from Athlone, a suburb of Cape Town, describes how she used to drive her son and "ten of his friends" to the park or the beach to play, but now that would never happen. "Because of safety concerns?" I ask. "Because all they care about now is the status of your car," she responds. "Everyone cares about status now." Discussing her concerns about South Africans' new tendency toward individualism and excess, another woman asks me earnestly, "Is it democracy that does this?" For some, democracy has brought a feeling of social dislocation, as communities of mutual support and collective struggle break down into individual competition—for jobs, land, housing, and consumer goods. Accusations of witchcraft, apparently motivated by jealousy, are on the rise.[21]

Joining the global capitalist economy under a neoliberal structure has meant that economic opportunity has arrived for some, but at the cost of driving a deeper wedge between the haves and have-nots. A teacher asks me, "Is this what democracy is all about? Is it democracy that makes some people wealthier and others poorer?" I suggest that what she's witnessing are the effects of a neoliberal capitalist economy. "But is that what democracy means?" she persists. As the elite class becomes multiracial, impoverished ghettos remain completely black, and South Africans see growing inequalities within black families and communities. The racial dimension of stratification is now more complicated, and without apartheid to blame for black poverty, neoliberal assumptions blame the poor for their inability to adapt and prosper in the new dispensation. And Cape Town, home to millions of people who live in the all-black Cape Flats ghettos, has plenty of poverty visible and undeniable to everyone.

Class and Poverty

> "Nothing has changed," says Khayelitsha resident Frank with rage. "I get so angry—all those lives lost [in the struggle], for nothing. Nothing."

Although there certainly has been black mobility, the reality of transformation is a growing wealth gap and the entrenchment of poverty. Under apartheid, anti-apartheid activists could use the international currency of democracy against the apartheid government. Since they had an internationally supported morality on their side and could argue that apartheid was wrong and illegal, those opposed to apartheid could commit illegal acts that adhered to broader global laws of democracy, equity, and justice. But now, under democracy, that ability to claim participation in a broader global morality that contradicts the present political structure is gone. As my friend and fellow anthropologist Susan Levine observed to me one day, "Democracy is terrifically disabling." The main issues people continue to struggle with in post-apartheid South Africa are materially based (financial insecurity and unemployment), and unlike the situation under apartheid, there is no universal or globally recognized position on the injustice or immorality of inequality and poverty. Rather, the neoliberal global environment produces inequality and accepts poverty as unfortunate but normal. There is no global front with which to challenge democratic governments on inadequate economic policies for overcoming poverty and insisting on an equitable distribution of resources.

Cape Town's poverty is far from hidden. The 2001 census indicates that 39 percent of Cape Town's households earn incomes below R19,200 per year (equivalent to around US$3,000).[22] A 2002 report, "Cape

Town's Economy: Current Trends and Future Prospects," undertaken by the Unicity's Economic Development and Tourism and Property portfolio, reveals that almost half of all Africans, almost a third of Asians and Indians, and a fifth of coloureds live below the household subsistence level. Only 4 percent of whites fall into this category. A quarter of blacks are unemployed (although in some townships the figures reach 70 percent); 3 percent of whites are unemployed. Per capita disposable income of whites is five times that of blacks.[23]

Such glaring inequalities prompted President Thabo Mbeki to suggest in his famous 1998 address to Parliament that South Africa is composed of two nations: one white and wealthy, the other black and poor.[24] Recognizing that wealth is no longer confined only to white people, journalist and political commentator Allister Sparks offers the image of a double-decker bus, with a successful, wealthy multiracial upper deck and an increasingly impoverished black lower deck. The bus lacks a stairway from the lower to the upper deck.[25]

The stories included in this book reflect the massive economic and opportunity divides that continue to characterize Cape Town. Take, for example, the coloured community of Lavender Hill, where several people featured in this book live and work. According to the 2001 census, about a third of the adults in Lavender Hill are unemployed and fewer than 1 percent have a high school diploma. (The official figure for unemployment does not include those who have given up looking for work.) Khayelitsha, where several young men featured in this book live, is 100 percent African, of whom 96 percent do not hold a high school diploma and 51 percent are officially unemployed. Another entirely black community, Nyanga, home to a project featured in this book, reports similarly high levels of poverty. Only 5 percent of the residents hold a high school diploma and 56 percent are unemployed.

In contrast are other neighborhoods in which people featured in this book live: the southern suburb of Newlands is 83 percent white and boasts 97 percent employment; the neighboring suburb of Claremont is 80 percent white and also reports 97 percent employment. Educational levels in these suburbs are vastly higher and wealth in the form of property ownership vastly greater.

Contradictions

The historian Achille Mbembe quotes the observation by South African artist William Kentridge that South Africans typically live contradictory lives running in parallel.[26] This is not a particularly South African dichotomy—people live with contradictory knowledges and lifestyles everywhere, especially in metropolitan areas characterized by great inequities—but the contradictions that many South Africans try to accommodate may be more baldly evident because of the close physical proximity of radically divergent material lifestyles and cultural backgrounds.

But, as anthropologist Christopher Colvin observes about South Africa, "the language of crisis competes with the language of recovery. Deep optimism and pessimism, often found in the same person, seem to shape-shift into each other."[27] He notes that most South Africans view things in terms of their local context, rather than siding with one or the other side of the reconciliation/chaos, optimistic/pessimistic polarities that many use to describe contemporary South Africa. Rather, most South Africans are engaged in strategies of contingency and creativity. Cape Town's liveliness emerges from such strategies, provoked by the contradictions so constantly and obviously on display in city life. A few examples demonstrate what I mean.

One of my first interviews with a prominent public figure in Cape Town was with Rhoda Kadalie, well known for her dynamic approach to political life and human rights activism. I requested the interview because Kadalie runs an impressive awards program through the Institute for Democracy in South Africa (IDASA, the national institute that promotes democracy). The Impumelelo Awards program identifies exceptional poverty-reduction projects and over the preceding years has honored several remarkable, successful projects all over South Africa. I went to Kadalie's office expecting frank but nevertheless laudatory remarks on the new South Africa. To my dismay, our long and wide-ranging interview was dominated by her critical commentary on South Africa. She chastised the government for corruption and for promoting the unqualified through affirmative action, expressed her deep concern about soaring rape and HIV infection rates in the country, criticized the press for bowing to the tyranny of political correctness, and argued that the forces of globalization cannot be blamed for the lack of economic progress in post-apartheid South Africa. "It's important that people like you don't come here and romanticize our struggle," she admonished me. "We were brutalized; we're ruthless with each other." As we concluded the interview, I asked her how she can reconcile her pessimism with the energetic optimism of the Impumelelo Awards program she directs, since its purpose is to celebrate hope and optimism. Smiling, she responded, "I'm a walking contradiction."

Two years later, I spent a weekend at a lovely oceanfront condo with two white South African couples. After our arrival, the women talked over tea in the dining room for several hours about the exciting new directions their lives have taken. One had joined a community-based project to develop a preschool in a black squatter camp near her wealthy gated community. She described her time-consuming work with residents of the squatter camp on fund-raising, publicity, bureaucratic organization, and teacher support, glowing with admiration for the pluck and courage of the women from the camp who started and sustain the project against tremendous odds. The other woman in our vacation group had begun volunteering at primary school in a coloured township as a counselor and literacy specialist. Her commitment to the school had grown from one day a week to several, as had her involvement in the lives of the children and their families. The two women spent the afternoon sharing their experiences of personal growth, commitment, and optimistic engagement in their respective projects. Meanwhile, their husbands sat a few feet away in the lounge, carrying on an entirely different conversation. Their afternoon hours were spent commiserating about South Africa's ongoing decline, sharing stories about the country's collapsing infrastructure, growing corruption, and bureaucratic incompetence. Overhearing their husbands' conversation, the two women chuckled at the contradiction in their views of South Africa's transformation.

Another example: Terence (not his real name) is a leader in the educational division of government in the Western Cape, widely respected by his peers as a humanistic innovator with the skills to successfully transform the apartheid baggage of the education bureaucracy. In his first year on the job he pioneered anti-violence programs in schools throughout the city and was responsible for implementing and overseeing new programs to change school culture and teacher conduct. Physical safety and mental health are high on his agenda of school reforms. One day in 2002, he arrived late and obviously distressed to a meeting with me and my university students to talk about educational reform in Cape Town. In his gentle manner he apologized for his tardiness and described the horrific situation that had dominated his morning. He had been called to one of the township schools in his anti-violence program because of an outbreak of rape assaults on school grounds. Apparently a boy who had been raped came to the school and started a campaign of rape against other students. Frantic, the school principal had called in Terence to deal with the ensuing trauma and crisis. "How did you respond?" we asked him, expecting a description of counseling services and rape awareness workshops. Instead, he shocked us by quietly answering, "The first thing I wanted to do was find the boy and kill him."

Obviously this response came from a place of deep pain, horror, and exhaustion, and he immediately clarified that he was joking and then embarked on the description we were anticipating. But the joke betrays the tensions of fighting violence with peace (and assault with counseling) in a new social order that emphasizes human rights over punishment.

This book explores these kinds of contradictory feelings and thoughts, held collectively and individually by many Capetonians as they work through the fraught business of transforming their society. Great creativity and innovation can emerge from such contexts, and Cape Town has many important stories to tell about liberation and the potential for personal and social change. To tell stories about the first decade of transformation in Cape Town, this book juxtaposes the social work of transformers and of retrogrades, the visions of cultural innovators and of traditionalists, the worlds of parents and of children, and the fears of employers and of their workers to expose what it feels like to live in city defining itself between the old and the new, white and black, wealth and poverty.

. . . . .

Over dinner at a Caribbean café during my last research visit to Cape Town in 2004, I ramble to one of my primary interlocutors, high school principal John Gilmour, about losing my focus and trying to cover too many stories at once. I'm tracking a number of different efforts at transformation in nonprofit, school, and community-oriented undertakings. Some are attempts to create new education or health initiatives based in partnerships built across apartheid-era boundaries, whereas others are efforts at self-transformation that draw on contributions from outsiders. The stories tumble and mingle in my research notes and my bulging packet of interview tapes; the participants' lives overlap in unpredictable and unpredicted ways. As I move deeper into these projects, my fascination with their details and cast of characters repeatedly hijacks and obscures my focus. I want to write a book about each of the initiatives, because each deserves it, and such a manageable focus (on one case study) makes lovely ethnography.

John reminds me that all of the stories I'm following are important to the central theme of this book, which is the space of trust and the different things people bring to that space that make them struggle to transform their society, that allow them to go forward or keep them from moving forward. It would be difficult to capture the story of transformation in Cape Town in a single case study—a jumble of case studies more accurately captures the slow yet frenetic, uncoordinated, amoeba-like grassroots efforts at transformation. A man in the tourism business who regularly traverses the city's many neighborhoods described Cape Town to me in 2003 as a city that appears frozen in (apartheid) time, yet when you look closer you realize that the ground is moving constantly. The disorder in my field notes emulates Cape Town's low-grade constant movement, some of which is like Brownian motion (with no effect), and some of which disintegrates boundaries and changes lives. It is a messy portrait.

None of the kinds of efforts toward transformation I chronicle is exactly new. Community improvement and support projects built by local visionaries have existed for many years in Cape Town's African and coloured townships. Whites as well have long participated in community projects in African and coloured townships, and multiracial networks that link churches and work in the interest of community health or skills projects have long existed. In 2003, at a civic club meeting where I was invited to speak about my research on white people's experiences of transformation, a member of the (all white) audience responded with annoyance to my description of the ways in which some white people are now attempting to change their lives and create new kinds of connections to black people: "You haven't talked about anything new! Nothing you talk about is new since 1994—this has all been going on here from way back," he claims, arguing that nothing really changed with the end of apartheid because white people had always "done community work" and interacted with black people. His irritation at my discussion of how some white people are struggling to overcome their racism is clear in his insistence that white people's engagement in charitable undertakings in black communities is old news.

My angry interlocutor is right that relationships between white and black people were normal under apartheid, although he neglects to mention that for most the relationship was of master and servant or, less often, charitable donor and dependent recipient. (The only woman in my audience that day disputed her colleague's remarks by noting that in her "very typical Afrikaner" upbringing, all the black people she'd had contact with prior to 1994 had been her servants.) While installing clear-cut racialized boundaries, apartheid policies also attempted to carefully engineer the terms of cross-race contact, making clear the lines of authority and control and making any hopes for equity dangerous. But the context of black-white relationships is now radically different. Equity, empowerment, self-help, and partnership are the buzzwords; dependency and white dominance are anathema. White people reaching out across old boundaries must actively redefine their power position and be ever mindful of what their whiteness means in the new South Africa. Black people are now free to pursue any dreams they wish, bound only (and hugely) by the structural confines of poverty and the ideological challenges of self-esteem and confidence. Under apartheid, cross-race linkages by definition implied partners came to the relationship with dramatically different means. While enraging to those of color, state policy upheld wealth and resource inequity as desirable, necessary, and non-negotiable. Since 1994, such material inequities between partners are unsupported by state and popular discourse and are thus awkward; there are no cultural or political guidelines for how to navigate the discomfort, guilt, and rage provoked by wealth inequities widely seen as illegitimate.

Hopeful partners now find they must renegotiate their mutual terms of engagement and understandings of reciprocity. What does dependency mean in the post-apartheid context of massive wealth inequities? How do those trained to think in inequalities come to see themselves as equals? What is involved in the emotional work of imagining and creating contexts of equity? At the conclusion of my talk that so provoked the man quoted above, another older white man in the audience approached me. "That's me you're talking about!" he said, visibly excited. He explained that his son had fled South Africa in disgust after growing up in Cape Town, attending the finest white schools, and completing his mandatory military service during apartheid, but he had returned with his wife after 1994 to settle in South Africa, where they adopted two black children. "Now I find myself with two black grandchildren. That's transformation! I'm transformation!" he exclaimed to me. He shared his concerns that perhaps he and his wife were overcompensating for their uncertainty by spoiling the grandchildren, fussing too much over them to prove that they accept them. He described their discomfort with their friends' hesitant attitude about their grandchildren and their guilt over wondering if they would behave differently—and more naturally—if the children were white. He asked if I would interview him and his wife, apparently eager and relieved at finding a way to talk about his situation.

This book chronicles the sentiments of transformation among those who are making significant efforts to change their lives, their neighborhoods, and their city. Since the efforts and projects I describe are all still unfolding, the descriptions are dangling and unresolved. Most of these efforts are characterized by a constant back and forth—usually a two-steps-forward-one-step-back kind of experience. I try to capture the optimism that propels the forward steps and the challenges that force retreat. Over dinner at the Caribbean café, John mentioned that the swing between success and failure so characteristic of community-level transformative projects mirrors the ongoing nationally televised and avidly followed conflicts regarding transformation within South Africa's national cricket team. A breakdown about race and incomplete transformation in the team occurs, and the team holds workshops, talks, and press conferences to resolve the issue, and yet problems continue to resurface cyclically. As John puts it, after each breakdown and reconciliation, the participants ask, " 'Okay, are we okay now?' and agree 'Yes! We're all okay!' Until the next thing comes along and suddenly they're not okay." The stories I recount here are about negotiating that space and sustaining the trust required to ensure ongoing forward steps.

THE BOOK

Chapters 2, 3, 5, 7, 8, and 9 present ethnographic research and analysis. Chapters 2 and 3 provide an overview of the legacy of apartheid's imprint on the urban landscape of Cape Town in order to explain the kinds of material and ideological forces that keep people segregated and ignorant about one another's lives. Historically rooted patterns of work and leisure that are difficult to change continue to define people's daily lives. Life in the city brings an awareness of those who live differently, of course, but not necessarily an understanding or empathy. How is empathy developed in a place like Cape Town?

Chapters 5 and 7 focus on the legacy of white supremacy in the construction of contemporary racial identities and highlight how patterns of white supremacy under apartheid created the basis for contemporary class hierarchy. Some may argue that such an overt focus on the apartheid racial categories is regressive in the post-apartheid era of nonracism and nonracialism, but as Sandile Dikeni wrote about Cape Town, the city is racist.[28] There is a distinct need to acknowledge, dissect, disarticulate, and investigate the planes and pathways of racism before race can be transcended. Chapter 7 grapples with questions about the legacy of whiteness and class consciousness for coloured Capetonians, the city's largest demographic.

Chapters 8 and 9 focus on the work of people I call "transformers," offering case studies of Capetonians who have embraced the transformation of Cape Town as central to their lives and fundamental to their well-being. Cape Town is home to many engines of change, from major government programs in housing and infrastructure development, black empowerment, and school reform, to internationally funded NGOs working on reconciliation and HIV and AIDS, to powerful activist social movements advocating for new policies on health, the rights of victims of apartheid, and other major issues. All of these initiatives are vitally important, but my focus is on ordinary people who have made some extraordinary choices to become part of the momentum of social change in personal, grassroots, and local ways. The people I profile as transformers are not politicians or policy makers, and they don't necessarily recognize themselves as politically engaged activists or organizers. Rather, they identify as people who have taken the imperative of social change to heart in very personal ways and have come to believe that being part of the celebrated new South Africa means a commitment to self-consciously developing new networks and new models for community building.

Reaching across racial and economic divides to build new networks is awkward and fraught; it requires a major investment of psychological energy, it is emotionally taxing, it is not economically lucrative, it can be dangerous, and it often meets with limited immediate success. Community organizing and building new interpersonal networks sometimes means spending time in dangerous neighborhoods, and in fact most of the people I profile here have experienced violence as a result of their work. The success of these undertakings is measured by the belief that they share, across race and class lines, a stake in the same issues of health, education, and security; a belief that is the essence of democratic culture. As Todd Gitlin observes, "The citizen puts aside private affairs in order to build up relationships with other citizens, with whom we come to share unanticipated events, risks, and outcomes."[29] Their stories are remarkable tales of hope and vision and offer lessons to others seeking to participate in Cape Town's post-apartheid transformation.

The other chapters (1, 4, and 6) play off against these ethnographic discussions by describing the process of anthropological fieldwork and ethnographic research. Chapter 1 explains how I ended up in Cape Town studying transformation. Chapter 4 explores some of the personal challenges of anthropological fieldwork, particularly fieldwork undertaken in South Africa by a white American. Chapter 6 describes how my research questions were shaped by those whose lives I document as they questioned my assumptions and views about life in Cape Town. Anthropology is profoundly interactive—Pierre Bourdieu once called it a combat sport—because anthropological research emerges from intense social encounters. One contribution I seek to make in this book is to demonstrate that the tools of anthropology are the tools of life—they enable a critical and constructive awareness of the terms on which people meet and engage, and they offer a model for connection in a dangerous, unstable world.

CHAPTER I

Seduction

There is an old joke in anthropology that asks, "What is a typical Navajo family?" The answer: "A husband, a wife, two children, and an anthropologist." Since 1994, Cape Town has had the same feeling of saturation by foreign anthropologists. The promise of South Africa's democracy, the excitement of transformation, the remarkable process of national reconciliation guided by two of the twentieth century's most authentic heroes, Nelson Mandela and Archbishop Desmond Tutu, brought anthropologists to South Africa in droves. South Africa in transformation promised to offer anthropologists a treasure trove of insights into some of our favorite topics: race, class, gender, violence, memory, identity, ethnicity, tradition, modernity. Africanist anthropologists whose hearty optimism had been challenged by African tragedies showed up in South Africa looking for positive models of change and optimistic trajectories toward the future. Suddenly it seemed everyone I knew was starting a new research project in South Africa.

I too joined the flood, eager for a look at the miracle. Colby College, where I teach anthropology, had joined with Bowdoin and Bates Colleges to establish a study abroad program for our juniors in Cape Town, and I was asked to serve on the steering committee to design the program. At the time, I was immersed in literature about violent state collapse, struggling to make sense of the civil war that had destroyed Somalia, where I had done fieldwork in the 1980s, and I was feeling a bit out of sorts with my discipline of anthropology. Ten years of studying and writing about Somalia left me wondering about the value of anthropology during times of war and crisis. While I promoted anthropology in my classes at Colby to help students dismantle their exotic images of foreign Others and challenge their assumptions about what is "natural" and "normal" in human behavior, I was puzzled by the absence at the time of anthropological expertise in the arena of public debate about the crises erupting at the conclusion of the cold war. During the 1990s, while political scientists and other pundits were influencing American policy makers with their assessments of the New World Order, and economists from the International Monetary Fund (IMF) were redesigning the economies of transforming states, anthropologists seemed to remain isolated in our ivory towers, talking to one another, quietly certain about our superior knowledge, writing books few would read and fewer would understand.

Every semester I worked to convert students to the worldview of anthropology, arguing that our critical analytical stance, our holistic and comparative approaches, and our ability to situate mundane local experience within the global world of transnational processes provide deeper insights into the world they would enter after college. But every term I found that I was assigning fewer readings by anthropologists and more readings by journalists, literary figures, essayists, and—yes—even political scientists. It was becoming increasingly difficult to convince my students that anthropology provides a superior analytical lens through which to view the issues of the day when few anthropologists at the time provided role models for how anthropology could contribute to national and international debates about capitalism, modernity, transformation, war, and peace. Instead, my students found anthropological writings— with a few notable exceptions—filled with jargon, self-obsessed, difficult to understand, and distancing. My parents, loyal to their daughter's choice of a profession, kept asking why they never seemed to hear about books written by anthropologists that could explain to a lay audience the changes taking place in the world.

Anthropology is a strange discipline, born of the colonial encounter, caustically critical of authority yet a child of privilege, uncertain of its merits while smug about its superior methodologies and theories. From today's vantage point, its colonial roots seem quaint and ignoble: mostly white, mostly male Europeans and Americans recording descriptions of the lives of "savages," looking for schemas to unlock "the primitive mind," documenting indigenous social structures in anticipation of the colonial takeover of those structures. Such an orientation lent anthropology an air of paternalism, as Americans and Europeans became "experts" on indigenous people: the Yanomami, the Igbo, the Nuer, the Tikopia.[1] The privileged position of studying the Other (always powerless in how they were represented ethnographically) came under severe challenge by late twentieth-century critics who questioned the discipline's claims to expert and factual knowledge and condemned our heritage of colonial complicity and paternalistic writings. Such criticisms—well deserved and long overdue—left a generation of graduate students uncertain about their calling. For some anthropologists, reflexivity and cultural critique became the domain of expertise: the only subject about which we could write confidently and authoritatively was ourselves.[2] Anthropologists began exploring alternative writing styles to avoid making truth claims about the lives of our "subjects." Ethnographies took on a tone of suggestion, thoughtfulness, and uncertainty rather than authority.

Forcing anthropologists to acknowledge our own subject positions and our own biases liberated anthropology from the rigid confines of scientific writing, but the emphasis on the deconstruction of reality cost us as well. Fin de siècle anthropology became the voice of critique, not authority, which meant an unwillingness to claim to know the truth, to be experts, to pick fights in public with IMF economists or international security specialists or domestic public policy wonks. But equivocation is quite a luxury, and relentless critique can become an easy lifestyle. By the late 1990s, I was struggling to identify the unique expertise anthropology could offer to a globalized world of transnational mobility and instant communications technology.

Arriving in Cape Town in 1999, I was quite clear in my own mind that I was there to help set up a study abroad program, not to do fieldwork. The local academics I met joked good-naturedly about being made into subjects in the research projects of foreign anthropologists, many of whom arrived to study the Truth and Reconciliation Commission (TRC), treating local academics as informants rather than colleagues. The fact that local academics felt few publications had resulted from the army of post-1994 foreign researchers only enhanced their fatigue with foreign anthropologists. In contrast, I could comfortably define my presence in Cape Town as part of a mission of tertiary education—to help create a study abroad program that would build bridges between Americans and South Africans and fight American stereotypes of the African continent.

But that first trip to Cape Town in June 1999 was far from comfortable. Cape Town is a fundamentally weird place in many ways, so saturated with the legacy of apartheid that one can't help but feel unsettled.

My American colleagues and I stayed at a little bed-and-breakfast rec-
ommended by the University of Cape Town that was straight out of the
English countryside: scones with cream and marmalade for breakfast;
floral chintz and porcelain everywhere; English landscape paintings;
lawn-bowling, English-speaking proprietors who dressed in white slacks
and sweater vests. A local Islamic group called Pagad (People against
Gangsterism and Drugs) had recently bombed Planet Hollywood—a
symbol of Western culture and imperialism—in downtown Cape Town,
and we were advised to avoid any interaction with Muslims for fear of
attacks on our American study abroad program. The white people we
met shrugged off apartheid as an unfortunate historical aberrance and
assured us that blacks hadn't really been that disenfranchised in the
Western Cape because they'd never owned any property there anyhow.
Many of the coloured people we encountered advised us to avoid African
townships and shared their anxieties about an African-controlled government. Some even expressed the shocking sentiment that things had
been better under apartheid than under the African National Congress
(ANC), whose leaders were corrupt and inept. Other than the local
friends of one of my American colleagues, we hardly met any African
people during that trip except on organized township tours. We spent
our time with lawyers, university officials, real estate agents, and tour
guides, who were practically all white. The restaurants in the suburbs
near the university catered to mostly white patrons, the other visitors to
the nature preserves we toured were white, even the student pubs were
dominated by white people. The university administrators with whom
we met were nervous about our intention to include a community service component in our study abroad program, which would require our
students to spend two afternoons a week in African and coloured townships. This would be much too dangerous, we were told; Cape Town's
townships are too "political" (which, I learned, meant "not docile"), and
the university administrators needed to make it clear that they would not
be responsible for what might happen to our students.

Where, I found myself thinking, is the famous rainbow nation?

One day during that visit, one of my American colleagues and I decided
to stop in at the District Six Museum, then located in the old Moravian
church left standing in the rubble of District Six. (District Six was Cape
Town's famous urban multicultural neighborhood, defined as a slum and
bulldozed by the apartheid government. District Six was never rebuilt as
a white neighborhood, which was the government's original intent, and
except for the construction of a technical college it remained vacant and

uninhabited until 2004.) We arrived to discover a workshop in session for former residents. The museum was packed and Father Michael Lapsley, the ANC activist and Anglican priest who lost his hands to a package bomb sent to him by an apartheid government "death squad" in 1990, was speaking, gesturing eloquently with the hooks which replaced his hands. After he finished, we were invited to the food tent outside, where samosas, koeksisters, and curry were being served. Someone introduced me to Father Lapsley, and in an effort to employ the universal symbol of introduction, I reached out and grabbed his hook. He looked perturbed. Feeling self-conscious and embarrassed—by being there, by my awkwardness, my foreignness, my voyeurism—I retreated, wondering if this was an affront, an attempt on my part to normalize something that should be recognized as abnormal. As we walked back to our car, a man stopped us to chat. "I can see you are foreigners," he began. "I'm a former resident of District Six. You, my friend," to my colleague, "I can see you are one of us. Your ancestors came from here. But you," he turned to me, "what is your family heritage?" Blushing, I responded, "British and Dutch." The man chuckled, although he wasn't joking. "Ah! So you are a colonialist!"

One evening another American colleague invited me to a birthday party at the apartment of a friend of his. Prompted by a new play in Cape Town we had all seen that explored the politics of being coloured, the party discussion turned to racial identities. An American colleague at the party recounted her treatment by white South African customs officials at the airport the previous week. Upon her arrival in Cape Town, the customs officials pulled her aside and forced her to wait endlessly in the arrival area with no explanation, while shunting her paperwork from one official to the next. Her narration of the hours she spent waiting to clear customs was raucous, hilarious, and outraged, as she imitated each official and repeated her escalating series of arguments with them. The audience was rolling with laughter—she is a master storyteller. When it came to the part where she recounted how she finally lost her temper at a white female customs agent, she chose me as her target in the reenactment of the scene, screaming, "You fucking Boer!" as she pointed her finger at me. I, the only pale face in the room, momentarily became the abusive customs officer. The party collapsed with laughter at her bravado and daring.

Although my visage was useful for bringing her story alive, being targeted to play the role of the white official left me pondering the question of whether being white, and of *Dutch* heritage no less, makes me, inevitably, "a fucking Boer" in post-apartheid Cape Town. How does one—anyone—transcend that category?

. . . . .

I returned to Cape Town the following year, in October 2000, to begin planning my term as program director of the Colby-Bates-Bowdoin study abroad semester. By this time, the colleges had bought a property to house our program—a lovely Mediterranean villa–style house at the foot of Table Mountain in the tony, leafy suburb of Newlands. It boasted a saltwater swimming pool, a rose garden, and a patio and deck area with a built-in barbecue, and it emanated an affluence befitting the colleges' status as expensive, elite institutions. A staff was hired, and our first group of American students was halfway through the semester, taking courses at the University of Cape Town (UCT) and at our center with their American program director, doing community service at a township high school, and living with local families. I had agreed to serve as program director for the second semester, which committed me and my family to relocating to Cape Town from January through July 2001. I considered the October visit—spent making arrangements for the following term—as "service to the college," since I had no intention of beginning a research project of my own. Rather, I was thinking of the coming semester as an opportunity to take some time off from anthropology while learning about the fascinating city of Cape Town, and to reconsider my commitment to the profession as I thought through alternative careers. I was pleased to avoid a Maine winter, excited to make the switch from small-town to city life, and happy to offer my children another opportunity to live abroad, in a different social environment than the one we had in Maine. We were looking forward to taking family trips around southern Africa—Lesotho, Botswana, Namibia, Mozambique.

A week or so after our arrival in Cape Town in January 2001, my children's school had a information night for new parents. We had enrolled our children in an English-language school that was widely touted for its progressive approach and strong academics. Although it was located in one of the predominantly white southern suburbs, it enrolled significant numbers of children from other parts of Cape Town and required students to study Xhosa and Afrikaans. Parents assured me that the school was committed to multiculturalism and diversity and that my children would find the atmosphere welcoming and tolerant.

At the new parents' meeting, the headmaster spoke at great length—nearly one and a half hours—on the school's philosophy, curriculum, governing structure, and extracurricular activities. The philosophy emphasized well-roundedness, which, he noted, included neat uniforms, a concern for personal security, and the need for physical exertion. Physical exertion was particularly important, he explained, now that South Africa had joined the modern world and everyone is so much busier. Now that "life has sped up" and "mommy must work too," aftercare programs or watching television at granny's house has replaced carefree afternoons of climbing trees and running around. Several other speakers, asking for service contributions (for a dinner put on by the school for local retirees, who, it was noted, are "not poor"), or suggesting parents join a weekend hiking club as a way to unwind, echoed this theme of the high stress brought on by "modernization."

About the curriculum, the headmaster assured the parents of the ease of the transition at the school from the old system to the new requirements adopted by the Ministry of Education, noting that the required changes were fairly insignificant. He affirmed the continuing emphasis on reading skills and math, recognizing that some parents had been concerned that these basics might be demoted in importance by the requirements of the new ministry guidelines. On the governing structure, he explained that currently the government provides state funding for twenty teachers, in keeping with the government mandate of a forty-nine-to-one student-to-teacher ratio. The state-supported teachers answer to the provincial educational authorities. Through school fees, the school raises funds to hire seventeen additional teachers, thus dramatically reducing the student-to-teacher ratio. These teachers are considered private employees, and they answer to the school's governing body. Several parents questioned the rationale for this structure. The headmaster explained that it resulted from the rationalization of education across the country and the fact that there are now so very many schools that come under the same educational system in South Africa. All schools are now treated the same, he explained, and the funding has to be balanced out. This means some schools that had more have lost some of their state-supplied resources, while other schools have gained. For example, the state no longer supports a music teacher, so now school fees must cover that kind of specialized subject. As an afterthought he added, "But of course, there were many schools that never had a music teacher under the old system." He explained that the school maintains a thirty-to-one ratio, which he thinks is fine, especially in comparison to other schools that have a fifty-to-one ratio. There are even schools in rural areas and some of the squatter camps, he added, where population numbers are impossible to gauge, and some classrooms reach a ninety-to-one ratio. There was an audible gasp from the audience. He concluded by noting that things have changed regarding education policy in the country, but the school is stable and able to maintain its programs and its standards.

As I sat there listening, it felt like the headmaster was speaking in code. I realized I arrived at the parents' meeting expecting to hear exciting news about how the school was continuing to transform: how it was tackling the hard questions of integration and multiculturalism, how it was addressing the mandated curricular changes that sought to deconstruct apartheid-era teaching practices, how it was eagerly redefining its mission as South Africa entered the twenty-first century as a dramatically different kind of nation. Instead, the emphasis of the entire evening was on how the school was *not* changing rather than on how it was welcoming change. There was no overt mention of the word *apartheid* and its legacy in relation to the curriculum, the student body, the composition of the (almost entirely white) teaching and administrative faculty; no mention of how the study of history was to be addressed. Rather than embracing new directions at the school, the emphasis was on how difficult things are now—much busier, less relaxed, more insecure (thus necessitating the construction of a fence around the school perimeter to ensure, joked the headmaster, that in the face of rising crime students "won't get caught in the crossfire")—and on how, despite this environment, the school was determined to maintain its standards.[3]

I returned home with my head spinning from the gulf between the excitement I expected to find about the possibilities afforded by living in a society undergoing transformation and the actual messages of "staying the course" and "maintaining the same standards" that were the evening's theme. That night, I started my first journal of field notes.

Almost three years later I was enjoying a sunny day at Kirstenbosch Gardens with my friend and colleague anthropologist Fiona Ross. As always, our conversation meandered through various topics: the legacy of Bantu education, what the low matric (for university qualification) pass rates at township schools meant for the future, the current situation of domestics in South Africa, the ongoing troubles in Zimbabwe, the future of anthropology in South Africa. I was remembering my insistence when I had first met Fiona that I was not in South Africa to do fieldwork, that I was not part of the foreign hordes arriving to scavenge Cape Town, only to return home and years later produce a book that promised a novel analysis of South Africa's transformation. And yet here I was, plotting the outline of the book I would return home to write, asking Fiona's advice about things I was struggling to understand, already planning the research I would need to complete during my return to Cape Town later that year. Feeling somewhat abashed, I complained to Fiona that I felt like Cape Town had seduced me; the initial attraction which drew me to South Africa as "a service contribution to my college" had grown into a love affair that took over my life and from which I could not seem to extricate myself. As I described the enlivening tumult of emotions I felt throughout each stay in Cape Town, and the longing I felt for the place when I was back home in Maine, a subtle smile played across Fiona's face. "Isn't anthropology always about seduction and desire?" she asked. (As well as, she continued, curiosity, hope, engagement, rigor, and many other things.)

Yes, I suppose it is. As anthropologist Hugh Gusterson once pointed out to me, anthropologists usually choose to do fieldwork among people whom they admire and want to be like.[4] Certainly, admiration for South Africa's supposed miracle had drawn me back to the country nearly twenty years after my first, deeply disturbing visit in the early 1980s. We as a world need South Africa to succeed and to pioneer a model for meeting the challenges of poverty and racism; one dimension of my desire is how badly I want South Africa to provide answers to the questions that haunt us and how seduced I am into believing that it can.

But my engagement with Cape Town also led me, unsuspectingly at first, into a long slow dance with anthropology. Initially imagining my time in Cape Town to be a break from anthropological research, I spent two years simply trying to figure out how to teach effectively about South Africa's transformation (after completing my first six-month term of teaching in 2001, I returned for another term in June 2002). I found I returned over and over again to anthropological tools for understanding and teaching about the dynamism and profound contradictions of post-1994 Cape Town. My students were encountering dramatic and opposing viewpoints from Capetonians during their six months in South Africa: ebullient optimism about the future and anxious dread; an uplifting sense of liberation and profound insecurity; horrendous criminal acts of violence and community workers who could qualify for sainthood; nonracialists and rabid racists; children with little knowledge of apartheid's realities and adults deeply traumatized by their memories; vicious anti-American sentiment and a desire to consume American culture. My students were swimming in a tide of contradictions and complexities, as was I, but I was the one being paid to help them make some sense of things. And, to my delight, anthropology showed me how to do it.

This realization began to take shape one day over lunch with University of Cape Town anthropologists Susan Levine, Sally Frankental, and Fiona Ross. Our conversation circled around what anthropology should be doing now in South Africa; in the post-1994 rush to pioneer new arenas of study, anthropology's areas of expertise had been quickly cannibalized by other disciplines and interdisciplinary programs. South African anthropology has a long, solid tradition of relevant research and critical commentary;[5] our conversation focused on its strengths in South Africa's current context. What does anthropology offer to the study of transformation that is unique? As we debated anthropology's merits, I realized I felt strongly, passionately about this: that our strength is our holism, our relativism, our humanism, our empathy, and our methodological rigor—all those backbone concepts of Anthropology 101.

Anthropology is the only discipline that provides a way to study complexity without reducing it to simple models, flow charts, and generalizations. It can take account of and explain contradictions in people's lives and the gap between people's ideals (such as the rainbow nation or nonracialism) and their everyday behavior (such as residential racial segregation and racism). It can successfully encompass the unique experiences of individuals and the communal experiences of collectivities. It is profoundly empathetic; anthropology is all about listening and striving to understand. Anthropology is about perception, trying to grasp what people's experiences have been and how they understand those experiences and behave because of those understandings. Anthropology takes the researcher into the intimacy of family life, into the workplace, and onto the street; it encompasses identity politics, gender politics, class hierarchy. It strives to grasp what it feels like to live in a township or a fortified suburb, what it feels like to be afraid of black people or to resent white people, what it feels like to live with the rage of poverty, what it feels like to be repudiated for challenging racist friends and family members, and it endeavors to communicate these feelings to people of different backgrounds. My lunch companions were among those South African anthropologists who were setting the standard for ethnographic work that was both intimate and broadly relevant;[6] our inspiring conversation set me back on the path of fully embracing anthropological methods and perspectives as the best way to understand a transforming society.

. . . . . .

People often ask, "How do you *do* anthropology?" The idea of moving into a community, getting to know people, encouraging people to talk with you and share their thoughts and sometimes secrets, proving that you can be trusted, maneuvering local politics, learning local norms and mores, joining networks of mutual care and support, and earning the right to tell stories about other people's lives is indeed daunting. Anthropologist Cris Shore writes: "Intensive fieldwork (or 'qualitative research') is a gloss that covers a vast array of promiscuous techniques and messy encounters."[7] Because anthropological knowledge encompasses the general context as well as individual experiences, it requires that the researcher learn about broad, dominant social structures and ideologies (how the economy works, how the political hierarchy is maintained, how the legal structure operates, what the dominant religious ideologies are, what conceptions are of family structure and gender roles, what the predominant categories are for defining personal and group identities, etc.) *and* develop intimate relationships with a variety of people.

Anthropology demands a lot of humility from the researcher, who often has to learn a whole social and cultural world; learning how to function in a new cultural environment presents a minefield of potential faux pas, embarrassments, and discomfort. It can play hell with your self-image and self-confidence.[8] But the rewards are a depth and breadth of understanding and human engagement unparalleled in other modes of research.

My work began with the task of figuring out how to present to my students as encompassing a picture of life in Cape Town as possible in a six-month term. Wendy (a pseudonym), the local study abroad program administrator, and I spent hours conferring on guest speakers, events, workshops, performances, and field trips. We attended political and cultural events all over town—plays, musical performances, poetry readings, public lectures, public workshops—researching themes to highlight during the semester and looking for guest performers and speakers. We chose a roster of speakers who could talk about topics like the TRC and reconciliation; religion and the role of the churches during apartheid and in transformation; inequality and the economy, housing, education, and sport; tourism; HIV/AIDS; human rights law; and crime. Our list included academics, activists, politicians, artists, church leaders, lawyers, and psychologists. Realizing that we needed to understand the face of tourism in Cape Town and the complex ways in which Cape Town represents itself, we binged on "township tours," taking nearly every township tour available (some several times to hear different guides) to compare and contrast their representations of Cape Town's history, geography, and social relationships. I spent hours in the car, driving around Cape Town because I wanted to feel comfortable finding my way around most parts of the metropolitan area. Because of my particular interest in the interface of cultural production and political life, I began making acquaintances with a handful of cultural producers—artists, musicians, comedians, dancers—who were gracious enough to grant me hours of interviews and who allowed me, over the next several years, to follow them around town to their workshops, performances, and fundraisers.

Gradually, as my semester of speakers, workshops, and performances took shape, and as I was finding my footing in Cape Town's social and material geography, I began requesting interviews with public figures and local experts on Cape Town's social and material realities. I joined a visiting family member at meetings around the city of his international service club. Since membership in this particular organization has remained mostly white businessmen in Cape Town, I was interested to learn about its community service projects and the club members' understanding of their role in the new South Africa. Over the next two years, I attended meetings of several branches of this club, spoke with dozens of members, and visited about a dozen of their sponsored projects. To learn more about Cape Town's youth and how public schools were contributing to transformation, I asked at several schools if I could spend time in the classroom. To my initial surprise, I encountered the stiffest resistance from my children's school, which seemed uncertain about the prospect of actually having a parent volunteer in the classroom. One of my daughter's teachers said to me, "What would we do if all the parents wanted to come help at school?" the implication being that this would be unmanageable and chaotic. Other than participating in school events, parents' meetings, and extracurricular school activities, interviewing school administrators and teachers, and spending lots of social time with my children's school friends and their families, I was only able to spend two days actually in the classroom on visits that were carefully defined and closely constrained (you may visit this teacher's classroom, but not that teacher's; you may observe this lesson, but not that one, etc.).

In stark contrast to the chilly reception from the formerly white school, the two township schools I approached not only welcomed my presence but immediately put me to work. Although I had asked only to be allowed to sit in on classes as an observer (with the offer to volunteer if there was any way I could contribute), my first days at both schools were identical: the principal introduced me to the teacher I would be shadowing, who in turn introduced me to his or her class and then took a seat (or, during later visits, left the room) after turning the class over to me. I quickly realized that my time in the classroom would be in front, in charge of the lesson, rather than at the back as an observer. Anthropologist Signithia Fordham reflects in her book about her fieldwork at a high school in Washington, D.C., that anthropology's use of the phrase *participant-observation* to describe our research technique doesn't clarify what we really do, which is *watching*.[9] Watching people interact and situations unfold is actually a much more threatening undertaking than the neutral-sounding *observing*, a fact often well understood by those we watch. Andy Dawes, a psychologist who has worked in Cape Town schools for decades, helped me understand why I was placed in front of the classroom rather than at the back, *watching*. Imagining I could sit in on a classroom simply as an observer was indeed naive; given the history in township schools of surveillance, control, terror, state intervention, and top-down authoritarian control, few teachers would be comfortable with being *watched* by a foreign researcher. Such concerns also undoubtedly influenced my reception at the formerly white school.

At a primary school in Lavender Hill I spent my volunteer days with the grade sevens; at a high school in Langa I was assigned to an English teacher who taught grades nine, eleven, and twelve. Our activities varied: we spent time talking about human rights, democracy, their local communities, their schools, life in the United States. The students' questions were informative: "Does your government pay for services, like water, or must the people pay?" "Do you have gangsters?" "Are many people in the U.S. HIV positive?" "Who pays for the fancy awards ceremonies we see on TV, like the Grammys, and where do they get the money?" and, from Lavender Hill's grade sevens to my grade-seven daughter, "Do you use condoms regularly in the United States?" I gave in-class essay assignments about students' hopes for the future and the issues of importance in their daily lives. The teachers took me to meetings and to lunch breaks and spent hours talking with me about the realities of townships schools, as did the principals, who also made arrangements for me to spend time with parents, and in Lavender Hill, in the after-school madrassas run by Muslim parents in their homes for their children's Islamic education. The teachers were patient with my mistakes and very, very gracious to surrender their classrooms to me; the students were delightful educators. Over the next several years I expanded my understanding of school environments in Cape Town by spending time in a number of other primary and high schools, as well as private schools.

The formal interviews and hours of informal conversation with colleagues; the township tours, public events, performances, and workshops; the days spent at schools with students, teachers, principals, and parents; the service club meetings; the hours spent driving; the masses of literature I waded through to prepare my classes; these ways of engaging Cape Town gave me an overall grid of perception, a backbone of understanding that was critical to grasping, anthropologically, how the legacy of the past continued to structure the present in Cape Town. But anthropological insights about the present draw as well on intimacy and close personal relationships; on, as anthropologist Clifford Geertz once put it, a methodology of "deep hanging out."[10] Once I allowed myself to recognize that I had been irrevocably seduced, that I wanted to learn intimately about South Africa's transformation, and that anthropology offered the tools to do it, I followed Geertz's advice. My acquaintances deepened with some of the host parents in our study abroad program, friendships grew with some of the parents of my children's friends, with neighbors, with colleagues, with teachers at the schools where I was spending time. I accepted invitations to dinner parties (joking with Wendy that I was doing "dinner party ethnography"), afternoon teas, morning coffees, hikes, picnics, and "sundowners."

As my relationships and friends' interest in my research agenda grew, people started inviting me along to witness their meetings, to visit their community service, community-building, or development projects, and to socialize with their circles of friends and family. I began intensive interviews with people deeply involved in both the personal and the institutional aspects of transformation. My time was stretched thin during my first years of research: I was equally enthralled by the phenomenon of township tours, hip-hop events, the meetings of my neighborhood association and the international service club, discussions with the township primary school and high school students and teachers, dinner parties with neighbors and host families, the demanding work of township community workers, and academic discussions with professional colleagues. What else but anthropology gives a researcher such breadth?

But I realized I needed to draw some boundaries. Geographically, I decided to ignore the northern suburbs, which have a character distinct from that of the southern suburbs and the townships (more Afrikaans speakers, more mixed working- and middle-class neighborhoods, more newly constructed neighborhoods). An ethnographic study that takes account of Cape Town north of the N2 highway would present quite different informative insights than my study does. Other than acquaintances and a few dear friendships, I cannot claim in-depth associations with the white Afrikaner, Muslim, or Indian communities of Cape Town. Over the course of my six visits over five years of study, my primary communities of association were coloured English- and Afrikaans-speaking and white English-speaking working- and middle-class people in their late thirties and forties (and often their children) in the neighborhoods stretching from Woodstock to Muizenberg and Athlone to Lavender Hill, and economically disadvantaged high school students in their late teens and early twenties living in Langa, Khayelitsha, and Guguletu. Thus, I should very clearly specify that my research focuses on linkages and barriers between the southern suburbs and townships from the point of view of individuals in these communities. Rather than an ethnography of a particular community, social group, or development project, this is an ethnography of connections and gaps that describes places where people come together across apartheid-era divisions specifically in order to deconstruct and overcome cleavages of race and class. In a sense, this is an ethnography of possibility and of the social imagination.

Topically, there are many arenas of transformation in Cape Town I did not fully explore. Primary among these are for-profit work environments and large NGOs, although in interviewing people about their work in such environments, I heard many stories of racism in the workplace, of the perils of affirmative action, and of the successful forging of collegial relationships. Such research would be fascinating for what it would reveal about shifting hierarchies, generational differences, and the minute, daily shifts in perception nurtured by a changing work environment. Religious institutions are another arena where radical transformation is occurring in some quarters (paralleled by conservative intransigence in others), but where I spent little time. The explosion of evangelical Christian churches provides possibilities for fellowship and worship quite different from those of apartheid-era churches. Religious orientation was an important topic in many of my interviews, and I accompanied friends to worship services on numerous occasions; a study focusing on spiritual transformation during the past decade would be fascinating.[11]

Although I interviewed several members of the South African Parliament, I purposely did not focus on the government, the political elite, or on transformation in political institutions. Many studies of democratization and transformation focus on such institutional arenas, whereas my interest is the commonplace, mundane, and personal experiences of change. Another arena of transformation I barely explored is gender and sexuality. Cape Town's reputation as a premier destination for pink tourism has encouraged public and private discussions of sexuality. Excellent studies explore the relation between South Africa's transformation and gender roles, some prompted by the chasm between the constitutional affirmation of gender equality and reality. South Africa's HIV/AIDS pandemic has focused much social science research on this critical arena.

These are substantial gaps, and it is quite possible that research in these areas will question my findings. If so, our understanding of the challenges, complexities, and contradictions of transformation will be greater, not less.

.   .   .   .   .

The challenge of attempting an ethnography of urban transformation is one of scale and complexity, so I need to be clear about my goals, which are relatively modest. Through vignettes, anecdotes, quotes, and stories, I aim to provide a glimpse of what it feels like, for some people, to be living in Cape Town during these exciting and uncertain times. These stories won't reveal anything that Capetonians don't already know about themselves, but seeing their experiences filtered through an outsider's lens might, I hope, bring new perspectives or insights. Anthropologist David Graeber once wrote:

> When one carries out an ethnography, one observes what people do, and then tries to tease out the hidden symbolic, moral, or pragmatic logics that underlie their actions; one tries to get at the way people's habits and actions make sense in ways that they are not themselves completely aware of. One obvious role for a radical intellectual is to do precisely that: to look at those who are creating viable alternatives, try to figure out what might be the larger implications of what they are (already) doing, and then offer those ideas back, not as prescriptions, but as contributions, possibilities—as gifts.[12]

The greatest challenge in this study is how to communicate the passion with which people live and dream for the future. How can one convey people's emotionalism about the most important things in their lives, their rages, their pride? Carolyn Nordstrom once asked anthropology for "theory that laughs and cries"; Ruth Behar asks for an anthropology that breaks your heart.[13] I echo this desire for an anthropology that communicates laughter and tears, that deeply explores the contradictory spaces within which most people live, breathe, and make their peace with life.

CHAPTER 2

Legacies

"There was a fundamental lack of appreciation by the new government of the extent to which the legacy of the past would continue to shape postapartheid South Africa and to haunt its future" (Mamphela Ramphele)[1]

In the *Mail and Guardian,* 23 February–1 March 2001, Louise Holman, head of the Holman Institute for Educational and Psychological Evaluation and Research, reports that her surveys in sixty-five schools across all provinces reveal that 73 percent of grade-seven students don't know what apartheid was and 98 percent are unaware of township grievances under apartheid.

In a history class at Pinelands High School in 2001, I mention the *Mail and Guardian* article to the young teacher and ask about his students' knowledge of apartheid. "Well," he responds, "it's not just white kids. It's also black kids from the townships who don't know anything about apartheid. They didn't really experience the effects of apartheid directly. They never saw 'whites only' signs, or couldn't enter a building or bus or train because of their color. And their parents don't really seem to tell them much."

Al Witten, principal of Zerilda Park Primary School in Lavender Hill, explains one of his goals as an educator: "I want to teach these children *why* they live in Lavender Hill, why Lavender Hill exists, why life here is the way it is, why the government would build a sewage treatment plant across the street from a primary school in the middle of the community. I want them to know it's not their fault that they live here."

.   .   .   .   .

Table Mountain as seen from the city center. Photo by Jorge Acero.

To the tourist, Cape Town may be the world's most beautiful city. The downtown sits snuggled between the ocean and the majesty of Table Mountain, lined on one side by the gentrifying "Muslim Quarter"—the Bo-Kaap—with its cobbled streets and candy-colored cottages. Residential neighborhoods tucked along the base of Table Mountain look out over the neatly gridded city, centered on a large public garden surrounded by colonial and modern government buildings and museums. The garden ends at a pedestrian walkway that cuts through the center of downtown, lined with cafés, shops, and craft markets where closed-circuit cameras ensure safety. At night, cosmopolitan restaurants and vibey clubs spill out into downtown streets, serving every kind of cuisine from Thai to Moroccan, Turkish to Austrian, Mexican to Xhosa, and offering jazz, reggae, hip-hop, heavy metal, spoken word, African drumming, and even belly dancing. Cape Town is a destination spot for wine connoisseurs, surfers, backpackers, sports enthusiasts, photographers, and those of varied interests. One can enjoy a proper afternoon tea at the historic Mount Nelson hotel, where the doormen still wear British colonial uniforms complete with pith helmets and white gloves, or the more adventurous can opt to be suspended from the ceiling by cables and hooks through one's flesh at one of Cape Town's more alternative clubs.

Cape Town's Atlantic seaboard. Photo by Jorge Acero.

Part of the city's waterfront has been developed into an upscale des-tination spot, with luxury condos along lovely canals, a huge shopping and restaurant complex patrolled by security guards, outdoor perfor-mance spaces with a rotating roster of musicians and dancers, a stunning aquarium, and an IMAX theater. Beyond the tourist-oriented waterfront complex, the Atlantic seaboard from Cape Town to the southwest boasts spectacular scenery, beautiful beaches, and exorbitant real estate prices accessible only to South Africa's elite and international jet-setters. On the other side of the shopping complex, the working part of the waterfront devoted to shipping and trade adds a touch of authenticity and evinces Cape Town's economic links to the rest of the world.

To the south and east from Cape Town's secure tourist- and business-oriented downtown and waterfront area are many of its residential neigh-borhoods: fortified elite suburbs flowing around the base of Table Moun-tain to the south, and townships and informal settlements stretching across the Cape Flats to the east, home to the majority of Cape Town's citizens. Cape Town's northern suburbs, not included in this study, stretch along the N1 highway to the north of the Cape Flats. Everyone en-tering or leaving the city center from these residential areas passes by the

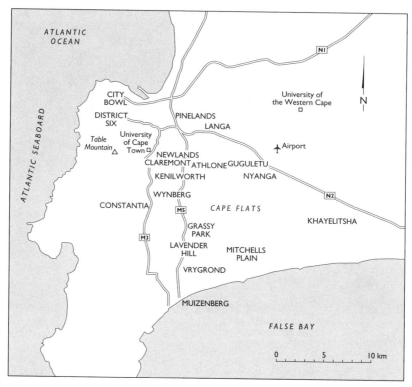

Cape Town

cleared area adjacent to downtown, dotted here and there with churches, where the multiracial urban neighborhood of District Six stood prior to its demolition by the apartheid government. Its scarred and barren landscape makes it one of the most visible reminders of the damages of apartheid's Group Areas Act, even though its demolition represents only a small piece of the much broader historical experience of displacement.[2] Because until very recently District Six remained largely uninhabited since its destruction, it is one of the few areas in Cape Town where debates about restitution for forced removals can actually focus on property rather than only monetary compensation. Reclaiming the property they lost under Group Areas is not an option for the tens of thousands of Capetonians whose former houses now have new occupants or were destroyed for private businesses or public facilities.

Continuing beyond District Six along the base of Table Mountain, one passes through the neighborhood of Woodstock, which retains some of the mixed feel that once characterized this part of the city. Ironically, gentrification has come to Woodstock, as young professionals attracted to the neighborhood for its multiracial character, charming architecture, and proximity to the downtown are driving out of the market local families who survived Group Areas removals. Following the lower slopes of the mountain, beyond Woodstock, one enters white space; one leafy suburb after another declared white under apartheid's Group Areas Act and "cleansed" of all black residents. The neighborhood of Observatory functions as the university district and thus maintains a transient bohemian student character, but the other suburbs—Rondebosch, Claremont, Newlands, Bishopscourt, Constantia—emanate whiteness. Further out toward the Cape Flats from the base of Table Mountain, separated from the ring of apartheid-era white neighborhoods by busy highways and strips of public land, are the suburbs designed by the apartheid government for coloured residents; communities of small, neat single-family homes adjacent to neighborhoods of overcrowded blocks of flats patrolled by local gangs. Further out still, on the southeastern sandy flats, are the densely packed townships and informal settlements that are home to the majority of Cape Town's African residents.

The way one moves through and experiences Cape Town has everything to do with where one was placed during the massive urban geography campaign engineered by the Group Areas Act of 1950. Prior to World War II, Cape Town was the least segregated city in South Africa. Although Africans had been legally segregated since 1890, Cape Town's southern suburbs were only half white, with the working-class neighborhoods stretching from the docks to Observatory being especially multiracial.[3] After Cape Town began implementing the Group Areas Act in 1957, all the southern suburbs except lower Wynberg were declared for whites only. By 1985, following the forced removal of 150,000 (mostly coloured) people from their homes, Cape Town had become the most segregated city in South Africa. Only 9 percent of coloured Capetonians remained "out of place" by 1985, mostly living in the Salt River, Woodstock, Rondebosch East, and Landsdowne areas.[4] Coloured families removed from the ring of white-designated space were relocated into a second ring of neighborhoods on the Cape Flats, separated from white neighborhoods by highways, open areas, railroad lines, and power stations: Bonteheuvel, Athlone, Grassy Park, Retreat, Lavender Hill, and beyond them, Manenberg, Heideveld, and the vast Mitchell's Plain.

Prior to World War II, Africans constituted a small minority of Cape Town's population because of laws controlling black population movement and property ownership; this demographic persisted because of the draconian limits on African immigration into the city emplaced by the 1954 designation of the Western Cape as a Coloured Labor Preference Area.[5] Africans legally resident in Cape Town were confined to Langa (Cape Town's oldest township, established in 1918), Nyanga (founded in 1948), and Guguletu (1958), but Africans entered the city illegally by the tens of thousands during the apartheid era, squatting throughout the metropolitan area in unused space, in backyard shacks on employers' land in white neighborhoods, and in between rental units in townships. The apartheid government regularly razed their camps until finally granting official recognition to the squatter settlement of Crossroads in 1976.[6] The desperate need for more housing prompted the government to designate Khayelitsha for Africans in 1983, although the housing and land allocation didn't come anywhere near meeting the demand.[7]

The combined policies of Group Areas, influx control, and Coloured Labor Preference resulted in massive housing shortages for black families. As the downtown and southern suburbs were purged of residents of color, those who could not afford new accommodation in coloured areas had to accept poor-quality dwellings in city council rental flats. But the supply of these flats was criminally low; by 1992, 42,570 coloured families were on the waiting list for subsidized council housing, most looking at a ten-year wait.[8] The housing shortage for Africans was even more acute because of the refusal to officially recognize the legitimate presence of Africans in the metropolitan area. No housing was built for Africans in the 1960s and 1970s,[9] forcing people to cram into existing dwellings in Langa, Guguletu, and Nyanga, to erect squatter settlements throughout the metropolitan area, and to build shacks in rented backyard space in townships.[10]

Today, over a decade after the end of apartheid, the racially segregated neighborhoods created by the Group Areas Act remain relatively unchanged; most people in Cape Town continue to live segregated lives and continue to be ignorant of the lives of people in other parts of the city. In the words of economist and urban planner Ivan Turok, "Cape Town remains one of the least altered cities in the country."[11] The southern suburbs remain mostly white and mostly well-to-do; the townships and informal settlements in the southeast remain completely black and mostly impoverished. During the day, schools and businesses in white neighborhoods and the downtown become integrated spaces; people of color from outlying areas commute in as students and workers. But at night Cape Town has, as Fanie du Toit of the Institute for Justice and Reconciliation expressed it, "nocturnal withdrawal." One Newlands

Informal settlement in Guguletu. Photo by the author.

resident, remarking on his frustration with the slow pace of residential desegregation, said, "We come together in public spaces, everyone intermingles, and then at night we all go home to our separate sections, our separate communities. It's terrible. Hard to see how it will change."

The careful apartheid planning that created elegant, well-serviced, comfortable white neighborhoods (with more houses available than families to live in them) simultaneously ensured massive housing shortages and overcrowding in the underserviced areas designated for black people and the proliferation of unserviced (and illegal) squatter settlements throughout the city.[12] Despite the projections (and fears) of white South Africans, few people of color have managed to move into formerly white areas, and the government has shown no political will to construct low-income housing in middle- and upper-class neighborhoods.[13] In stark contrast to the rainbow nation image so popular with foreigners, the slow pace of residential desegregation in Cape Town is one of the city's most notable features.

The enduring legacy of racial segregation and class formation as a result of apartheid policies in Cape Town is both profound and overlooked. It is profound because many coloured Capetonians still experience the emotional and psychological scars left from the destruction of their communities and extended family networks. Because the Group Areas Act and other property control laws created high-value white neighborhoods and low-value neighborhoods for black people, the children of those dispossessed by Group Areas continue to suffer economic discrimination because such policies ensured that black families amassed much less wealth to pass on to their children than did white families. It is also profound because poor young people of color inhabit an urban landscape clearly marked by class divisions, and their poverty ensures their exclusion from the opportunities and pleasures available to those living, working, and studying in formerly white—and now privately policed—space.

The legacy of apartheid-era racial segregation is overlooked because the self-sustaining geography of apartheid makes residential segregation seem natural and normal, and in comparison to the horrible and violent acts perpetrated by the apartheid government, property alienation and forced resettlement don't seem to register in the public consciousness as appalling and atrocious. But because the psychological and material damages of alienation and resettlement were left unaddressed by the Truth and Reconciliation Commission, and because restitution, desegregation, and new home construction have moved so slowly, the wounds left by the enforcement of Group Areas policies emerged in my research as a critically important part of Cape Town's post-apartheid story. This chapter and the next highlight some of the enduring emotional, psychological, and financial implications of apartheid-engineered residential segregation in order to demonstrate why apartheid racial barriers remain so difficult for many to cross.

. . . . .

During the 1990s, Cape Town's governing structures were deracialized, and in 2000, they were reorganized into a single metropolitan municipality called the Cape Town Unicity. The Unicity model offered the promise of integrated development planning specifically oriented to dismantling apartheid's racial and residential divides. Unfortunately, the record since 1994 has not been good for township dwellers. The development objectives of achieving global competitiveness and eradicating poverty have cohered around the neoliberal perspective of evaluating people as consumers, which in practice reinforces rather than reduces apartheid's geographical divisions. Although the government expanded the provision of basic services to historically excluded communities, treating people as consumers meant that thirty-five thousand Capetonians had their water supply cut off for failure to pay at some point during a three-year period following post-apartheid restructuring.[14] The first "City Improvement Districts" to be developed after 1994 were the downtown area and the Claremont business hub, and their targeted consumers were clearly in the business, tourism, and leisure arenas (mirroring the orientation of the glitzy new waterfront complex and the Century City shopping/ business/theme park complex). Apartheid-era white space, far from opening up to poor black Capetonians, has become increasingly exclusive as private security firms have assumed policing functions in shopping malls, gated communities, and leisure spaces, and spaces that seem open to the public are regulated by private owners through security and surveillance structures.[15] People access these spaces by, in effect, buying their way in. Those unable to pay, or those who don't feel entitled to enter privately policed, consumption-oriented spaces, are excluded.

Since the end of apartheid, private-sector investment and jobs have been concentrated in the affluent north and west, whereas the construction of low-income housing has been focused in the poorer southeast. The southeast has few business centers because of historic restrictions on black business, low skills and education levels, perceived insecurity, poor access to capital, poor infrastructure, redlining practices by financial institutions, community suspicion of outsiders, and local community politics such as barriers created by "traditional gatekeepers" that can hinder development initiatives (as one woman involved in community development in the southeast bluntly told me about the local bureaucrats whose support was essential for her project, "They are thugs!").[16]

The obvious initial solution to the growing divide between still largely white middle-class residential areas close to economic centers and the increasingly impoverished all-black communities of low-rent flats, backyard shacks, and informal settlements distant from economic centers is to construct low-income housing in areas close to centers of economic activity and to facilitate development of economic centers in the lower-income southeast. Although policy makers are aware of this, and planning documents since the early 1990s reiterate the need to direct development toward urban integration, the city has been unable to effect such changes. Residents' resistance to low-income housing in middle-class neighborhoods has been strong, and the political will to target low-income areas for economic development has been slow to develop. This contradiction is recognized in city planning documents; the March 2004 Draft Integrated Development Plan produced by the city of Cape Town states "policies and practices toward managing the city have been largely reactive, in that they have simply and continuously reinforced historical investment patterns. Little effort has gone into, and little success has been achieved, in creating significantly new patterns of opportunities. As the City has grown outwards it has become increasingly inaccessible, inequitable and inconvenient for the majority of people."[17]

.   .   .   .   .

I have the right to live wherever I want.

We have a right to live anywhere we like no matter if it's a white or black community.

Black people have the right to stay in the community of white people.

If you want to live in a white town that's your right.

We are humans, we have our own rights, and everyone is equal. So why can't we have things like suburbs?

We have the right to go anywhere we like.

Essay responses by secondary students in Langa on their
understanding of the concept of human rights

.   .   .   .   .

The right to make choices about where one lives emerged as a central theme in a group discussion about basic human rights I had in 2001 with high school students in Langa. But despite the knowledge that apartheid is over and black people can live anywhere they like, the reality is that few can afford to move into the formerly white suburbs. After emphasizing their right to live anywhere in the new South Africa, the students quoted above were also quick to note that although legal apartheid may have ended, economic apartheid continues to dominate their lives. (One girl argued that apartheid still exists because white people want it to and they have the power.) Although a middle-class coloured woman explained that "the blacks continue to live in townships because they like it there. It's their culture," the truth is material rather than cultural: poverty keeps township dwellers from moving into suburban spaces.

In addition to the obvious things that maintain poverty (namely, high unemployment and low educational achievement and skills levels), the patterns of property ownership created under Group Areas continue to determine who can live where. The urban geography of apartheid in Cape Town produced such massive inequality in property values that post-apartheid suburban integration has been slow and difficult and the material barriers that keep black people in townships are too great for many to surmount. Despite lots of complaints about the declining middle-class standard of living, no one is moving from suburbs to townships.

Since the end of apartheid, property values in the southern suburbs and Atlantic coast have skyrocketed. A friend's house in Newlands rose in value from R270,000 in the 1990s to R2 million in 2003. Similar stories flow from real estate offices throughout the southern suburbs and are widely reported in local and national newspapers. People forbidden to buy into the real estate market in white neighborhoods under apartheid (or those forced under Group Areas to sell their homes in areas designated for whites) have become, in the decade after apartheid, unable to move because of market factors. People of color who achieved a comfortable lifestyle during the apartheid years, but who were unable to buy or retain their property in the southern suburbs, often invested in homes in middle-class coloured neighborhoods and now sit with over-capitalized residences they cannot sell at a profit because their beautiful homes are not in "desirable areas." Their resentment about this fact often remains unspoken—compared to the grievances and bodily harms suffered by others under apartheid, unfair property valuations for middle-class coloured families seems relatively minor. But for those families, this historical fact is ever present and affects their relationships with white colleagues and friends who live in neighborhoods with high property values from which coloured families were evicted and excluded. Wendy, the study abroad program administrator, and her husband, Peter, describe how a white couple with whom they worked in multiracial church networks bought inexpensive property in Constantia thirty years ago when both couples were newlyweds. Wendy's and Peter's families had been evicted from their southern suburban homes by the Group Areas Act, and after their marriage Wendy and Peter lived in a community designated for coloureds. The white couple encouraged Wendy and Peter to buy the property adjoining theirs in Constantia, unaware or forgetful of the fact that people of color were purged from Constantia under the Group Areas Act. Thirty years later, I spent an evening with both couples during which we toasted the white couple on the upcoming sale of their Constantia property, which would provide them enough income for a comfortable retirement. No one mentioned the circumstances under which they bought the property or the fact that the properties available under Group Areas for Wendy and Peter to buy would only net a fraction of the sale price of the Constantia property.

In a separate conversation, another successful coloured businessman compared the property value of his nice home in the coloured middle-class community of Grassy Park with those of his white friends in Constantia and angrily reflected to me, "Oh, how we forget! Apartheid made them rich and us poor!" In addition to reading Cape Town as a landscape of lost communities and disrupted family histories, middle-class coloured Capetonians understand the long-term economic impact of this history in a way that seems to elude their white counterparts.

Unlike in other parts of South Africa, Cape Town township property prices have not improved, meaning that the severe price gradient separating southern suburban homes and township homes continues to widen. Turok suggests home prices in more affluent parts of Cape Town are up to one hundred times greater than in formal townships, a gap which has widened over the past two decades as housing prices in the former areas have more than doubled in real terms while housing prices in the townships have increased by only a few percentage points.[18] Augmenting this trend is the fact that the number of households and the average household incomes in the northern and southern suburbs have been rising, because residents' skills are desirable in the new economy of infotech firms and its demand for professionals, whereas incomes in the southeast are dropping because of residents' low skills and education and reduced manual employment as manufacturing has declined in the face of international competition.

Many white people dismiss such residential inequalities as trivial. While the claims that coloured people never lived or owned property in the southern suburbs is not true, such remarks reveal the level of ignorance many white people have about the economic legacy of Group Areas in post-apartheid Cape Town. Another point of ignorance is the unfair historical pattern of property taxes that worked to white people's advantage and the creation of a real estate market that ensured that property in white neighborhoods maintained a high value. Residents in these neighborhoods continue to assume their entitlement to these properties and to their right to bequeath their property to their children. When the process of revaluing land for tax purposes got under way and people in exclusive neighborhoods realized their property taxes would escalate, local newspapers were flooded with letters to the editor about this newest post-apartheid outrage. One angry homeowner in upmarket Hout Bay wrote to complain that his glamorous villa, built for R27,000 in the 1960s, was now being valued at R1.5 million, resulting in a dramatic increase in his property taxes. He is outraged at this "wealth tax," arguing that his family arrived in the cape in the 1600s and contributed to building the area, that he built his Hout Bay home where there was nothing, and now these "Johnny-come-latelies want to come and change everything!" Again, the role of apartheid policy in granting him access to a stunning piece of property, guaranteeing him cheap labor to construct a mansion, protecting its value, and ensuring low taxes is utterly ignored in his assumptions about his rights and entitlements.

Similarly, in conversations with white people who were distressed about the rising costs of real estate in Cape Town, I came to realize that my interlocutors almost always limited their consideration of where to live to just a few formerly white neighborhoods. The possibility of buying a home in a formerly coloured neighborhood, or a mixed neighborhood, did not enter their consideration. Listening to their complaints, it was apparent that they felt *entitled* to be able to purchase homes in the elite formerly white neighborhoods—other areas were simply unimaginable.

For most people in Cape Town, rather than protecting their property values, apartheid property policy ensured they could not enter the real estate market. Although some people of color who managed a middle-class status under apartheid were able to avoid being forced to settle in a township area, the majority of people displaced by Group Areas found themselves banished to distant township locations in the southeast, which few have managed to leave. Council flat accommodations, backyard shacks, and informal settlements grant their residents no place in the real estate market. Apartheid's economic legacy is starkly visible in Cape Town's townships, where poverty severely constrains people's efforts to raise their children in safe environments and to achieve a higher standard of living in the "new" South Africa.

. . . . .

Thirty-year-old Salomie grew up in her mother's council flat in the economically depressed, gang-ridden township of Lavender Hill, formed following the forced removals from District Six. In the three-room flat, Salomie shared a room with double bunks with her infant daughter, her ten-year-old brother, her sister, her eldest brother, and three others. A severe asthmatic, Salomie struggled with illness from sleeping in a room with so many other people. Desperate for a place of their own, she and her daughter's father, Ismael, bought construction materials for a shack for R140 ($20) from a friend, which they constructed in 1992 in the cramped yard space between the council flats and the street. Salomie paid her mother R200 ($28) per month for the use of the backyard space, shared with several other shacks, and for access to running water inside her mother's flat. Shortly thereafter Salomie lost her job as a housekeeper because she refused a request that she live with her employer, which would have required her to leave behind her infant daughter. Salomie's mother helped them with food until Salomie found a part-time job working as a housekeeper at Wendy's office. Salomie's mother had been Wendy's char-woman, and the two women had known each other for years.

After Salomie gave birth to a son and married Ismael, her living con-ditions continued to deteriorate. Her brother was murdered by a gang leader in the street outside her home, and bullets came through her walls with terrifying frequency. She found herself all too often huddled on the floor on top of her children, shielding them from gunfights on the street outside her shack. Her other brother, a gangster, twice broke into her house to steal; her neighbors in the adjoining backyard shacks were in-volved with gang activity. She feared their influence on her young son.

Deciding she had to move, Salomie approached the city council in 2002 about renting a council flat and was told there were "something like eighty thousand names" ahead of her on the list, so her turn wouldn't come up for over a decade. She began scouring the newspapers looking for something to rent or buy outside of Lavender Hill, but she found the prices beyond her means. In frustration, she explained: "There's nothing in there for me, and I get cross and miserable and angry with myself."

Finally, Salomie approached Wendy and another employer to ask for help in locating a new home. They began touring homes for sale in her price range (R45,000, $6,428), but they were shocked at the appalling state and dangerous neighborhoods of many of the available homes. The repossessed houses in her price range were far away, and land on which she could build her own home was not available unless she was willing to relocate almost twenty-five kilometers away from the city.

When, after almost a year of searching, it became apparent that mov-ing out of Lavender Hill to a safer neighborhood would not be an op-tion, Salomie finally found a suitable home in another part of Lavender Hill for R45,000 through a real estate agent. She learned she could apply for a government-sponsored first-time home owner's subsidy from the bank for R12,700, and she applied for a bond through a bank for the balance. It seemed her fortunes were turning.

To Salomie's chagrin, however, the bank turned down her application because she had been blacklisted for unpaid debts. Salomie had run up debts many years earlier, before losing her job when she had been un-willing to become a live-in maid:

> When you're young, you go into shops. You have a job; you just want to
> open accounts. I created my debt in one year because I was thinking, "I

have a job. I can afford to pay them." I never thought of what would happen if I lose my job and am sitting at home. When you're young, you don't think like that. I did domestic work for a lady in Southfield for five years, but when she wanted me to sleep in, I refused. My husband was working at the time as a contractor, so I wasn't worried. But I couldn't pay my debts. They sent me letters which I ignored. But then the gunshots began, and the murders, and I realized I needed to move. I phoned the shops and told them to come get the things. Some did come, but I was left with three debts: MNET [a cable company], Edgars [clothing], and furniture. That's the biggest mistake in your life that you must never do.

Salomie concludes, weeping: "It's a habit. It's a bad habit."[19]

That Salomie's debts were relatively small demonstrates how difficult it is for people who work as domestics and casual laborers to acquire basic items like clothing and furniture. Salomie's outstanding debts totaled R10,500 (about $1,300; inflated by interest from the original amounts), and she had been afraid to tell her employers she was blacklisted. She described her feelings of being caught in the middle of a dark swirling mass: "The blacklisting was surrounding me—it was whirling around me. Being blacklisted is a thing you can't get out of. It can destroy your whole life." She was becoming ill with worry about her debts.

Salomie lost the chance for the house and realized that banks wouldn't even consider her for other loans. The credit bureau debt collection agency discovered where she worked and began bringing her bills to the office. Wendy explained that she was going to have to find a way to repay her debt and overcome her blacklisted status if she ever wanted to get a loan for a house. Given her poverty, Salomie felt there was absolutely no way she could manage to pay back the debt. She felt that she'd learned her lesson from being blacklisted and was humiliated and overwhelmed: "I'm blacklisted. Why must I pay you—you already blacklisted me! I've got a bad name and bad credit." Salomie found her blacklisted status deeply traumatizing because she wanted so much to maintain a reputation as "a good person," both at home and at work. She knew her employers found her responsible and smart and was proud to be respected by her neighbors and coworkers.

In addition to feeling overwhelmed by humiliation and poverty, Salomie was influenced by the rhetoric at her church, the American-based Church of Power, which preached that she needed to hand her problems to God and that if she donated 10 percent of her income to the church, she would receive a tenfold return. She prayed fervently for God to intervene but received no response. Just when she was ready to give up her dream of moving, a teenager drove a car through the wall of her shack, destroying one of her three rooms and smashing her remaining furniture to bits. She and Ismael worked until midnight to close the opening, and that night someone was killed in the street just a few feet from the opening left by the car. In desperation, she consulted a religious coworker, who counseled her that God was waiting for her to take the first move, to take responsibility, and then he would help with the rest.

Salomie worked out a payment plan and accepted donations from several people at work to put toward her debt. Wendy negotiated with the shops to lower their interest rate. When another house in Lavender Hill became available for R52,000 ($7,428), one of her employers paid off the R6,000 ($857) balance on her debt to clear her name, accepting no-interest monthly payments from her until the debt is repaid.

But even after Salomie cleared her debt problems, the next bank to which she applied for a loan rejected her application because the property is in Lavender Hill. Redlining practices used by banks and financial institutions mean an additional barrier to home ownership for township residents.[20] The most they would consider was a 70 percent bond for that area. Salomie, who is ashamed of the stigma attached to Lavender Hill, normally tells people she lives in Retreat to avoid being tainted with Lavender Hill's notorious reputation. But admitting residence in Lavender Hill is unavoidable on a bank loan application.

Finally, after several years devoted to the process, Salomie was able to obtain a loan from a specialty bank that had been established to help people in her situation, and at last she moved into her own home. Of her R2,200 ($314) monthly salary (although she earns an occasional R110 per week when she takes on additional housekeeping jobs at private homes), she must pay R400 to her employer who covered her debt, R800 to the bank to repay her loan, R20 to the government for unemployment, and R260 transportation fare for her and her children. She is left with about R720 per month (about $102) for all her other expenses. But for her, the sacrifice is worth it: "It was always my dream to have my own house. I dream the whole time when I walk by other people's houses. . . . It's a sacrifice to have a home. If you have porridge at night [because you have little money left from the purchase of your home], no one knows because it's inside your own home."

For Salomie, who has a steady income as a housekeeper, moving out of the township was an impossible dream. Even buying her own home within the township was difficult, and only possible because of the assistance and intervention of both of her employers, who helped her repay

New Rest. Photo by the author.

loans, look at available properties, and negotiate with banks and real estate agents. Many township residents do not have sources of support outside their communities to help them manage the financial and bureaucratic hurdles characteristic of the real estate market. They are multiply burdened by constraints they do not control: their poverty, the stigma attached to the places they live, the redlining practices that financially imprison stigmatized neighborhoods, the steep gradient that separates insecure township dwellings from safe middle-class neighborhoods, and the legacy of government policies that created impoverished townships in the first place.

.   .   .   .   .

When I met him, Siyabonga Knowledge Shwala, a engaging, friendly competitive runner and high school student, inhabited a tiny shack in the informal (squatter) settlement of New Rest, built over a swampy area alongside the township of Guguletu below the busy N2 highway. About five thousand people make their homes there, in an assortment of ramshackle dwellings made from bits of old wood, plastic bags, cardboard, and salvaged pieces of tin. A few dirt pathways—soggy in winter, dusty in summer—wind through the settlement, along which are a couple of outdoor spigots that provide potable water and a few bucket latrines housed in individual cement cubicles.

Siyabonga's late mother in their shack, New Rest, 2003. Photo by the author.

Due to escalating tensions in his father's household in KwaZulu-Natal, Siyabonga ran away from home at age sixteen and made his way to Cape Town to join his mother, who had left him as a six-year-old child in the care of his father when their marriage failed. When he found his mother in New Rest, Siyabonga learned that the intervening years had not been easy for her: "My mom had a very bumpy ride. She lived and worked places I don't even want to mention."[21] Their home consisted of two tiny rooms, each able to hold little more than a bed, constructed of cantilevered sticks of wood lined with plastic bags and bits of cardboard. The rooms leaned perilously to one side, so that Siyabonga and his mother—both tall—had to maintain a constantly bent posture to maneuver between the two damp and sometimes flooded rooms.

After he arrived in Cape Town Siyabonga enrolled at a technical college, but after a year switched to grade ten at a secondary school in Langa, where the fees were more affordable at just over one hundred rand (fourteen dollars) per year. Every day Siyabonga commuted from Guguletu to Langa, where he became a model student well regarded for his leadership skills, maturity, and strong sense of pride and integrity. He received good grades and excellent evaluative comments and was chosen to participate in several school activities and volunteer projects, including the peer mentoring program with my American students, which is how I came to meet Siyabonga early in 2000. For the next several years, Siyabonga was a regular visitor at the Colby-Bates-Bowdoin Centre, sometimes attending classes and workshops, using the computer lab for his e-mail and for school projects, always making his presence known with his deep resonant voice and confident presentation of self. When I first visited Siyabonga's home in 2003, he showed me through the two little rooms and then said with his disarming smile, "So this is where I come home to after I leave the center up in Newlands."

Halfway through his senior year, Siyabonga returned home from school one day to find that his mother had suffered a stroke. His sole source of emotional and material support, she had become incapacitated and had to remain in the hospital for a month and receive in-home care following her release. He tried to hold things together for himself in order to get through high school, "but I was really in trouble. I had no one whose shoulder I could cry on. I had to pretend I was all right, I was coping, but inside I was in shock and couldn't let anyone see. My mother is my only family and I didn't know what to do. It was like my mind went blank and I lost the ability to think." Siyabonga had been chosen by his teachers to participate in a two-week exchange program to the United States following the end of the school year, and he pushed all his problems aside in excited anticipation of the trip.

After his return from the trip, Siyabonga received the shocking news that he had failed his matric (graduation) exam, which means he is not considered a high school graduate:

> Everything began to unravel with my mother's stroke. I kept focusing on the trip to Seattle, thinking I could forget what had happened and that it would somehow go away. But of course, when I returned, it was all still here. And I was falling apart. When my exam results came and I saw how I had totally failed, the shock was too great for me. My mother asked me about repeating my matric [senior] year, but I couldn't return to that school. They destroyed me. I had to find something else I could do, so I thought to get a job and make my goal to build a house. I decided to put everything I had into building a house. I couldn't think about school, because my heart wasn't healed and my head was in the mist.

Siyabonga showed me his portfolio of term results, which showed his consistently good grades as well as handwritten remarks from the teachers: "Excellent results. You are doing a great job." "You are a great pleasure to have in class." I learned that, despite the fact that he received excellent math marks for grade eleven, his class was without a teacher for most of that year. Their teacher never returned after the midyear break, leaving the students on their own for the remainder of the year. The principal, who couldn't get funding from the department for another teacher, tried to arrange extra Saturday classes and (unsuccessfully) to find somebody in the community willing to volunteer as a part-time math teacher. When the students entered grade twelve, they were severely handicapped in math. Siyabonga and another classmate, Frank, described the efforts they undertook to locate another math teacher during grade eleven. "We even said we would go on strike!" Frank recalled, laughing. "But we realized it wouldn't do us any good—we'd just get behind in our other classes." Siyabonga recalled how they tried to "hijack" a teacher from another grade: "We begged him to teach us. But he refused. He didn't have any time."

Siyabonga's failure demonstrates the terrible legacy of inferior "Bantu education," the companion policy to Group Areas: a dedicated student with strong grades is so failed by the situation at his school that he cannot manage to pass the national matric exam. For some, education might seem to be a way to overcome the barriers of township poverty, but no one living in townships or involved with township schools to whom I tell this story is surprised.

Siyabonga had little or no control over the circumstances that constrained his life: his mother's poor health and consequent lack of an income, his inability to pass high school (due to a variety of factors, including his interrupted schooling, his stress over his mother's illness, and chronic teacher absenteeism), and the encompassing poverty of the informal settlement in which he and his mother live. Unable to change his mother's health, and emotionally too damaged to return to school, Siyabonga turned his attention to the one thing he could change: his immediate living environment.

During 2003, Siyabonga began constructing a new home for himself and his mother, to replace the dilapidated shack. He wanted a sturdier dwelling without leaks, constructed of two-by-fours and nails, with a poured cement floor, larger rooms, and a higher ceiling. When I asked how old he was when he built the shack in which they currently reside, he responded with dismay, "What? You think I would build something like that? How can you think that I would build something like that?" I realized I was doing the white liberal thing, trying to protect Siyabonga by pretending to normalize something which any idiot can see is a disaster of a place to live. I laughed and said I didn't want to hurt his feelings by telling him he'd done a bad job the first time around—I was relieved to learn the shack was not an indication of his carpentry abilities. "I know what I'm

Siyabonga in front of his new house, New Rest, 2004. Photo by the author.

doing," he said. "This one will be a proper house." With small amounts of money earned here and there, he bought pallets (which he pulled apart to build the frame), nails, and corrugated tin for the roof, and a high school principal arranged a full-time summer job at a large corporation. His modest salary paid off his mother's debts and allowed him to buy small household items: cooking pots and utensils, some furniture, a few new clothes, and one personal luxury—his pride and joy—a music system.

While Siyabonga's dream is a small flat in the southern suburbs, where rents run about R3,500 ($500) per month, his hand-constructed home (which now boasts three rooms, high ceilings, electricity, glass windows, and burglar bars) cost him under R1,000 ($143) and a lot of labor time. But because he lives in an informal settlement—courtesy of Group Areas and influx control laws—his property has no market value and can never be traded up for something better. The legacy of apartheid's educational and residential policies—policies that were abandoned when he was a young child—continues to utterly impact his life as a young man.

. . . . .

In their masterful analysis of how, in the United States, race-based inequalities accumulate over generations, tying white accumulation to black disaccumulation, the sociologist Michael Brown and his colleagues note: "Most of the current gap in life chances and various measures of performance between blacks and whites reflects the legacy of past decisions—decisions that cumulatively resulted in a profound imbalance in the most fundamental structures of opportunity and support in America. In housing, in education, in transportation, in employment policy, and in income support/social insurance policy, the choices that systematically disadvantaged black Americans were also ones that, by design or otherwise, benefited white Americans. These policies, in combination and over generations, have had enormous and pervasive consequences. . . . The majority of white Americans today do not comprehend the multiple ways in which their lives are enhanced by a legacy of unequal advantage."[22] Urban planning, development initiatives, and economic policies during Cape Town's first post-apartheid decade have ensured exactly this pattern.

The social scientist Jeremy Seekings poses the question of why the landless poor have not spearheaded massive land invasions onto prime unused land.[23] He suggests that the poor believe the state has the ability and the desire to keep them out of middle-class areas. Indeed, the poor can see very clearly that the development initiatives and new gated communities and leisure spaces on the waterfront and in the southern and northern suburbs are not for them, and they are aware that the state will intervene to protect middle-class interests if necessary. During two of my stays in Cape Town, I lived in the southern suburb of Newlands, where I witnessed firsthand the protection of middle-class interests. For example, gatekeeping issues continually dominated the newsletters over several years from the city councilor representing Newlands: an obsessive concern with policing graffiti, always assumed to be the work of those outside the neighborhood; efforts to obtain public funding to repair a decorative gateway demarcating a historic neighborhood boundary; and assurances that the councilor was working to permanently remove the few homeless individuals who made their homes in the lot of a public building on Main Road.

The neighborhood association repeatedly reacted strongly against the possibility of introducing mixed-use or denser residential patterns into the area. Newlands contains one of Cape Town's original estates—a large tract of wooded land used recreationally by the neighborhood association and by parliamentarians. In 1996, a major South African businessman who was awarded a contract by the government to develop the area announced plans to subdivide the property for luxury housing, but

a group of coloured land claimants who had been evicted from Claremont during Group Areas also identified the property as suitable for redistribution to victims of forced removals. Newlands property owners
vehemently objected to either form of residential development of the
area, arguing that its history as a rural estate and the special character
of the neighborhood must be respected.[24] Similarly, when a property
owner in wealthy neighboring Bishopscourt proposed to subdivide his
enormous property into two lots, the residents association of Newlands
objected, arguing that the proposal "threatened to change the unique
character of Bishopscourt and would set a precedent."[25] The Bishopscourt Residents' Association acknowledged the need for higher residential densities within the city but argued that "a well-balanced city
should have a range of densities." Despite their claims to support "sensitive densification" of the city, the authorities deferred to the neighborhood association protests and denied the request.

What is unclear is how long the poor will be willing to wait for the
state to get around to making real its rhetoric of inclusiveness and urban
integration. While many in the older generation may be unwilling at the
moment to forcefully challenge the residential status quo created by
apartheid policies, those I interviewed in the younger generation speak
with intense anger and growing impatience about ongoing residential
segregation. People of color deeply resent the continuity of apartheid
space.

The statistics and facts on forced removals, housing shortages, and
squatter demographics do not convey much about the experiences they
so neatly summarize. Nor do they convey the ignorance of many economically comfortable Capetonians about the ongoing impact of the
legacy of apartheid-era property controls. How do people navigate the
social and physical spaces that endure as apartheid's legacy? In a society
self-consciously trying to transform, how do people build new kinds of
relationships and social networks across apartheid's racial boundaries
when neighborhoods remain segregated and development initiatives reinforce rather than transcend old boundaries? How do people come to
terms with the immensely unjust legacy of the past, indelibly written into
the landscape of residential neighborhoods, schools, and churches?
What does it feel like to live in such a landscape? How do coloured families respond to the claims of white residents of their former neighborhoods that "no evictions happened *here*"? How does a black woman
who lives in a shack in an informal settlement and works as a maid respond to the comment of her white employer that blacks can't really

claim any right to property in Cape Town because they never had any right to own land in the first place, that now if they want land, they have to acquire it "just like everybody else," through the real estate market? When the maid earns only ten dollars a day, with no benefits? What real estate market will let her in?

.   .   .   .   .

Having decided to take some visiting relatives out to the wine country for a few days, I found a nice bed-and-breakfast in Stellenbosch, "now restored to its former Victorian glory" according to the brochure. The chatty owner, a young white man, explained that he and his siblings had converted "the family home" into an inn. All four sons were raised in the home: "you can still see our family's baby high chair in the corner of the parlor where breakfast is served to our guests." The daughter, working at the reception desk, was for some reason left out of the narrative. We were assigned to one of the lovely family cottages adjacent to the original home, which the owner described as "the original slave quarters." Back at work in Cape Town after the trip, Wendy, the study abroad program director, asked me where we stayed and told me she had tried to reach me before I left to suggest I drive by her family's ancestral home, where she spent the early years of her childhood before her family was evicted during Group Areas. As I described the charming inn I found on Ryneveld Street, she got a funny look on her face and questioned me carefully about its location and appearance. The inn is her family's home. "Slave cottages!" Wendy exploded at my description of the current owner's "our family home" narrative. "Those were my aunt's cottages!"

The home and adjoining cottages had been owned by Wendy's maternal grandfather, who also owned the surrounding land, which he farmed. After the family was forced to leave the property in the 1970s (after being made to pay rent to the city for several years before ultimately receiving a pittance in compensation), later owners sold off the farmland and gardens to developers and turned the house and cottages into an inn. The location near Stellenbosch University and the downtown makes the property extremely valuable and popular with visitors. The loss of the property was shattering for the family, particularly for the surviving elderly aunt, who still lives in the coloured area to which she was removed. In 1995, Wendy's brother filed a land claim on her behalf for the loss of this property, just as he had already done for the loss of his father's parents' land. By early 2004, the claim had made no progress through the inefficient land claims bureaucracy, but the family emphasizes that for them the claim is symbolic rather than economic. They are aware of how much wealth the property brought to those who acquired the property after they were forced to sell it and realize they will never be able to recoup that financial loss. But, as Wendy says, "It's to get the truth, so that whoever is out there knows the truth, so that the guy who tells the story about his family house and the 'slave quarters' knows the truth."

The "truth," while perhaps recognized in some bland, general, abstract way by white people who now occupy homes that once belonged to coloured families, seems to remain quietly unacknowledged and even delegitimized. The constant refrains "Well, they never really *owned* the property" or "No coloured people ever lived *here*—it's always been a white area"[26] deflect the truth and steer the conversation away from uncomfortable topics at dinner tables and cocktail parties. But for people whose lives were detrimentally transformed by the forced removals under Group Areas, Cape Town's landscape reads like a geography of lost homes, disrupted communities, and painful memories.

Many of my early journeys around the southern suburbs were accompanied by stories of loss: Tracy drove me through Claremont's Harfield Village, where three generations of her family occupied two rows of adjoining cottages and she grew up playing in the streets with her cousins, watched over by an army of aunts, uncles, and grandparents. When Harfield Village was declared for whites only, her family was separated and sent to different locations farther out on the Flats. Lynn drove me past her childhood home in Observatory, discussing her concern for her aging parents, removed from suburban Observatory to dangerous Bonteheuvel. During the memorable first drive through Newlands on my very first visit to Cape Town with my two American colleagues, our South African associate Bernard Dudley, and a white real estate agent to look at properties that might house our study abroad program, I was wedged in the back seat between Bernard and one of the Americans, who innocently asked the agent about forced removals in the Newlands Village area. She benignly replied, "Oh, no, that didn't happen here. These were always white-owned properties." Bernard became apoplectic, straining against his seat belt toward the front seat to tell his family's story. As we happened, at that very moment, to be driving by Dudley Street (named for his family), he began shouting, "That's my father's street! That was my father's house!" The alarmed real estate agent, trying to safely maneuver the narrow streets, studied Bernard in the rearview mirror—did she not know his apartheid racial classification was coloured? Could she possibly not know the history of forced removals in Newlands? "Oh!" she retreated. "I didn't know. Of course, it was all terrible."

I realized, over the next several years, how pervasive "not knowing" is in the white southern suburban communities. Whereas the obliteration of District Six is undeniable (even though many white residents argue that "it was just a slum" and those who were evicted "didn't actually *own* property there"), the whiteness of the southern suburbs appears to many as natural and orderly, underscored by an unwillingness to acknowledge how much effort went into creating such ordered residential landscapes—landscapes that residents feel are now threatened. Remarks like "Well, they have no claim because they never owned property here" obliterate both the historic coloured presence and the memories of community and belonging people retain for the areas from which they were evicted.

During our stays in Newlands, my husband regularly jogged by a stone church situated at the end of a small park adjacent to some stone cottages near Kirstenbosch Gardens and used by the botanical society. Noticing that the church congregation included coloured people coming from other communities, he questioned our neighbors about the history of the area around the church. People were vague, focusing mostly on its use as a nature park. Only when the District Six Museum began its project on the history of Protea Village did we learn that the park had once been part of a community of 110 families, evicted in the 1960s under Group Areas. Rather than acknowledging the injustices of the removals, or the pain of a destroyed community, the first neighborhood response to the land claim filed by former Protea Village residents focused on the importance of retaining the natural environment of the area (as opposed to supporting a return to the area of former residents). None of my neighbors attended the opening of the Protea Village exhibit at the District Six Museum, nor did any representatives from the well-organized neighborhood association join in the speeches of public acknowledgment that marked the opening ceremonies.

In contrast to the tendency of white residents to obliterate coloured history in their neighborhoods, coloured people removed from the southern suburbs during Group Areas have an excruciating awareness of the old borders and can recite exactly where the borders were drawn in their old neighborhoods. Whereas my neighbors in Newlands avoided any acknowledgment of a historic coloured presence in their neighborhood, the former residents of Protea Village who attended the exhibit at the District Six Museum excitedly pointed out their former homes and gardens on the maps and photographs that made up the exhibit.[27]

When different understandings of the past collide, the result can be dramatic. The angry accusations and public arguments reported in the newspapers in 2002 surrounding land claims made by coloured families evicted from downtown Claremont—now developed into a busy, upscale shopping mall—demonstrated the ongoing deep anger on the part of people who feel their historical experiences of loss are being trivialized.[28] Similarly, exclusive schools in white neighborhoods face challenges when residents who were evicted from their catchment areas under Group Areas appeal to these schools to accept their children. Tracy, the woman whose family had been evicted from Harfield Village, had wanted to send her child to the excellent primary school that serves the Harfield Village neighborhood. The school rejected her child's application, however, on the grounds that priority was given to siblings of current pupils, residents in the catchment area, or children whose parents were alumni. Tracy and her husband did not fit any of the criteria. Although she knew several other coloured couples whose applications were similarly rejected, and who accepted this outcome, she decided to take the school to task for its willful ignorance of the past. Tracy recounted how she and her husband attacked the school's criteria for acceptance in an angry letter to the school's governing board: "The only reason we don't live in the catchment area and aren't alumni is because we were thrown out of the area under Group Areas! You can't use this as criteria for admittance. It smacks of elitism!" The school, chagrined, revisited its policy and accepted Tracy's daughter, as well as the children of several other couples with similar historic ties to the area. Reflecting on this experience, Tracy observed how hard it is, even now, to feel entitled to make such a challenge—to think outside of the old categories.

Alternatively, the experience of colliding histories can be painful silence and disengagement. Johanna, who lives in Kenilworth, had a contractor visit her home one day to make a bid on a small job. He walked silently through the house, studied the area to be renovated, and then told her he wasn't interested in the job. His family had been evicted from this very same house during Group Areas—forced to relocate to Mitchell's Plain—and on principle he refused to work there. Johanna tried to talk to him about his experience during that time, but he was unwilling to engage. "Or at least he was unwilling to engage with *me*," Johanna observed. "No, I can't imagine he would be," commented Wendy's husband, Peter, when Johanna recounted to him this conversation. Peter's family had been evicted from another street in Johanna's neighborhood, and he can well understand the pain of chatting over coffee with the stranger—even an empathetic stranger—who now lives in your family's former home.

. . . . .

Of course, some families of color have managed to cross apartheid's geographical boundaries and reintegrate wealthier neighborhoods reserved for whites under apartheid, although the number of interracial property transfers in the 1990s—mostly coloured families moving into white neighborhoods—was shockingly low.[29] Black families and young professionals are integrating southern suburban neighborhoods, but at a much slower pace than many had anticipated. Stories about white reactions to new black neighbors circulate throughout Cape Town as party jokes, such as the time someone called the police on a black (university professor) jogger, who turned out to be a neighborhood resident, or the time a white man mistook his new black neighbor (a prominent judge) for the gardener and told him to ask his master if he could also work next door one day a week.

In addition to enduring such ridiculous expressions of racism, people of color integrating white space carry a distinctive burden, familiar to those charged with the task of integrating everywhere. Coloured families integrating white space not only suffer the ignorance of their neighbors about the unequal legacies of apartheid, but also become compelled to take on the role of educators. Working closely with Wendy over several years made me a witness to the unending explanations of the past she must provide to her white friends and associates, and the unending patience she must bring to ignorant comments about the present. Shortly after my return from Stellenbosch, for example, I overheard her talking with another white coworker about a landlord-renter conflict. The coworker was saying, "Why does this government make eviction so difficult! It doesn't make any sense!"

"Well," Wendy responded, "we have a history of unjust eviction. My family was evicted." Surprised, the coworker asked to hear the story, which Wendy recounted yet again. But after decades of cross-racial engagement, Wendy and Peter are getting tired of playing the role of educators. They find they've retreated into themselves a bit because they are tired of being conciliatory, tired of being responsible for whites' education, even well-meaning white friends who claim "they didn't know." But, generously I think, Peter suggested to me that white people *don't* know, really, the incredible pain and suffering of dislocation. They know about forced removals—"but it was a slum"; "but they didn't own the buildings"; "yes, it was terrible, but that's all over now." But their "experience" of apartheid was "whites only" signs. To them, apartheid meant separateness (yes, all right, inequality too) and not knowing each other. As one of Wendy's coworkers said, "I feel anger about the friends and relationships that I might have had but were denied to me by apartheid." They didn't *know* the humiliation and terrible trauma of losing a home and a neighborhood community, the stresses on the family, or the severe and enduring material consequences of unequal tax burdens, unequal access to property ownership, to transportation, to business districts, to workplaces, and to schools.

These insidious issues continue to affect the consciousness of Capetonians of color as they go about their lives in the post-apartheid city. These are issues that few people talk about publicly, yet they are personally significant in how Capetonians orient themselves to the city and to each other.[30] When compared to the horrible human rights abuses of the apartheid security forces, these issues seem minor and less important, yet these are the mundane things that matter to people and that contribute to underlying resentments and disappointments at the individual level and within families.

. . . . . .

"The most devastating aspect of the legacy of racism and sexism is the poor human and intellectual resource base our society has to contend with. . . . The most tragic area of poor performance is education. . . . The inherited legacy of a disabling educational philosophy, poor quality of the teaching corps in many areas of South Africa where the majority of black people continue to live, as well as poor national and provincial leadership have perpetuated the inequalities of opportunities between the 'haves' and the 'have-nots.'" (Mamphela Ramphele).[31]

Apartheid rules forbidding blacks to develop skills is "the worst of all apartheid's crimes against humanity. Its legacy is now the new democratic regime's greatest liability." (Cyril Ramaphosa)[32]

. . . . . .

The apartheid policies that structured racial residential segregation also provided dramatically inferior education in the townships. Education statistics from Cape Town's African townships are shocking and reflect, even more than housing and residential segregation, apartheid's most tragic legacy and democratic South Africa's most pressing challenge. Education was not compulsory for black students until the 1990s; poor teacher training, extremely limited subjects of study, and few educational resources ensured a radically inferior education for black children who did attend school. In addition to the official impoverishment of black schools enforced by Bantu education, the role of township schools as sites of resistance during the anti-apartheid protests of the 1980s has ensured, according to Jane Hofmeyr, the national executive director of the Independent Schools Association of South Africa, that "many urban black schools are still no-go areas, where school hours are meaningless, pupils do not attend class (or at least not for long), teachers do not teach, and principals do not manage."[33] Today many of Cape Town's township schools struggle with chronic teacher absenteeism, drunkenness, and sexual abuse—challenges that exhaust those teachers who remain highly committed to their vocation—and many of Cape Town's black children experience an education of humiliation and failure. The deplorable state of some of Cape Town's township schools is well documented. For example, in her book on childhood in Cape Town called *Steering by the Stars*, Mamphele Ramphele describes her horror at the conditions at Nyanga's only high school—which she bluntly calls "a caricature of what an educational institution ought to be"—staffed by demoralized teachers broken by alcoholism and unable to communicate effectively in English.[34]

Certainly, my experience at township high schools confirms such reports. Day after day during my research in township high schools, I watched students sit in classrooms waiting for teachers who never arrived; I watched as students strolled in and out of classrooms at will, regardless of the schedule; I watched as students attempted to access the consistently locked media resource center; I listened to teachers' frustrations with rebellious and inattentive students, to students' frustrations with absent or abusive teachers, to the frustrations of the principal with the whole disastrous system.

Siyabonga's high school experience is far from unique. In 2003, slightly more than half of the 650 matriculants at five different schools in Langa passed the matric exams, and only six of these with exemption status, which is the minimum qualification for university application. None of the six passed with math and science exemptions on the higher grade, which is expected for gaining entry to engineering, medical, or business studies at any South African university. According to one source in the Western Cape Education Department, only fifty-five African-language-speaking black students in the *entire Western Cape* passed with an exemption that included math and science in 2003.[35] As the sociologist Alan Morris observed, "In contemporary South Africa, the possibility of a child from a poor home who attends a historically

black school succeeding academically is remote."[36] In a shifting economy
with dwindling opportunities for sustainable low-skilled and unskilled
employment, the implications of this statistic for the growing population
of poorly educated black youth are staggering.

The integration of formerly white schools clearly contributes to a growing democratization of education. But the relative number of these schools
is tiny, and even for black children whose families arrange their entry into
formerly white schools, the history of white accumulation and black disaccumulation cannot be minimized. Black and white children in grade one
may share the same classroom, but their parents' situations may be critically different. Wanga, for example, was a bright and motivated grade one
student at a formerly white school whose parents valued education so
highly that they moved their family from Guguletu into lower Wynberg to
ensure easier access to good schools, despite the major financial challenges
of such a move. When Wanga was eight years old and in first grade, the
family of five occupied a small three-room flat from which Wanga traveled
alone every day a distance of several miles to and from school. Wanga was
often responsible for caring for his two younger brothers (aged three and
six) while his parents worked. During the summer between Wanga's first
and second grade, several members of the family died in Guguletu, and
their funeral expenses devastated Wanga's family, who lost their telephone
service and had to cut back in every imaginable way. Although I do not
know the detailed family circumstances of each white child in the class, I
do know that every single one lived in vastly more comfortable economic
circumstances in neighborhoods adjacent to the school. Many of the other
African children in the grade one class commuted from distant townships,
some traveling almost an hour each way. There is absolutely no way that
these children can be imagined to have the same opportunities simply because they attend the same school.

. . . . .

There are clear legacies everyone knows about. Everyone knows that the
1913 Land Act destroyed black property rights, that the Group Areas
Act created racially segregated neighborhoods, that the Immorality Act
and petty apartheid policies kept people of different races apart, and that
Bantu education was inferior. The corresponding pieces seem to remain
largely unacknowledged though: what the creation of dramatically unequal property values means for the post-apartheid real estate market, the
impact on young people today of apartheid's unequal tax burdens and
unequal access to economic opportunities, the truth about the devastation

wrought by Bantu education on today's youth, and the reality of living in crushing poverty. Because material and cultural capital run hand in hand, these enduring legacies of apartheid make reconciliation profoundly difficult.

One night, I got into an argument with a visiting American friend—a very successful business owner—about poverty in Cape Town. He kept pushing me to agree that a kid born into poverty in a township has the ability now, in the "new" South Africa, to get out of the township and get an education and make a good living. Of course it's possible, I conceded; there are many such stories. But I am so sick of the American dream myth and the assumption that because a few can climb the ladder to success, anyone can.[37] The important story, I argue, isn't the few who "made it." The important story is the huge barriers that continue to constrain young people, that continue to make the climb out of poverty so very, very difficult, that produce hopelessness, rage, and self-loathing in young people who are aware that their country considers them dispensable, who are aware that their schools are substandard, their communities neglected, and their futures uncertain. The important story is to recognize how insurmountable these barriers are for most people, and how shattering they can be. The important challenge is to ensure that South Africa does not follow the example of the United States, where the legacies that created and entrenched inequality are ignored and impoverished people of color are blamed for their poverty.

CHAPTER 3

Ignorance Is Not Bliss

Many Capetonians recalled for me the euphoria that swept over Cape Town in 1994, when white people realized they weren't going to be murdered in the streets, and black people could, at long last, claim South Africa as their country. Those early years of democracy, at least in people's memories, are characterized as a time of curiosity and excitement about the chance to finally get to know "other" kinds of people. The Institute for Democracy in South Africa (IDASA) even organized "one-city tours" that were designed to show Capetonians how apartheid structured Cape Town and to enable locals to travel to parts of town they'd never before visited. Given the common lament that apartheid enforced ignorance and kept people from making friends across racial boundaries, one might imagine that the decade following the 1994 election was filled with a human crosscurrent of discussion, dialogue, partnerships, and relationships. In fact, many Capetonians were already involved in these kinds of multiracial networks—through their churches, schools, and civic organizations—in the decades prior to 1994. The expectation that many held was that these networks would quickly grow and intensify following 1994, as schools, neighborhoods, working environments, and public spaces integrated, and that many new kinds of relationships and communities would form across former boundaries as ideological barriers broke down. The rainbow nation image of racial harmony, cultural richness, and mutual respect held a compelling appeal.

To the contrary, however, apartheid's powerful legacies of fear, mistrust, and suspicion severely challenged the actual willingness of many Capetonians to rush across apartheid's old borders, and many of the early attempts at border-crossing and -crashing have withered. Several friends and acquaintances recounted to me their astonishment and frustration at the fact that, once apartheid's legal restraints were dismantled, many of their friends and neighbors retreated *further* into their homes and insular social worlds rather than seeking out spaces of integration and possibility.

I heard many such stories from school administrators, for example, whose efforts to open doors and provide partnership opportunities for youths fell victim to parents' fears. The principal of an elite, private high school with an entirely white student body recalled how he tried to introduce an ethic of community service in 2000. He brought in speakers to teach about volunteerism and chartered a bus to transport his students to Khayelitsha for a day of interaction. Not one single student from his school showed up on the appointed day. The parents, he discovered, were simply too terrified. "It was terrible," he recalled, "but that's our reality." A principal of a township high school recounted how she had received a phone call in 2002 from a white boy at Westerford High School in Newlands who wanted to establish a relationship with her school. The day before his first scheduled visit, he phoned to say his mother refused to allow him to come. The principal asked to speak to the boy's mother and finally managed to overcome the mother's fears by promising to personally transport the boy from Newlands to Langa, closely supervise his time at her school, and return him home again each day. The principal of a primary school in Lavender Hill recalled how he had sent out dozens of letters to white schools asking if any were interested in forming a partnership with his school; he did not receive a single response. Black parents whose children attend formerly white schools described to me how difficult they found social interaction with other school parents and school administrators, and how they were thus choosing to minimize their personal involvement with their children's schools. In the words of one parent, "this school is for my children, not for me."[1] The African township youths who joined our study abroad program's peer mentoring program, which encompassed evening and weekend social activities in addition to after-school tutoring, faced disparaging taunts from their classmates that, by hanging out with a group of white kids, they were "fakers" who were "playing white."[2]

Whereas the previous chapter described some of the material forces that maintain racially distinct neighborhoods and constrain the life options of township residents, this chapter and chapter 5 explore the kinds of forces and fears that constrain people's ability to imagine and actively form integrated personal networks. The ideological barriers to crossing old borders exert a powerful constraint on the imagination, especially for the affluent.

.   .   .   .   .

The setting was a historically exclusive private club in Newlands; the event, a dinner meeting of a local service organization based in the southern suburbs. The club's members are successful professionals who gather once a month over drinks and dinner to hear speakers, conduct club business, and plan charitable undertakings. I had been asked to speak during dinner about why American students come to study in Cape Town and about the community service projects in township schools required by our study abroad program. The club members listened politely, despite the inevitable oddness of dining elegantly (complete with white linen, china, and fine wine) while hearing about the poverty of those living just a few miles down the road.

At the conclusion of my talk, several club members asked questions about the logistics of our community service undertakings, such as how we found the school in Lavender Hill where we placed half our students. I explained that our program administrator had seen an article in the local newspaper about a national award the school won for its innovative attempts to strengthen school-community bonds. She telephoned the principal and asked if we could visit the school to discuss the possibility of offering some American student-volunteers. A club member asked, "You just phoned the school? How did you know who to phone?" Unsure what he was asking, I responded that one can simply dial the phone number listed for a school in the phone book and ask to speak with the school principal—an anonymous approach that clearly seemed surprising to many in the audience. In the car driving home after the meeting, another club member explained to me that although the club members would like to begin establishing relationships with township schools, they don't have any idea how to connect. "We're white, we're wealthy, and we're elite, and we don't know how to get involved in the townships," he lamented. They fear being targeted for only their money; they want to help but don't want to be perceived as bottomless money bags. "We're tired of the begging bowl approach," he told me at least a dozen times, helping me understand why I, rather than a township school principal, for example, was asked to speak at the club that month.

. . . . .

One day at his kitchen table as we prepared dinner, my friend Adrian talked about his financial situation and his struggle to know how to situate himself, a beneficiary of apartheid, financially, as part of the transformation. He and his family help support several homeless people in the neighborhood; they employ a full-time (unneeded) charwoman and offer employment in their tiny garden to her grown children when they are between jobs; they pay the school and uniform fees for the children of another struggling family; Adrian's wife, Johanna, volunteers several days a week as a counselor and reading specialist at a township school, buys all of her teaching materials herself because the school has no budget for such things, and gives financial assistance to the families of some of her students. Feeling the financial pinch of these obligations, Adrian asks, "How much is enough? How do you know when you're doing enough?"

. . . . .

My husband and I attended the June 2002 show at the Armchair Theatre in Observatory to see Sky189 perform for the Cape Comedy Collective's celebration of its 150th comedy night. It was a mixed young crowd, except for two older white couples sitting right up front in one of the theater's few couches. Comedian Fred Strydom opened the evening with jokes about coloured stereotypes and coloured identity—joking that after all those years of oppression coloureds don't have any idea who they are. Suddenly, he pointed at the older white couples on the sofa and yelled, "For fifty years of apartheid, fuck you!" Then he returned to his comedic tone, joking that all the whites you meet these days talk about how they were anti-apartheid activists, but if they were all activists, then who was in charge of apartheid? Maybe it was all a figment of black and coloured imaginations, a product of internal mental domination. We did it to ourselves! The audience rolled with laughter as he performed a little skit showing how this might have come about.

In Cape Town, one seldom hears anything like, "For fifty years of apartheid, fuck you!" in public or mixed forums. Comedy provides one of the only venues where the unspeakable is voiced. As Kagiso Lediga, a black South African comedian, explained to a reporter, "When black comedians speak their minds to a white audience, it's a first time experience for them. That's got to count for something."[3] Of course, South Africa's famous and beloved Pieter-Dirk Uys used comedy to challenge apartheid oppression and injustice for decades. Notably, his ability to avoid arrest while delivering mocking commentary on apartheid policies demonstrates the unique space that comedy offers to speak uncomfortable—and even treasonous—truths.[4]

Other than in comedy clubs, the legacy of white oppression and Victorian mores—of what must not be said, of not challenging the customs and ideologies that uphold inequality and hierarchy—has normalized a kind of culture of civility, where people avoid talking about injustice, domination, and the unfair lasting effects of apartheid. Johanna, a friend of Afrikaans background who is deeply committed to working toward an integrated South Africa, recounted her frustration during a recent family hunting trip to the Karoo in which she got fed up with the ongoing complaints about the current government and state of affairs in the country. She kept trying to challenge her family members to think more critically and more reflectively, finally bursting out, "Don't you know it's because of apartheid that you are all here for a hunting holiday on this farm with your new guns and nice cars?" Her sister-in-law tried to shush her, saying they were supposed to be enjoying a family holiday, implying that this was not the time to talk of such things. Johanna retorted, "It's never the time to talk of such things!" In a later conversation Johanna remarked with a chuckle that she seemed increasingly to find herself at the receiving end of what she calls "the look," a loaded glance directed at one who is speaking uncomfortable truths in public. Despite her decision to be more forthright about acknowledging the abuses of the past and the necessity of transformation, she says she nevertheless finds herself all too frequently phoning with an apology the next day.

Wendy mentioned that speaking of the past, of the Truth and Reconciliation Commission (TRC), of apartheid legacies is simply not done in their integrated circle of middle-class professional couples; people become too uncomfortable. John Gilmour, an educator who has long partnered with educators in Langa and who in 2004 opened a private school for African-language township students, joked that he can empty a room of his white peers by talking about his Langa partnerships. "People's smiles freeze. 'Oh, how nice.' Then they quickly move on to the next subject." Merle described the novel experience of talking to a roomful of white people at a therapeutic weekend retreat about her lifelong struggles to define a positive personal identity by overcoming her family's persistent orientation to deny their coloured heritage and "act white." "I can't believe I had the strength to say those things to a roomful of white people!"

Repeatedly I hear stories about how people who attempt to talk of such things feel silenced and apologetic for mentioning uncomfortable topics.

Greg explained to me, with a sardonic smile, that his move to the southern suburb of Rosebank from the huge, apartheid-created coloured community of Mitchell's Plain was not motivated by a desire to integrate or create an integrated social community. "It was an act against the system, which worked to keep us in Mitchell's Plain." After moving to Rosebank, however, he said he thought he should return to Mitchell's Plain, "where you know who the criminals are," unlike in Rosebank, "except for the fact that apartheid created Mitchell's Plain to keep us far away from town and from opportunities." Hip-hop artists, like Greg, from Mitchell's Plain and Grassy Park, who hold performances at the Waterfront and parties in downtown clubs, clarify to me that their motivation is not integrating apartheid-era white space—they are not interested in creating a "new South African" social scene. Rather, performing in these venues nets the resources they need for their projects in their home communities. One hip-hop artist of color teases a fellow hip-hopper who holds regular "Boogie Down Knights" parties downtown by renaming his parties "Boogie Down Whites," because the downtown venue provides a comfortable zone for white youth to enjoy hip-hop music. But then he retracts his critique, acknowledging that the parties bring in enough money from the white kids to enable the artist to hold lower-priced or free hip-hop functions in townships as well.[5] He mentions a locally famous DJ who plays no local music during his shows because the audience wants American stuff: "It's what they know. [The gangster association is seductive and enticing] to white kids who like to live the fantasy and then return home afterwards to the safety of their expensive homes."

. . . . .

Wendy and I had decided at the beginning of my first term as faculty director of the study abroad program to host evening events for host families, students from the University of Cape Town (UCT), and township students from our peer mentoring program. We hoped that our roster of well-known public speakers would pack the classroom, providing opportunities for people from different backgrounds to come together and talk about South Africa's history and its future. Several host parents had indicated that an incentive to join our program was to expand their social horizons by meeting families of other races. As our semester got under way, however, few host parents were showing up to listen to the speakers, which included Father Michael Lapsley, TRC commissioner Glenda

Wildschut, artist and former Robben Island political prisoner Lionel
Davis, and filmmaker Lindy Wilson, who showed her searing documentary *The Guguletu Seven*. In response to my confusion about why the
same host parents who complained that we didn't have enough events
never came to the events we did have, Wendy gently suggested that the
speakers were perhaps too intimidating for our host parents, who might
be afraid of feeling uncomfortable. In other words, I learned that while
some host parents might have joined our program in order to meet families of other races, they wished to do so in a "safe" environment, and my
seminar topics were scary rather than safe. As one obvious clue, a white
host mom later told me that she had dubbed my course on transforming
South Africa "Why Wicked White People Destroyed Everything."

Finally, almost at the end of the semester, we managed to attract about
a dozen parents to hear Mary Burton, TRC commissioner and former
president of the Black Sash.[6] The evening was disastrous. Mary Burton,
poised and reflective, talked of white people's fears of democracy and the
resounding success of South Africa's first democratic election, of the successes and failures of the TRC, of the burden of white guilt and the need
to give something back, of the need to pursue compensation and development initiatives for apartheid's victims. Several white parents objected,
arguing that apartheid victimized white people as well, that no one benefited from apartheid except for perhaps a few white men. One white
woman spoke of domestic violence, which she blamed on the patriarchal
structures upheld by apartheid ideologies. Other host parents of color responded to the "we were all damaged by apartheid" view by recounting
the unjust and direct constraints apartheid placed on their opportunities
and life choices because of their race. As the discussion heated up, voices
rose in anger and indignation as it became clear that opinions sharply di-
verged about apartheid's victims and beneficiaries, and where responsibility lay to fix the problems left from the past. In one exchange, a white
host mom argued, "It's *their* government now! *They* have their government now! And they've lost five hundred thousand jobs! It's *their* job to
equalize things!"

"Why are you saying *them?*" retorted another host mom of color.
"*We* must all jump in and work together. Not *them,* but *us,* collectively!"

The evening disintegrated, as people became deeply angry with one
another and a palpable tension pervaded the room. I couldn't imagine
why I had thought this would be a good idea. As the evening concluded,
I thanked Mary Burton for her calm, steady control of the situation,
apologized to Wendy for opening a Pandora's box with the host families,

and went home to unwind. The next morning the phone started ringing, as host families called to thank us for the stimulating evening of debate. "We never get to talk openly like that!" one host mother said. "It gave me so much to think about."

. . . . . .

One evening at Johanna's house I was introduced to a visiting couple as an American anthropologist. In response to the usual question about what I was doing in South Africa, I mentioned that I am interested in studying integrated spaces in Cape Town, where people from different backgrounds can talk about their country, their past, and their future. The man who asked the question looked at me blankly and responded, "But we never do that. We never come together in the same place and talk." He clearly thinks my research is pointless.

. . . . . .

An omnipresent reality in Capetonians' thoughts as they move about the city is physical security. Fear of bodily harm—bolstered by a barrage of crime reports in the media, rumors, and firsthand accounts of robbery and assault—is hugely significant in keeping people from physically crossing neighborhood borders. My American study abroad students received constant warnings from their white and coloured middle-class South African acquaintances about traveling to African and coloured townships, and whenever my daughter missed school to accompany me to a township school, her classmates joked that she would get out of having to do her homework that evening because she wasn't going to make it home alive. Coloured friends also expressed fright at the thought of traveling to the African townships that adjoin their working-class neighborhoods. While such fears may particularly characterize white and coloured middle-class people's views of traveling to townships, youths from Khayelitsha expressed their discomfort about traveling to the southern suburbs, where they feared police harassment and white hostility.[7]

. . . . . .

These representative vignettes suggest a range of ideological barriers to integration and post-apartheid border-crossing. For people who are white, not knowing *how* to cross borders is part of the problem: not knowing whom to call or how to call, feeling uncertain about the expectations that might follow from new contacts. For those who live in material comfort, the possibility of being irrevocably drawn into a relationship with the impoverished can be unsettling; the need is so great, one's contributions are never enough, so to protect oneself perhaps it's best to carefully limit one's associations and contributions. The fear of being confronted with uncomfortable truths—anger, rage, resentment—looms large. Fears of physical harm add to the list of challenges.

These issues affect white people's perceptions of post-apartheid social and physical geographies. People of color, as we will see in further detail in later chapters, experience an enduring legacy of mistrust of white people's motives and commitment and a resentment of ongoing white privilege and white ignorance or denial of past abuses. For many people of color I interviewed, their desire to redefine the ownership of apartheid-era white space is motivated more by accessing the material benefits available in white space than by the desire to build new, integrated communities. For many Cape Town residents, the emotional and psychological challenges of crossing old ideological and geographical boundaries are enormous and will require active, committed work to overcome. Transformation is not a passive undertaking.

. . . . .

One effect of ongoing racial segregation is that few Capetonians really know much about the experiences of other groups under apartheid, and they remain ignorant of how the structures of apartheid, legally dismantled but persistent in their effects, continue to constrain people's options—particularly people of color—a decade into the new democracy. Racial segregation bred massive ignorance, that useful compost for racism. The twin legacies of apartheid—ignorance and inequality—saturate life in Cape Town today because spaces to overcome the former are rare and filled with fear and uncertainty, and opportunities to overcome the latter are few and constrained by past government policies and the current adherence to neoliberal policies. The assumption that neoliberal market forces will normalize social life by allowing integration of middle-class suburbs and schools to occur "naturally" utterly disregards the fact that there is nothing natural about the racialized class structure that democratic South Africa inherited from the apartheid era. It also ignores the reluctance South Africans may have to enter into relationships of intimacy with those of different and thus unfamiliar backgrounds. Ignorance about apartheid's legacies means that few discourses are available for analyzing and challenging persistent inequalities.

Apartheid worked brilliantly to enforce ignorance, while allowing people to think they knew things about other groups. I often heard white women, for example, remark on the close relationship they share with the family maid who has been with them for the past twenty years, and who lives in "the township."

"Which township?" I would ask.

"Ummm," comes the inevitable uncertain response. "Is it Guguletu? Or Khayelitsha? One of those. Anyway, we're very, very close."

This lack of awareness and knowledge of how other people live allows middle-class Capetonians to criminalize black township dwellers for their poverty, such as when black shanty dwellers refuse to pay for city water because they have no funds but demand that the city provide water. Middle-class Capetonians who have no understanding or experience of such extreme poverty say things to one another like "Imagine what would happen to me if I decided not to pay my mortgage but insisted on keeping my house! I'd be arrested! Why do those people get to demand water but think they don't have to pay?"

"Wanting things they can't pay for" is a regular theme at white gatherings in the southern suburbs. At a dinner party, for example, the conversation turned to the white hostess's distress that her family maid had acquired credit cards, because the hostess believes black people don't know how to manage debt. But she does not acknowledge that the family maid, like Salomie, wants to be able to buy her children clothing and furnish her home with the basics but cannot afford to do so on her salary. Just like middle-class people in the United States who maintain middle-class status by buying cars, furniture, and summer vacations on credit, Salomie and others like her use credit cards to buy necessities as well as modest luxuries. For people living in townships, trying to acquire modern consumer goods may be one of the only ways to feel part of the new South Africa. But such debts can become disastrous in an uncertain economy for those without job security, as Salomie learned. And the problems with debt faced by many of Cape Town's underemployed residents allow those of secure middle-class status to imagine the debt problems of their housekeepers as the result of personal weakness and not poverty.

Several years after that evening, I sat in a meeting with a man from a wealthy local service club who oversees international student exchanges. He acknowledged that the vast majority of students sent abroad from South Africa by his organization are white. "You see," he explained, "blacks here are either very rich or very poor. The blacks who get chosen are very rich. You can send the wealthy black students on these programs, because they're used to Model C [formerly white] schools and a middle-class lifestyle." He continued, explaining why they do not send township students on exchanges: "It's not fair to them, you see, to take them from a township environment and put them into a Westernized context where there is a high material standard of living. They cannot adjust when they return to the township and have to live there again." The man has no problem imagining that township environments are not "Westernized" and that township dwellers, who watch television and work in the homes of the middle and upper classes, are unaccustomed to material plenty.[8] For him, clearly, township residents occupy a completely separate, bounded world, culturally as well as materially.[9]

Another effect of apartheid is that people don't know how much they don't know. Ignorance fosters assumptions, which in turn stifle curiosity. I listened to countless descriptions of the behavior of other races from people who, adopting the role of educator, would reiterate their own assumptions about how others live: black people cannot handle debt; white people still want to uphold apartheid; black people are noisy and like to cook outside and yell at one another in conversation; white people are stingy. The need to feel certain about one's knowledge may be particularly potent in a time of flux, when all the rules are changing. The flip side of uncertainty and transformation is rigidity and close-mindedness, an insistence that one really does know the lay of the land, and an unwillingness to acknowledge the lacunae in one's worldview.

In addition to fear, another thing that keeps white and middle-class people from entering townships and acquainting themselves with "how the other half lives" is that, unlike people of color who enter white neighborhoods to work, shop, and attend school, they have no reason to go into poor communities. One evening, while visiting with some close white friends, a tense discussion developed about this issue that culminated with the mother challenging the adult daughter about why she lacked black friends. "What am I supposed to do?" answered the daughter. "I don't work in a township like you do. How am I supposed to go there to meet people? Drive my car into the middle of Khayelitsha and say, "I'm here to make friends. Does anybody want to be my friend?"

Recalling their first venture into an African township, the members of the hip-hop group Black Noise, primarily from the coloured communities of Grassy Park and Mitchell's Plain, can now laugh at their own early post-apartheid naïveté. Famous in Cape Town for their socially conscious orientation and talent and for their ability to cross all borders and engage any kind of audience, the group decided to begin taking their message into African townships in the late 1990s. Emile YX?, Black Noise's founder and leader, described their first time in Khayelitsha; after arriving an hour early because they weren't sure where they were going, some members of the group decided to get out of the car to get something in a store. The newest Black Noise member freaked out: "You're going to get out of the car *here!*" But it was fine, of course, and now they travel around African townships on a daily basis. This is what people need to learn, Emile explains: that the old borders can be crossed, that if people rejected the typical attitude toward crossing borders ("What for? There's nothing there for me"), they would be less nervous, less scared, and less susceptible to slanted news coverage and stereotypes. Emile pointed out that the same people who walk around in Mitchell's Plain are afraid to go around in Khayelitsha, noting that more people from downtown Cape Town have been to Khayelitsha than from Mitchell's Plain, even though the latter two communities share a common border.

Having a reason to cross racialized residential borders can begin a process of "mind-blowing education," to quote Evaron Orange (also known as Sky189), Cape Town's well-known graffiti artist, comedian, and emcee (now relocated to Switzerland). Evaron told a poignant story about his recent experiences in Guguletu. After growing up in Athlone, he made friends across race lines in his personal and professional life; he dismissed race talk as uninteresting and increasingly irrelevant in contemporary Cape Town. But during 2003 he began teaching graphic arts at a technical college in Guguletu and came away profoundly moved by what he witnessed. "I thought I knew a lot and was pretty well informed about a lot of things in Cape Town—I felt pretty knowledgeable—but teaching in Guguletu made me feel like I'm back in grade one again. I realized I didn't know anything."

"Like what?" I asked.

"About people just across the border!" He responded. "About their lives. I realized I didn't know anything about how people just across the border live." He told the story of one of his students, a girl, who also studied ceramics. She was born with a growth-stunting genetic problem and was tiny despite being an adult. Consequently she couldn't manage handling some of the heavy work of the ceramics workshop, even though she had worked hard to master the technical components. Evaron was asked to attend a meeting at the school about this student because her granny, who paid her fees, was struggling to meet the fees. She had signed a contract promising to pay the fees because she really wanted the girl to be able to enroll, but she lived on a pension of only R500 ($71) per month. The granddaughter's school fees were R3,000 ($428). There was no way she could pay this sum, so she scrambled and tried to find bits and pieces of income here and there. Evaron was stunned to learn of this level of deprivation. Then one day Evaron overheard another colleague at the college ask the girl if her mother was feeling better. Evaron had seen the girl's mother on occasion—a beautiful woman, he thought—and so he asked the student if her mother had been ill. The girl explained that her mother was dying of AIDS. Evaron was shocked: "I mean, you know about this, you read about it, hear about it, but suddenly it's right in front of you, someone you know and see everyday." He couldn't imagine managing with the challenges of ill health and poverty his student had to face.

.   .   .   .   .

Over the course of five years of research in Cape Town, I was repeatedly struck by how often those I was interviewing would ask me what other Capetonians thought about the things we were discussing. After asking about my research project, my interlocutors would question me about how others live in Cape Town. For example, I was asked a poignant question over dinner in New Rest, the informal settlement in Guguletu where Siyabonga lives alongside the N2 highway. Siyabonga's neighbor told me of his shock at discovering that one of the white men with whom he was coordinating in New Rest's community development process signs his name on professional documents with the AWB symbol, indicating his membership in South Africa's notorious white supremacist movement, *Afrikaaner Weerstandsbewegung*. "What can he be thinking?" the New Rest community organizer asked me, flabbergasted. "Why would white South Africans continue to support the AWB? Do they think they are Europeans? What are they thinking about the future of South Africa?"

.   .   .   .   .

During a spirited discussion with high school students in Langa on culture and racism, the teacher asks students to define *culture*. After producing a list (rituals, customs, religion, beliefs, dignity, values) and avidly discussing aspects of their cultural practices, the teacher asks the (entirely black) class, "Do white people have culture?" The students momentarily quiet down, and everyone looks confused. Finally, one boy turns to me and asks, "Do you?"

.   .   .   .   .

Siyabonga's and Salomie's regular commutes from, respectively, an informal African settlement and a coloured township to predominantly white upper-middle-class neighborhoods place them among the minority of Capetonians who regularly traverse such boundaries in the city. Only those with jobs move daily from townships to the city center or the suburbs, and few with homes in the city center or the suburbs travel to the townships. Although the demographics of some schools, work environments, and public spaces in Cape Town's formerly white neighborhoods are changing, the vast majority of people in Cape Town don't seem to be crossing old borders, and effective challenges to apartheid-nurtured ignorance are sorely lacking. IDASA's one-city tours lasted only a short while, and all the township tour operators I interviewed—who offer a structured, safe, contained way to cross old boundaries—said white South Africans were an insignificant percentage of their clientele.[10] Ongoing residential segregation and class distinctions, in addition to the lingering terrors created and sustained by apartheid ideologies, ensure that people in Cape Town find few opportunities to come together in meaningful ways across the boundaries erected by apartheid.

By their own admission, Capetonians describe the social scene in Cape Town as "very cliquey." "Once you're in, you're in," one young man explained to me at an all-white party in Claremont, "but it can be bloody hard to get in." Social circles form around family, school, and church and tend to be small and exclusive. "Cape society is tightly cliquish," explained a man at another all-white gathering in Newlands. "Most likely one's circle agrees with one—you make certain of that." Describing the tension he feels pervades Cape society, he imitated a nervous person peeking out to size someone up: "You surround yourself with people who will agree with you and leave it at that." The part of my research I jokingly called "dinner party fieldwork" confirms these observations; spaces of integration and open debate certainly don't seem to be happening in people's living rooms. So where are they?

The Institute for Justice and Reconciliation's Reconciliation Barometer Surveys conducted in March/April and October/November 2003 and April/May 2004 show that more than half the South Africans interviewed say they never socialize with people of other races. This number grew by 10 percent between 2003 and 2004. A higher percentage of blacks report no involvement with people of other races. Around 60 percent of respondents report that they find it difficult to understand the customs and ways of other racial groups.[11]

One avenue across apartheid's old barriers that might combat stereotypes and provide information is the media. To the contrary, however, black friends and acquaintances often complained that the media portrayal of their communities does much more harm than good. Indeed I found that after the first few months of each visit to Cape Town, I would stop reading the newspapers because they were so depressing and terrifying. "103 gang killings in the Cape Flats" screams a typical morning headline. In my interview with him, Ray "Skillz" of Black Noise decried media representation of black communities:

> What about all the good things people are doing in the Cape Flats? What about the mother who leaves each morning very early in the cold to take the train a long way to work, returning each evening late, tired, cold, all to support her family and bring up her kids well. Why isn't this mother from Mitchell's Plain in the paper? . . . Why not? People who own the papers don't know anything about what's really happening. . . . Emphasizing all the negatives, like showing a photo of a gang killing but never a photo of the mother who works hard for her family, desensitizes people to black death.

Such a negative barrage of media images is impossible to counter when white people seldom or never travel to black communities. The journalist Allister Sparks notes that many South Africans are dissatisfied with their media but "cannot quite put their fingers on what it is that they find unsatisfactory. I suggest it is an absence of context. We are living in one of the most fundamentally transforming societies in modern times, a hugely exciting process of transition, yet our newspapers fail to capture the essence of what is happening."[12]

. . . . .

Despite the reality that old stereotypes live on, old patterns of association persist, and fear and uncertainty trump curiosity and opportunities to meet new people, there are spaces in Cape Town where people do actually come together in meaningful ways across apartheid's old barriers. But each of these arenas is limited in scope or vision. Discussions hosted by IDASA and by the Institute for Justice and Reconciliation, both nonprofit organizations dedicated to researching and fostering reconciliation, democratization, and open dialogue, provide one arena. After attending several meetings, I realized that the same crowd seemed to show up each time, and several faces in that crowd belonged to—why was I not surprised?—other anthropologists. While these organizations' work contributes in important ways to transformation and is regularly covered in the local newspapers, their meetings did not seem to attract many beyond a small group of elite intellectuals and researchers.[13] A somewhat different approach is offered by the Institute for Healing of Memories, which offers weekend retreats for self-selecting individuals to share their memories of apartheid in a facilitated group workshop. The goal of the workshop is to help people cope with painful memories in order move forward into a different future. The anthropologist Undine Kayser, who worked for several years as a workshop facilitator, argues that while the workshop offered participants a way to safely confront the past and imagine new kinds of relationships in the future, the reality of material inequities and social barriers in Cape Town frustrated the hopes of workshop participants to effect a newly imagined sociability. The hopeful imaginings made possible in the closed, intimate workshop space could not easily be put into practice in the context of Cape Town's rigid divides.[14]

One popular venue for open discussion across old boundaries has been the radio, specifically the *Tim Modise Show*, during which people phoned in to share their views on every subject imaginable. Everyone I know except for teenagers listened to Tim Modise (until his program went off the air in 2003 and he moved to another radio program) and talked about it afterward. Because of the anonymity of the radio, the safe space that Modise managed to create was unique. "White people love Tim Modise because he lets anyone say anything," a white woman told me, although I heard the same sentiment from people of color. Tim Modise didn't require last names; all contributors could remain utterly anonymous and removed from the uncertainties and discomforts of face-to-face interaction.

For the younger crowd, nightclub venues provide a privileged minority who can afford it access to multiracial environments. Yet my forays into clubs and my interviews with club goers and musicians who perform in Cape Town's clubs suggested they were multiracial rather than integrated—a "Why are all the black kids sitting together in the cafeteria?" kind of setting.[15]

Formerly white schools may provide a promising arena for integration. While expensive private schools remain exclusively or overwhelmingly white and African township schools remain entirely black, most formerly white government schools have been rapidly transforming their school bodies, and some schools in coloured areas are enrolling more African students. Yet, the process of integration has been predictably rocky in many schools. For families who live in townships who would like to send their children to formerly white schools, the challenges of transport and school fees pose significant barriers. For example, while the fees at a high school in Langa are relatively low (although still unaffordable to some), the school fees at neighboring Pinelands High School are *fifty times* higher. Expensive schools offer little financial aid; my children's' school offered only two full scholarships to a student body of over seven hundred, although a few other students, such as children of domestics who worked in the school's catchment area, received some financial assistance from the school. When I asked if the domestics' employers helped pay school fees, a school administrator laughed at my naïveté and told me about the law that mandates free schooling if school fees are more than ten times one's salary: "Employers know this and so ensure that they pay less than that amount so the children qualify for free schooling." Nevertheless, few domestics understand this law, she continued, and very few attempt to enroll their children in schools in the wealthy neighborhoods where they work (nor do such schools reach out to domestics in their catchment area).

In addition to the financial barriers, familiar themes dominate social interaction in integrating schools. Black children who live in townships but attend formerly white schools talk about how their white friends are not allowed to visit them at home, about birthday parties where none of the invited white children attend. Students from Langa attending high school in Pinelands remark that their white friends have never even come to Langa to meet their families, even though the white and black students live less than a mile apart (but, thanks to apartheid planning, are separated by a highway, a railway line, a power plant, a large stretch of vacant land, and a concrete wall encircling the Pinelands neighborhood). Formerly white schools that maintain traditional European uniform standards struggle with the question of allowing girls to wear Muslim headscarves or African braids, which don't conform to the white traditional hairstyle regulations. White children complain that their Xhosa classmates talk to one another on the playground in Xhosa, which excludes the non-Xhosa speakers. Formerly white schools, all of which have a tradition of Christian education (which includes prayers and Bible passages as part of school assemblies, Christian religious hymns as part of the music curriculum, Christian symbolism and imagery, and academic lessons taken from Bible stories), struggle with how to accommodate Muslim students while not alienating Christian parents who are opposed to ecumenicalism. Christian parents at one integrating formerly white southern suburban high school were so disturbed by the growing presence of Muslim students that they began holding weekly Christian prayer meetings at the school to pray for the ongoing supremacy of Christian values.

I also interviewed African children who were attending coloured schools, who reported very similar experiences of marginalization and alienation. A very bright girl from a squatter camp who attends a large coloured high school in order to access a better academic environment told me, with great clarity, "I know who my friends are," namely, her neighbors rather than her classmates. At another school I watched as coloured township children mocked and berated African children who attended their school from a neighboring squatter camp. The township children claimed the African children stank and refused to sit next to them.

School administrators and teachers in formerly white schools express a range of contradictory understandings of the complexities of integration. In interviews I was repeatedly struck by two prominent discourses. The first concerns how African students are seen as a "problem" for former white schools because of their poorer English-language skills; their lack of access to a home computer, electricity, and a quiet place to study; their greater need for special services; and even their cultural views of childhood as a time of play rather than work. One administrator/teacher told me, "They don't worry about tomorrow. Their work ethic is the most challenging. But they must conform to our expectations for deadlines and homework." This attitude defines African students as a problem to be solved; because of their cultural and material limitations they need extra attention in order to be assimilated to the school's norms and standards. Another school administrator at a southern suburban school told me, "It's the township kids who cost the school the most in terms of their needs. They travel huge distances to get to school, doing their homework by candlelight—no computers at home. This is really a problem because they aren't like the other children, they don't have the same resources or lifestyle, and some become very resentful." She continued: "Perhaps the child from Khayelitsha is being harmed more than helped by being at our school. Perhaps he or she is not receiving a favor. They should be at school with their own people in their own place, close to home, where everyone has the same resources. It's not fair to bring them to a place like [this]." She concluded: "There's got to be a limit on what we do."

A counselor at a southern suburban boy's high school who has worked in white and black schools for decades remarked on this theme in the course of many conversations, explaining that the students who struggle become convinced that their poor performance is their own fault. They internalize this message, which is reaffirmed by many voices at the school: "They are told they don't work hard, they don't prepare, they are disciplinary problems, etc." He observed that the parents of such children are ignored, recalling one boy who was referred to him for counseling because of disciplinary problems in the classroom. The boy had been selected to attend the school because of his sporting potential, but after attending the school for nearly three years, "silently suffering his lack of academic foundation," he had begun acting out because of a feeling of not coping and not belonging. When the counselor asked what contact the school had made with the parents, school administrators responded that there was none; they assumed there were no parents in the picture. The counselor asked the boy and learned that he did indeed have parents, who when contacted were distressed and surprised. They had never been aware of any problems their child had experienced at school, because the school had never contacted them. This example illustrated, for the counselor, one of the many ways in which students of color become problems and are treated as "different" in formerly white schools.[16]

The second discourse concerns the formerly white schools' approaches to multiculturalism, summarized in John Gilmour's parody: "We're multicultural—we even started a marimba band!" Notably, black students attending white schools often complained to me about their school's reluctance to introduce soccer, a sport with a strong black history in South Africa. In schools that insist on the preeminence of rugby, the sporting centerpiece of apartheid white South Africa, black student athletes to their frustration find themselves relegated to unfunded intramural teams. For formerly white schools, one of the central questions around integration seemed to be how to become multicultural while ensuring the ongoing supremacy of white values and traditions. I spoke to literature teachers who insisted that they would continue teaching exclusively European and American novels because African novelists were simply second rate; I spoke to music teachers who, while acknowledging the benefits of an extracurricular school marimba band, refused to include African music in the school curriculum because they felt it was so obviously inferior to Euro-American musical forms.

After one of Cape Town's most elite private schools announced in the local media a plan to "Africanize" itself in order to better prepare its graduates for professional life in South Africa, I interviewed the headmaster about what changes he anticipated making. He suggested that changes in school hymns, poetry, orchestral music, dance, languages, and sport would be desirable, although these changes would come about through the decisions of individual teachers rather than as part of an overall program of retraining or curricular revision. While the school's customary traditions (from Anglo-Saxon culture) will be retained, as will an insistence on protecting values and standards, he hoped that teachers would make the choice individually to add additional, African-based material to their curriculum—multiculturalism as a set of add-ons rather than a curricular transformation. Furthermore, the cost of school fees will continue to mean an overwhelmingly white student body for this elite school, although over the next several years the school hopes to admit sixty fully funded black students to the student body of 1,250, a number that would account for less than 5 percent of the students.

The turn to multiculturalism is thus not materially based and is not politically oriented (although the elite school mentioned above recently formed a relationship with a new independent school for African township students). I found very little interest expressed by the dozens of teachers and principals I interviewed at formerly white schools in revising the curriculum to teach about current history. Teachers at the primary schools told me it should be part of the high school curriculum, whereas high school teachers and principals emphasized cultural expressions of diversity rather than political history as their preference for embracing diversity and integration. Even here, though, many teachers expressed reservations about how far to go in introducing non-Western cultural forms because of their unwavering belief in the superiority of European literature, poetry, and music. In the interests of multiculturalism and diversity in the new South Africa, non-Western cultural forms could be acknowledged (usually as an after-school extracurricular activity), but only in such a way that made it clear that these art forms took second place to the European-derived forms of cultural expression taught as part of the core curriculum.

Cape Times columnist Sandile Dikeni writes of the lack of reciprocity in such attempts to introduce multiculturalism: "I cannot help but fear that many of the arguments made for classical art forms are not Eurocentric but South African and come from the narrow-minded elements in our white community. Black people in South Africa have opted to take the many good things that came from Europe while the mainstream of white society still needs to show me what elements of the African existence they have internalised. By God they even laughed at Johnny Clegg. And when he succeeded overseas in a Zulu costume it was a novelty right under their noses."[17]

Dikeni captures the experience of many of Cape Town's black artists and musicians who feel that they receive much more recognition from fans abroad than at home in Cape Town, a sentiment felt even by one of Cape Town's most prominent traditional African musicians, who holds a post in a university music department, has been invited to perform all over the world, and has released over a dozen CDs. An American jazz group was visiting his university to give some workshops, and during the visit they began jamming together in the music department's courtyard. On his instruments (kudu horns, gourds, marimbas, and other traditional African instruments), he would begin a melody and the Americans would join in on their trombones and saxophones. He described how as they were playing, a large crowd gathered, and "the listeners went crazy—they loved it." The next day, some of his colleagues in the music department sought him out in his office (located in a little outbuilding set behind the main music building) to ask if he would play with them sometime, as he had with the visiting Americans. He says he looked at them, thinking, "For thirteen years I've been right here, playing everyday, and you could have asked me any time. But it took Americans to come here and play with me for you to see it was not only possible but incredible."

In many formerly white arenas, particularly schools, the message of transformation is this: "We are embracing ideals of multiculturalism but insisting on conformity and assimilation. You can join us, but don't expect us to conform to you. We will accommodate some of your art, but it will not become a central component of our curriculum since it is inferior to our traditions, and because we care about standards, we will not waver from our commitment to these traditions." Since a number of studies suggest that schools offer the most promising arena for racial integration in contemporary South Africa, the emphasis in formerly white schools on assimilation and white cultural supremacy is particularly disturbing. In her 2005 review of the state of South Africa's schools, Linda Chisholm writes:

> The defining feature of South African schools and schooling is arguably the politics of race and racism. It is one of the central fault lines of South African society, intersecting in complex ways with class, gender and ethnicity. Race is historically inscribed into the functioning of everyday life through those institutions in which the majority of children spend the greater part of their lives: schools. Seen as one of the principal generators, justifiers and vehicles of racialised thoughts, actions and identities, the challenge has been, and continues to be, whether and how the roles, rules, social character and functioning of schools can change to challenge the retrograde aspects of such formation and stimulate new and diverse identities and forms of acknowledgement and social practice.[18]

.   .   .   .   .

Anne, an artist and art teacher, charts her students' emotional states and political awareness through the art they produce. One night in 2001 she presented to me and a small group of family and friends a stunning slide show of the art created by her white students in the late 1980s. It was a poignant evening because the story told through the students' art was suffused with sadness, desire, and longing. She began with art produced by her pupils in 1985–86, when the Carnegie Institute on Poverty asked high school students in white schools and township schools to draw a picture of their street. White students produced lovely peaceful pastorals—a quiet street lined with trees, a garden filled with gorgeous flowers. Although Anne did not have slides of the township students' art, she showed slides of works by black artists of the time that she said was similar in theme, showing township streets with Kaspirs (armored vehicles used by security forces), fires, flying bullets, and bodies. The art was hung together as a show at UCT but was closed down by the security police within three hours; Anne managed to rescue her students' pieces, but the police destroyed the pieces by the township students.

Motivated by this experience, Anne started indirectly exploring poverty and apartheid in art classes with her students. She pointed out that whites really knew very little about township life because they weren't allowed to travel freely within townships and because of media censorship. Living in an age of ignorance but with the knowledge that things were wrong, her students painted empathetic portraits of black people, a theme they extended to other nonprivileged social categories like the elderly and the sick. The portraits avoided sentimentality and showed the students' awareness of the emotional terrain of their country. One was of a beggar whose hand is coming straight at the viewer. The artist had written along the edge of the painting: "Give the beggar a penny. (But he hates you.)"

Within a few years, the students' art had become more emphatic and politicized, as they began trying to portray black rage. Showing a few slides of renditions of township streets, Anne commented: "We got the township here, despite being unable to go there, but we missed the violence: the Kaspirs, the police presence." Many of the paintings from this time capture anger: one is of a crowded train car with three black adolescents—one in a school uniform—jammed into the doorway staring at the viewer with level, cold glares. Anne remarked that her students during this time were very aware of anger: "The end was near and no one knew how it would come, just that it must." Occasionally during this time, police would phone her school and other white schools to warn them that black students were going to try to march downtown in protest and some white schools might be targeted. The school would implement security measures, lock up the whole place, and the teachers and pupils would hunker down inside. During these moments she recalls hoping that when the black kids arrived (which never happened) the art on the walls would provide a message of solidarity.

In the waning days of the 1980s, a theme of self-loathing emerged in the students' art. White artists of the time were making protest art that explored what was wrong with white society. Anne's students began creating haunting and stunning works about excess—one is of several gigantic-sized pastries painted in what looks like frosting. Written below are the names of the pastries interspersed with words and phrases like "sickly" and "lots of it." Another painting shows a sunlit, peaceful bedroom with white children sleeping in twin beds, curtains ruffling in the breeze, a charming country cupboard between the beds, a hooked rug on the floor. But the serenity is disrupted by horror: dozens of snakes are cascading across the floor and slithering up into one child's bed. The slide show concluded with her students' art after Mandela's release: euphoric images that exude optimism, hope, and unity.[19]

In 2002, over a decade after Anne's students created the paintings she showed us in her slide show, an exhibit of student work went up at the Castle of Good Hope in recognition of the Sustainable Development Conference in Johannesburg. In honor of the theme of recycling, Cape Town's art teachers instructed their students to create things out of found, used, and discarded materials. The students (most, as far as I could tell from the labels, from privileged, predominantly white schools) designed things like rooms, chairs, outfits, lamps and even a life-size replica of a shebeen (township tavern).[20] Strikingly, this art was being exhibited as artistic/aesthetic novelty, yet township dwellers do similar things with found and used objects all the time (well, they don't make clothes from bubble wrap or electrical tape). So why not an exhibit on how township communities *are* the epitome of recycling? How *everything* gets reused and reformulated there, including things discarded elsewhere (scrap iron, wood, rug fragments, bits of wallpaper, magazine pictures, etc.). Instead, kids from primarily privileged schools "play" with used objects to create art. And why a shebeen (which may indeed utilize recycled materials in real life) and not an upscale coffee shop? Since people in townships incorporate recycled material into their living spaces and into their commercial art (such as the ubiquitous wire sculptures and objects made from soda and beer cans), why is it only exhibited when privileged kids do it as art? How does this compare to ten years earlier, when white kids tried to capture black emotion and experience, as a form of solidarity? Should this be troubling?

. . . . .

The appropriation of the creativity of the impoverished by the comfortable is troubling because it is not necessarily accompanied by greater understanding or opportunities for community building. The work of Anne's students of a decade ago showed an effort to reach across the divide; it challenged the divide and offered a self-critique. The post-apartheid art on exhibit at the Castle of Good Hope suggests an appropriation rather than a reaching out; it contained no self-critique, no challenges to poverty or inequality. It ignored the context of inequality and made the necessity of recycling into an equal-opportunity art form. The desire for intimacy, mutuality, and understanding has been replaced by aesthetics appropriation. In the same year as the exhibit at the castle, a glossy coffee table book called *Shack Chic* made a media splash with its arresting photographs of the recycled interior decor of township shacks.[21] The exhibit and the glamorized representation of poor people's homes in the book suggest a new aesthetic—poverty fashion?—that celebrates the innovative creativity of the poor while saying nothing about the injustice of poverty.

The colonization of the aesthetics of the subjugated by the dominant is a troubling feature of a postmodern world. One sees it in tourism, where indigenous art forms are presented for tourists as an emblem of authenticity and beauty, even though the indigenous people who create the art live in poverty. One sees it in national festivals which celebrate the art of indigenous groups living on the margins of national society. What does a privileged art student who constructs a life-size shebeen out of recycled materials learn about real-life shebeen owners and patrons? How close does a coffee-sipping patron come, flipping through the pages of *Shack Chic* at Exclusive Books in the Claremont Mall, to the people portrayed in the book's stunning images? Multiculturalism as a set of aesthetic add-ons accessible to all contributes very little to personal, political, or economic transformation.

Apartheid's legacy of fear and mistrust created ideological barriers that are sustained by uncertainty about how to imagine building an integrated community, about how to conduct oneself in order to cross borders, by discomfort in the face of poverty and rage in the face of wealth, by fears of physical security, and by shallow reporting in the media. Such barriers nurture ignorance and reinforce stereotypes, particularly dangerous stereotypes that criminalize the black poor and demonize the wealthy white. People who have managed to cross apartheid's old barriers in all directions are few, as are arenas of empathetic mutual understanding and interest. The challenge will be to sustain and grow these arenas in ways that avoid paternalistic definitions of multiculturalism and the bullying tactics of "traditional gatekeepers" (across the color spectrum).

CHAPTER 4

Fieldwork Discomforts

By the middle of my first term in Cape Town, after embracing the choice to undertake anthropological research, I needed to make some decisions about my focus within the broader theme of transformation. The urban ethnographies I had read generally focused on a *community* defined by a neighborhood, a residential block, or even just a few families, allowing the urban context to provide a background rather than a focus. I was trying to focus on a *process* unfolding in an urban setting but was very much interested in how the urban setting provided opportunities and constraints for that process. Since my early circles of association were primarily middle-class white and coloured professionals and their families, and since my particular interest was racial politics, it seemed that a lot of my early conversations on transformation circled around the issues of white identity, white privilege, and the ideological and material legacy—particularly for people classified as coloured—of white domination. I was also excruciatingly aware of my own whiteness and the need to identify the baggage attached to that status in post-apartheid Cape Town.

Doing anthropology in an apartheid city—even a city in transition—poses a number of challenges to the white researcher. Never before had I felt my position was so fraught; never before had I felt that I needed to constantly, vigilantly monitor everything I said and did. In my previous fieldwork experiences—in Catholic, conservative northern Portugal and Muslim southern Somalia—the personal challenges I faced were much more about my gender and appropriate gender roles. Could I talk privately with a man, just the two of us, alone? At gender-segregated village feasts, should I accept the invitation to sit with the male elders, or should I sit with the women (whose feast foods included chopped up organs and intestines rather than the savory roasts reserved for the men)? Did I have to obey orders from a male neighbor who occasionally demanded I prepare coffee for him, or could I tell him to take a hike? Should I aggressively intervene on behalf of a neighbor when her husband beat her? How should I respond to jokes that since I'm a worthless wife who is too skinny and hasn't produced a child, my husband should take a second, teenage, wife? How about Halima, two huts over? She looks fertile and healthy and needs a husband. How should I respond to the obnoxious government official, on whose good will I am dependent for a visa, when he forces me to sit through lectures on the perils posed by women like me who are not subservient enough?[1]

In Cape Town, the issue was less my gender than my race, class, and citizenship. During my first period of research, I decided that as a white person I should limit myself to studying white people's experiences of transition. The neighborhood where I lived and the location of my children's school were in formerly white areas, and in the face of Cape Town's segregated reality, where a steep wealth gradient separated the southern suburbs from the Cape Flats, it seemed anthropologically fraudulent to write about, for example, people's experiences in a township if I wasn't actually living there myself.[2] The old traditions of participant-observation (or, to adopt Signithia Fordham's phrase, "participant-watching") and cultural immersion still resonated, overlaid with closer attention to the dynamics of inequality and power. The baggage of being white in post-apartheid, racially segregated, and highly unequal Cape Town sat heavily on my mind as I tried to fashion a study that avoided the twin evils of romanticizing and patronizing black people's experiences.

Furthermore, I was influenced by discussions in anthropology about the need to "study up," to focus our analytical lens on the elite and the dominant in addition to our traditional interests in the marginalized and subjugated. Additionally, a research focus on white attitudes and identity would help illuminate issues about whiteness back home in the United States, since both countries share a history of legally enforced white dominance and institutional and cultural structures that perpetuate white privilege.

There was a third reason why I initially chose to identify "whiteness" as my research topic. While limiting my study to white experiences of transformation and legacies of white ideological domination was defendable on one level, it also allowed me to avoid some of the discomfort of being white. It allowed me to imagine myself as different from many white South Africans, and although I spent much of my time in Cape Town's townships, it allowed me to avoid dealing intellectually with the kinds of emotional uncertainties faced by those whose hesitance to cross borders I described in the previous chapter. White liberalism, Cape Town–style, was looking pretty problematic because of its patronizing approval of assimilationist multiculturalism—a view that echoed similar white approaches to diversity initiatives at home in the United States. While still working through the symbolic and political baggage of being white in both contexts, initially it felt easier and more honest to reflect on white sentiment and experience in Cape Town. I didn't come to terms with the shortcomings of this approach until my third year of research, when challenges from colleagues and friends of color forced me to reevaluate my assumptions.

Interestingly, in 1999 the sociologist Gay Seidman noted: "The dynamics of race remain perhaps more unexplored in South Africa than anywhere else, and South African scholarship is only now beginning to problematize questions around the racial identities, racial politics, and racial formations that would appear so central to a divided society." Whereas Seidman attributes this reticence to the desire on the part of progressive scholars "to avoid any link to the scientific racism so rampant in South African science,"[3] the sociologist Ran Greenstein offers a harsher view, noting "the threat felt by dominant white academics (particularly those of progressive political persuasions) from any open discussion of racial concerns, in which they are likely to be seen as part of the problem rather than part of the solution."[4] Looking back on the early years of my research, I realize that in not wanting to naturalize apartheid's racial categories, and in not wanting—as a white person—to be seen as part of the problem, I didn't know how to situate myself within the awkward post-apartheid politics of racial identity, just like some of the white South Africans I interviewed.

When I explained to Fiona Ross my initial feeling that my whiteness made it legitimate for me to study only white people, she arched her eyebrows at me and commented, "That's a pretty shocking statement." Although I came to abandon my position (Fiona's voice ringing in my ears for the next several years), during my first two years of research a focus on themes of "whiteness"—how white people were experiencing and thinking about the transition and how so-called coloured people were reflecting on the ideological legacy of white domination—provided a context and a coherence to my work and is thus the subject of the next two chapters.

My citizenship status was another identity marker of significance. As I read my students' applications for the study abroad program, it became clear that one of my tasks was going to be addressing who we all, as Americans, were in South Africa. My students' comments about their upcoming semester of study abroad suggested their hopes for an experience packaged for their consumption, comments disturbing in their self-centeredness: "I am hoping for a real multicultural experience"; "I want my experience to show me all aspects of Cape Town"; "I want an authentic African experience." Early on in the term, the students objected to being called tourists, which they felt trivialized their six-month commitment and their desire to become immersed in Cape Town life. So, then, who were they in Cape Town? *Academic* tourists? Travelers? Or just privileged Americans? "Americans studying abroad in Cape Town" seemed to be a special category that locally carried a load of symbolism: of privilege, wealth, and snobbery. One guest speaker for our program made fun of an American study abroad program ("It isn't your program, is it?") that housed its students, according to him, in a walled, private, secure compound in Langa so that the students could claim to have had "a township experience." I phoned a local researcher to invite him as a guest speaker, and he shot back: "I have no time! All these American study abroad programs want workshops and presentations and guest lectures. Don't you know how much time this takes? If I accept, then I have no time to do any of my research!" A request for a meeting with a research group at the University of the Western Cape was denied, and we were told that they don't want anything to do with teaching Americans. Who do we think we are, asking them to give *us* their time? Many who do accept our invitations cannot avoid commenting on the lavishness of our facilities, a truth that the students simultaneously recognize and resent. Coming from an elite school that ensures they eat well and have access to fine facilities, they have a certain set of expectations about how they will be treated, yet they are also chagrined to recognize the privilege of these expectations.

Nick Shepherd, of the University of Cape Town's African Studies Centre, stunned my students into silence during his guest lecture when, after leading them through a complex discussion of class, status, privilege, hierarchy, and inequality in South Africa, he asked, "Who, in South Africa today, has cultural power?" My students responded, a bit hesitantly, "White people?"

"Isn't it you?" Shepherd threw back at them.[5]

Indeed, my students noticed and were bothered by what they felt was the constant carping on the United States by people who love to consume American products. "How can they complain so much about our country when they love American pop stars, American food products, and American designer clothing?" one student asked angrily. The role of the United States as global bully and cultural trendsetter, as gluttonous over-consumer and prolific symbolic exporter complicates our status as citizens of the global behemoth.

We come under constant scrutiny for being American—asked to justify our government's policies, rhetoric, and imperial approaches to international relations. We're asked to explain everything from our farm subsidies, which are killing third world agriculture, to our consumption levels, which are killing the world's natural resources. We're often asked about race relations in the United States—should we have had a Truth and Reconciliation Commission after the civil rights era? Wouldn't that have helped our (not very successful) reconciliation process? As Americans, we are held accountable for our government's decisions but also excused from personal accountability by more generous souls. A former MK commander, for example, remarked kindly to me that a country's citizens cannot be held responsible for the murderous actions of their government;[6] he suggested I look at the example of Robert Mugabe in Zimbabwe. Are Zimbabweans all responsible for his reign of terror and corruption? Yet, at my friend Merle's fiftieth birthday party, held at my house, I was called to account. One of the guests worked internationally on trade and conservation. Her parents are well known in activist and intellectual circles in South Africa and abroad for their engaged progressive politics. As we discussed American politics and the horror many South Africans feel about George Bush's presidency, she asked about the atmosphere at home: how are Americans reacting to his policies and his perspectives? Jokingly, in a party mood, I answered: "That's why I'm here. Our political scene is so depressing at the moment, I'm running away!"

She responded, with a wry smile, "Ah, just like a white South African."

.   .   .   .   .

My friend Johanna asked me if living in Cape Town had made me think differently about things. I immediately answered yes, and in reflecting later on her question, I identified several things that continually cropped up in my classroom discussions in Cape Town. One is understanding and thinking about complicity. Studying the attitudes of white South Africans and the questions many struggle with about their past behavior encourages one to think about what it means to be complicitous with systems of oppression, injustice, and inequality. Americans visiting Cape Town so easily judge and make fun of white South Africans who now say "I never supported apartheid" or "I've never been a racist" or even the slightly more complicated "we were all damaged by apartheid." When listening to racist diatribes, it's hard not to feel shocked and superior; yet the reality of where I come from constantly intrudes. The racism might be more veiled, but it is no less present in the structures of our society. How are Americans different from the racist, head-in-the-sand white South Africans whom we easily make fun of? When our history of white wealth accumulation and black wealth disaccumulation has been so carefully documented?[7] When we consume massive quantities of natural and synthetic resources and choose to ignore the effects of our consumption on our darker global neighbors? When we choose to overlook how our comfort and consumption levels are dependent upon cheap and exploited labor throughout the world? When we ignore the fact that we are utterly dependent upon the manual labor performed by undocumented workers within our borders who lack the legal rights we take for granted? We know this, yet we don't know it, too. So doesn't this make Americans, collectively, as complicitous as white South Africans were under apartheid? Being forced to recognize the parallels between the behavior of white South Africa and white America is unavoidable and uncomfortable.

Furthermore, the American students realize that when they criticize white South Africans for their ignorance of and unwillingness to travel to townships, they often behave similarly at home. One student asked the class how many fellow suburban-dwelling white classmates regularly traveled to or were familiar with the ghetto neighborhoods of their local cities. He remarked that he didn't know anything about the black inner-city ghetto just a few miles from his exclusive white suburb and elite private school. Others—in fact almost all the students (both black and white) in the class—sheepishly agreed. Indeed, the authors of the comprehensive study *American Apartheid* remark: "Blacks living in the heart of the ghetto [in the United States] are among the most isolated people on earth."[8]

Among my group of American students a theme began to emerge by the middle of the semester: as they moved back and forth from their volunteer work in townships to their elite study abroad villa, recognized their enormous privilege compared to the material realities of many, and felt pampered yet realized that they expect and count on a certain minimum standard of luxury, a burden of guilt began to seep over the group. Yet guilt is the most useless emotion of all.

. . . . .

One night after a particularly difficult interview I awoke in distress from a nightmare. I had dreamed that I allowed a hairdresser to bleach my hair white. When she was finished, I looked in the mirror to discover I had become entirely white, as white as flour. My face, my eyebrows, and my eyelashes had been bleached, and my hair had been straightened into long wisps of white thread. I looked deathly and dreadful.

One danger of anthropological fieldwork is how easy it is to become obsessed with a particular subject. The way we do fieldwork is so complex and so encompassing that the anthropologist is forced to filter the daily barrage of conversation and interaction in favor of a few themes that center the research. One colleague who has written several books on Native American aesthetics, symbolism, and language use recalled his boredom when men's conversations on the reservation would turn to reminiscences of their war experiences ("Oh God, war stories again"). Belatedly realizing how important these memories are to the men with whom he works, he finally began paying attention and couldn't believe that for several years he had just tuned out these discussions. The same thing began happening to me in my search for spaces of racial integration and active transformation. Because my teaching orientation was on cultural transformation and the cultural expression of racial/identity politics, I focused almost obsessively on ferreting out spaces where one could witness "transformation" under way, and specifically transformation that effectively challenged and dismantled white privilege.

But one day I was brought up short by a woman's story on the playground at my son's school. She was an older white woman who brought a first grader to school every morning, a plain woman with a worn face, not elegant and professional like some of the moms. She would sit on a bench in the small enclosed playground for the first graders and watch the children. I was doing the same, because my son was struggling with the transition to a new school and wanted me there until the bell rang and the children galloped into their classrooms. She and I—the only adults on the playground—occasionally exchanged pleasantries about the weather and the children's exuberance.

One day we walked out of the playground together after the bell rang, so I ventured a more personal question: "Is it your granddaughter you bring every day?" She responded with a flood of tragedy. The child is her granddaughter, who came to live with her when the child's father—the woman's son-in-law—died unexpectedly during an operation at a very young age. The child was two months old, and the distraught twenty-two-year-old mother "couldn't handle her." It took the mother a long time to pull herself together, and now she visits every few months from Durban, where she lives. Three months earlier, the grandmother's husband had died: "Suicide. Went into the garage and shot himself when I was dropping off the child at preprimary school. Very, very sick. He was a very depressed man." The child was a wonderful crutch to have during a difficult time, she explained. She could have gone to live with her mother but didn't want to go because she didn't really know her mother.

The grandmother's story, which took only a few minutes to recount, left me stunned and reminded me of the personal pain and tragedies of people's lives that have nothing overtly to do with racial politics. It sounds ridiculous, but this woman's story wrenched me into realizing that as I listened to people talk, I had been filtering everything through the lens of politics, race, and "transition"—the categories I'd been using to apprehend contemporary South Africa. I had been giving priority and attention to the politics of the past in every encounter, trying to situate everyone in a racial, political, and class grid of the past and the present. How unanthropological. Listening to this woman's story, I realized that I needed to loosen up my categories of perception and listen emotionally rather than simply analytically; furthermore, I had to listen empathetically to the personal stories of those who occupied what I saw as the "privileged white" category.

. . . . .

Anthropology is about spending lots of time with people, while finding a balance between the urge to interview and the need to deeply hang out, the inevitability of intense emotional connection and the absolute necessity of a sustained critical awareness. Johanna told me that Adrian, her husband, was becoming exhausted by all our intense late-night political discussions, reminding me that levity is an important part of friendship. It's wonderful to sit and laugh, frittering away time, meandering with conversation, telling stories, enjoying the pleasure of companionship. I reigned in my impulse to analyze, critically reflect, talk about the difficult, the uncomfortable, the political. I felt like I almost had to relearn the art of conversation with my growing group of South Africa friends. What do we talk about until late into the night? I can barely recall: books

we've read, music, spirituality, tradition, poetry, raising teenagers, cooking, movies.

. . . . .

Crime. Insecurity. Fear. These are the most pervasive narratives I heard
in white households; my fieldwork journal is filled with pages and pages
of notes recording conversations about crime. Many white South
Africans professed astonishment that I was willing to come to their country and bring my children along. "Aren't you terrified?" "Don't you
know about the crime levels?" Since my (rented) house was the only one
in the neighborhood without any kind of front wall or gate (I was cau-
tioned by many that " 'anyone' could walk right up to the front door!"),
I was warned to always keep my door chained and my windows closed
and to never, ever open the door to strangers. Some of the mothers of my
daughter's friends were appalled that I regularly traveled around metropolitan Cape Town alone at night. By my fourth stay in Cape Town, I
had begun feeling a bit smug and rather mocking of these fears, which
seemed so self-absorbed, racist, and disproportionate.

Toward the middle of that fourth stay, my husband and children were
scheduled to return home for the start of the American school year, while
I remained alone in Cape Town to finish my term with the program. A
few weeks before my family's departure, a woman a few doors down was
attacked in the middle of the day in her home by armed men who
climbed over her garden wall and entered the house through an open
window. They tied her up with her children and made off with the family car and valuables. A week later, the elderly woman and her equally
elderly housekeeper who lived next door to our study abroad center were
attacked at eight in the morning, as we were all arriving for work, by several young men who rang the bell and shoved their way in when the
housekeeper opened the door. The elderly women barely survived their
savage assault, carried out in front of the terrified three-year-old grandchild. That same evening, our security alarm went off at home, and neither security guards nor neighbors came to investigate. After a long wait,
I phoned the security company, who breezily promised that a guard was
on the way. A nervous young security guard finally arrived and reluc-
tantly crept around the house, only investigating the upstairs—where the
security panel indicated the alarm was set off—upon my insistence. Feeling unnerved, we decided to take the children to sleep elsewhere that
night; we were awakened at 3 A.M. by the security company phoning my
cell phone to say our alarms were going off again and asking what we

wanted them to do. Should they go to the house again? My faith in the security company evaporated.

A few days later, as I pulled out of my driveway on the eve of my family's departure, I noticed my neighbor outside watering her hedge. Since she was rarely outside her house—a fortress in miniature, with barred gates in every doorway throughout the interior and exterior ("My husband is absolutely neurotic about security," she had told me on the one occasion when I was invited inside)—I paused to say hello. She knew my husband was about to leave, and commented, oddly: "Well, if I hear screams in the night, then, well . . ." Leaving her sentence dangling, she stepped away from the car to return to her watering. I drove away, wondering what on earth she meant and feeling no comfort in having her as my neighbor. Within the space of two weeks, my smug sense of condescension toward fearful white South Africans had begun to disintegrate as I felt increasingly less confident about my own security as a woman living alone.

In fact, I began to realize that it wasn't only white South Africans who talked about crime all the time. All South Africans that I spent time with talked about crime; crime in townships was rising, and guns were replacing knives, according to the township high school students I spent time with. The high school teacher I shadowed in Langa was hijacked; one student in our peer mentoring group got shot, and two others were robbed at gunpoint. Our program's van was hijacked at gunpoint in Langa and then hijacked again later that year. Friends in Athlone and Grassy Park were robbed by thieves who axed in their front doors when they were at church; another friend's son in Steenberg was robbed of his clothes and shoes one evening as he walked home from the neighborhood convenience store. Parents in Lavender Hill who felt under siege by gang violence argued with me that South Africa needed to reinstitute the death penalty—human rights be damned. "The only people in this country with human rights are the prisoners!" I heard time and again (and this despite the fact that most families in Lavender Hill had family members in prison). Johanna and Adrian in Kenilworth invited me to stay with them after my family left (they had been attacked in their home the previous year by men posing as police officers); Merle, another friend, who occupied a tiny flat in Muizenberg, offered to come stay with me. Although I felt childish and ridiculous, I accepted both offers and divided my remaining time in South Africa between rooming with Merle and staying at Johanna and Adrian's.

The following year, one of Langa's high school principals and I were talking about her perception of increasing danger in Langa. Several teachers and principals had been attacked on school grounds in Langa, and she was beginning to reconsider her routine of arriving very early at school for some quiet working time before teachers and students arrived for the day. "Sometimes you don't know how careful you can be. What does being careful mean? Do you not go to school unless other teachers are there?" I realized this was exactly how I felt, and, it seemed, many Capetonians concurred. What does it mean to be careful? How do you know if you are being careful enough? As my friend Johanna observed, feeling insecure is a normal part of transition, of flux. People's behavior is unpredictable, rules are suspended and under negotiation, and each person has to find a way to read surroundings and assess security. I wasn't very good at it, and I was never entirely sure that I was making safe decisions, but I realized I had no right to judge others for their fears and feelings of insecurity.[9]

. . . . .

Talking with a colleague over dinner about how to write about transformation in Cape Town, we discussed the challenges of telling stories about a situation characterized by so much flux and uncertainty. This is, of course, a constant challenge in anthropology; ethnographies have the unfortunate tendency to freeze the unfolding dramas of life into a static portrait. The challenge strikes me as particularly significant in Cape Town, where the contradictions of daily life are so precariously balanced and unconfidently straddled, and where a person's perspective can change dramatically from one month to the next. Identifying patterns and themes, illustrated by vignettes, interviews, and observations, will have to be the form of my ethnography, with lots of questions left uneasily dangling.

Hoping for inspiration, I attended a talk given by an American anthropologist at one of the universities about the uses of storytelling and narrative in overcoming trauma. He talked of the gap between the therapeutic value of telling one's experiences of trauma and the ability of the bureaucratic realm to provide material compensation for that experience. He asserted that although storytelling is empowering, the path forward after telling one's story is uncertain. It was an interesting and thoughtful talk, but punctuated with fieldwork stories about the struggles the anthropologist had with being accepted, "getting access" to victims, and dealing with their expectations. By the end of the talk, I was completely put off by his smirking tone and condescending attitude toward those whose world he was working to enter. Is this what we sound like?

The presentation reminded me that anthropology can too easily project a patronizing, omnipotent ethnographic tone. During the first years of my research in Cape Town, when my interviews focused on white attitudes and legacies of white supremacy, I realized that I would have to deal with the question of how to write about the racism of those who gave me so much of their time and spoke to me so honestly of their fears, concerns, and beliefs. I came away from these interviews a shaky mess of emotion, feeling gratitude for the honesty of those willing to share their thoughts with me mixed with a horror at their words, a sadness about the circumscribed worldview provided by their parents, their churches, and their government, and shock at the ongoing force of these beliefs. How does one reconcile these emotions? Is it unanthropological to condemn the worldview of those I interview?[10]

This book situates anthropology's analytical home in the broad borderland between description and judgment, where we explore both the development of people's worldviews and the consequences of those views. Cultural relativism, that old core concept in anthropology, does not and cannot apply to situations of domination and racism, because the consequences of subjugation are dire.[11] Thus a fundamental assumption in this book is that if transformation is to be real, racism can have no future in South Africa (or elsewhere) and an utter rejection of racist views is essential. The most dynamic, optimistic, exciting people I met in Cape Town were those engaged in breaking old boundaries and working toward transformation. The most challenged are those struggling with poverty, who deserve all that transformation can bring, and those fighting against transformation, who must overcome their fear of the future. In the following chapter on white attitudes in Cape Town and the legacy of white supremacy, I am trying not to be mocking but to explain, clearly, what these fears are in order to contribute to public debates on how to challenge and overcome racism, white supremacy, and poverty.

CHAPTER 5

Still Waiting

The 2002 Reconciliation Barometer Survey of the Institute of Justice and Reconciliation (IJR) reveals that only 29 percent of whites, compared with 75 percent of blacks, 68 percent of coloureds, and 57 percent of Indians, agreed that whites profited from apartheid and continue to benefit today. Commenting on these statistics, IJR's Karin Lombard reflects that political compromise was successful, but now the time has come for economic compromise.[1]

Meredith tries to explain to me, over tea one rainy afternoon, why the white race is superior. She describes their achievements: they built a modern South Africa out of a tribal backwater; under apartheid they provided a good life for blacks; every white person in South Africa today supports eight black people; blacks are much worse off now, under a black government, than they ever were when the Nats [members of the National Party] were in power, because the ANC [African National Congress] government has ruined the economy and destroyed the previously stable black standard of living. The "idiots" in power are destroying the country, she concludes, quoting her friend who likes to say, "No African country ruled by blacks can be civilized."

Johanna says that she feels like she is just now waking up. "What was I doing all those years?" she asks, reflecting on her acceptance of the apartheid status quo and her timidity during her childhood.

"We didn't know," Susan says of the horrors of apartheid. "We just knew what our parents told us, what the church told us, and what our government told us. And we believed them. Why wouldn't we? It was all we knew."

"Everyone had a choice," Ilze says angrily. She rejects the claims made by white people that they didn't know what was happening during apartheid. "Everyone knew. They made their choices. And they received the benefits."[2]

A coloured man I'll call Trevor recounts to me his accusations against white friends who claimed they didn't know what was happening during apartheid.

> *Trevor:* [I said to them,] "On what continent were you when it hap-
> pened? What country were you in? What city were you in?
> What newspaper did you read? What newscast did you watch?
> And you *never* questioned? . . . Where were you, when all these
> things happened? You can't say you didn't see it. When you
> went to a school and you saw only white faces at the school."
> One poor girl who had become a dear friend of ours was in
> tears about the way I spoke to her. I said, "You went to an
> all-white school. You didn't think?" You know, we found it
> very difficult to accept. [My coloured friends] still battle with
> it. I find it very difficult to accept.
>
> *C. B.:* That people could say, "We really . . .
>
> *Trevor:* "We really didn't know." I found it difficult to accept. How
> could you not know! *How could you not know!* When you got
> into the train to go to school, you sat in the front of the train;
> why are all the other people sitting in the back? When you went
> here, you knew you had to look for signs to go in here. When
> you went to the loo, you knew which loo to go into. When you
> went to the post office, you knew which door to go into. And
> you're telling me you didn't know? Somehow, well, I'm now
> beginning to accept that. I learned that I must accept that. It's
> something of human nature that I will never understand, but in
> fact it did happen. And then I say, did I know everything that
> was happening in Khayelitsha? No I didn't. No I didn't. You
> know? I was so busy carving out my thing in life, battling the
> issues I had to face. We had friends down there and so on, but
> it was also another world away.

. . . . . .

Political conversation in Cape Town is filled with disagreements about what white people knew about the abuses of apartheid, the choices they made during the apartheid years, their ongoing entitlement to the bene-fits granted them by apartheid, and their role in the new South Africa. White attitudes in Cape Town are extraordinarily varied, and although stereotypes of white people abound and provide funny comedy fodder, trying to present a synopsis of "what white people think" would be fool-ish. I met white people who spoke without batting an eye about Africans as dogs and monkeys, and I met white people who so identified with the new possibilities for nonracialism in South Africa's future that they had undertaken massive life changes in order to fully participate in forging a new South Africa. Cape Town is home to white Afrikaners from staunchly conservative, National Party, Dutch Reformed Church backgrounds who are now at the forefront of transformation, and to English speakers who had always positioned themselves as anti-apartheid liberals, yet who are finding it very difficult to embrace post-apartheid transformation. Some white people deal with their guilt over apartheid policies by indulging in stories about the doubts that plagued them during apartheid's darkest years, while others vigorously reaffirm their apartheid-era ideologies. Some white people are deeply depressed about South Africa's transformation; tens of thousands have fled. The end of apartheid allowed some white South Africans to feel liberated for the first time in their lives, while others now feel imprisoned by their whiteness. To be white in Cape Town today is to occupy a fraught social location marked by complex and varied emotions, including fearful insecurity, uncertainty, guilt, relief, excitement, and liberation.

This chapter draws on hundreds of hours of interviews and conversations with white people in Cape Town's southern suburbs. The southern suburbs are historically home to Cape Town's English-speaking white residents, who have tended to define themselves as liberals in opposition to National Party/Afrikaner attitudes and political views.[3] As will become evident, such claims to historic anti-apartheid sentiment, however, do not sit well with many in the post-apartheid context of ongoing white racism, entrenched white wealth and widespread black poverty, and white opposition to redistribution. Furthermore, such claims are also contradicted by historians of colonialism in Africa, who argue that apartheid was a variant of colonial rule elsewhere in the continent, and an extension of the policies enacted under British rule in South Africa.[4] In other words, these studies challenge the idea that apartheid in South Africa was an aberration introduced by maniacal Afrikaners whose racist views and policies contrasted with (in the eyes of some) more benign or well-intentioned colonial ideologies and policies elsewhere in Africa or under the British in South Africa.

Furthermore, apartheid in South Africa lasted beyond the end of colonial rule elsewhere on the continent not because of an intransigent Afrikaner grip on power, but because, in part, the National Party had successfully managed to consolidate the interests of Afrikaners and English-speaking whites. South African social historians have documented how much work over a very long period of time went into the creation of "white" as a unified racial, cultural, and political category in South Africa.[5] Successive South African governments found ways to ameliorate Boer-English antipathy, tiptoe around anti-Semitism, and accommodate non-English, non-Boer pale immigrants from Lebanon, southern Europe, and Japan in order to draw boundaries around and consolidate a national understanding of whiteness that could be starkly contrasted with and affirmed as superior to native blackness.[6] The political scientist Anthony Marx writes, "The initial polarization between Afrikaners and English was brought to a head by the British Empire's victory in the Boer War. Reconciliation of the warring parties was conceived in terms of mutual agreement to discriminate legally against the black majority; 'intra-white' division was healed through reinforced racial domination."[7] Marx argues that white unity was effected, in part, by bringing the standard of living for Afrikaners in line with that of English-speaking South Africans, and gaining the latter's support for the Afrikaner National Party through promising modest reforms that appealed to English liberal ideas. Indeed, the growing white support for the National Party during the final decades of apartheid demonstrates the apartheid government's success at consolidating white interests. Despite this history, and despite the fractures that remain in the edifice of white unity, there is very little public dialogue about the construction of whiteness as a category and set of cultural practices and assumptions.[8]

Thousands of scholarly pages have been devoted to analyzing the tools used to consolidate apartheid ideology and generate a collective agreement about the legitimacy of enforcing white domination over the black population. Looking back on their upbringing, the white South Africans I interviewed spoke of the impact of their schooling, their churches, the media, and the state security apparatus. Under the state policy of Christian National Education, schools taught a version of South African history that glorified the role of white settlers in building the country and denied the legitimacy of a historic black presence. Churches preached a doctrine of racial separatism, patriarchy, and white supremacy. Media censorship (television was not introduced until 1976, and the entry into the country of foreign books, films, and music was tightly controlled) ensured a constant, uniform message that placated whites, ignored black grievances, and during the cold war, increasingly portrayed blacks and those opposed to apartheid as communists and terrorists. "We were fed poison, dripped into our brains," laments one middle-aged white man. "We were brainwashed," I heard time and time again. One might wonder how a population can so easily allow itself to be brainwashed by "poison," but as the world has seen time and again, a unified, constant set of messages disseminated via schools, the church, and the media is breathtakingly effective in consolidating public opinion for those who stand to benefit from those messages.

Several white people recalled their awakening during their first trips overseas, when they realized for the first time how the rest of the world viewed their country. Others reminisced, laughing, about the absurdities they were taught in Sunday school as they tried to reconcile the contradiction of legal racial inequality with the doctrine that God loves all humans equally. John Gilmour remembers asking why churches were segregated, if both whites and blacks have the same God. In a rollicking discussion at my house over dinner one night, John and Adrian, both of whom left their churches long ago, remembered asking whether, if there is only one God, all people go to the same heaven, and how can that be allowed? "We were told that we are all given new bodies in heaven," recalled John, "because there is no color in heaven." Adrian, chuckling, reports he was simply told, "Stop asking such questions!" I heard many descriptions by white people of their "awakening" from the years of apartheid misinformation as they tried to understand how they could have remained so ignorant and unaware of their society's injustices. White people's willingness to acknowledge apartheid's abuses are far from uniform and span the spectrum from utter denial ("apartheid was an excellent system that benefited blacks") to severe depression at the realization that one had happily subscribed to a worldview that was a contrived and harmful pack of lies.[9]

. . . . .

An evening early in my first term in Cape Town with one of the local branches of an international service club impressed me with what it revealed about the consolidation of whiteness. The evening was a club "fellowship" social gathering rather than a business meeting, hosted in a club member's home in a wealthy suburb on the Atlantic coast just beyond the downtown. Club members were a varied group and included a retired German cook who had immigrated to South Africa in 1951, a middle-aged Afrikaner real estate agent, a former judge in the Ministry of Justice, a young Afrikaner lawyer couple born in Stellenbosch, a retired Australian-born stockbroker, an older English-born ophthalmologist, and an assortment of wives and other members. Although they lived and worked in far-flung parts of the metropolitan area (downtown, the Atlantic suburbs, the southern suburbs, the northern suburbs), they had been gathering for years. Their personalities seemed wildly at odds: the German cook was loud, raucous, and sloppy, singing Waltzing Matilda at the top of his lungs; the real estate agent was dapper in a pinstriped suit and monocle, with an oddly affected way of holding his cigarette; the young lawyers talked thoughtfully about new changes in the labor laws and the role of advocates in defining labor law in the new South Africa; the stockbroker, whose retirement years are devoted to community service, was guardedly optimistic about South Africa's future. One woman, sadly suffering from dementia, was parked in a corner and kept trying to enter various conversations with nonsense sentences. Before dinner, I chatted with a club member's wife who explained to me that white South Africans who have emigrated are now returning to South Africa because of the weather and the availability of domestic help. "You can't live abroad and have a gardener and a maid. It's so much more comfortable and luxurious here, and we're used to that." One of the young advocates responded, quietly, "Not everyone has a maid and a gardener." As our conversation meandered, I mentioned how I was training my ear to understand the variety of accents in Cape Town. The club member's wife asked if I'd ever had occasion to talk to "one of the new South Africans."

"The who?" I asked.

"The new South Africans. The blacks. They're hardly understandable! You can't make out a word they're saying. Impossible to understand." She went on to describe the new black elite that "we're now seeing here." She now has black people, expensively dressed, wearing designer labels, coming into her clothing shop, and when they speak—here she paused meaningfully—"they're Americanized. I see their Gucci shoes, their designer jeans. I can tell. They've been away. They've got money."

Before I could clarify her meaning (Blacks have to go away to achieve financial success? Black South Africans who travel abroad are no longer African?), our conversation was interrupted by a drunk young club member who began loudly telling racist jokes ("What's the difference between a coloured and a donkey?" "About four beers.") and maligning the black newscasters on television for their success ("They may earn good salaries here, but in England they'd be nothing! They wouldn't be able to live on what they earn!"). The young lawyers shut him up by telling a long string of anti-lawyer jokes. After several of these, the drunken man reprimanded them harshly, saying, "That's terrible! You shouldn't run down your own profession. Stop it!" I wondered if the lawyers had launched into their barrage of jokes in order to derail his racist monologue, which had been vicious and shocking. This commentary was particularly noteworthy since the club member who drove me to the party had been lamenting the lack of black members in the club, musing that black middle-class professionals had yet to develop a service ethic.

The evening continued with a long, serious conversation about South Africa's future; except for the stockbroker, the group's sentiments were far from positive. The real estate agent emphasized South Africa's promise but argued that "the rest of Africa is a disaster, and South Africa is tarred with the same brush" in the eyes of investors. One of the young lawyers kept repeating that South Africa is "in a nosedive, down the tubes, falling apart," while flinging his hand in a downward trajectory as if imitating a crashing plane. The multinational companies are raping the country and the continent, he argued, and South Africa is falling victim to the same forces of globalizing capital as the rest of the continent. "And nobody cares," he persisted, offering the example of Mugabe's destruction of Zimbabwe and his use of a private army to protect his gold mines in Congo. "The international community sits back and says, 'Oh, you bad boy. Don't do that!' Whereas look at what they did to South Africa during apartheid. They made us into a pariah nation! Sanctions! A bunch of outcasts! Look at what they did to South Africa, and now no one's doing anything to Mugabe." The stockbroker noted that no one cares now about Zimbabwe, whereas during apartheid the rand was stronger than the dollar and the United States was just emerging from dealing with its own racial issues, so apartheid came under a lot of pressure. Now the United States is rich, she argued, and couldn't care less about what's happening in Zimbabwe. She suggests South Africa will follow the pattern of Mozambique, which, she argued, was successfully engineering a development strategy out of the ruins of its prolonged, violent civil war. "But *we're* down the tubes," repeated the lawyer. "In a nosedive."

The evening concluded with the entire group singing nationalist Afrikaans songs, with obvious emotion and longing. I left the party trying to imagine what brought this disparate group of people from different neighborhoods and backgrounds together month after month; what tied the young lawyers to the racist joke teller and the retired baker, and the English-born ophthalmologist from the southern suburbs to the Afrikaner real estate agent from the northern suburbs. Perhaps the collective singing revealed the clue; as the young man quoted in chapter 3 had explained to me: "You surround yourself with people who will agree with you and leave it at that." Perhaps the obvious differences among the party guests in home language, religion, place of residence, age, profession, and educational levels receded in the face of the desire to come together as white people who share an adherence to the sentiments expressed through apartheid-era (thus racially marked) nationalist songs.

The apartheid-era doctrine that whiteness and blackness are naturally discrete biological and social categories continues to pervade social life in Cape Town, even though apartheid's separatist policies, created to uphold and ensure racial distinctiveness, are discredited. The conviction that white people and black people are inherently culturally distinct has enormous force, underscored in the minds of some by an ongoing belief in biological and evolutionary distinctions as well. White people often expect to feel comfortable with other white people and to feel uncomfortable with people of color. In a commentary published in the South African *Mail and Guardian,* Bryan Rostron writes, "One of the greatest illusions of apartheid was that it deluded most whites for nearly another half-a-century that they lived in a virtual European society. Many still cannot wake from their dream." The idea of an urban white European culture in Cape Town that is different from African culture has emotional force that resonates deeply with white people uncertain about their future in a black-dominated African country.

The young lawyer's pessimistic insistence that South Africa is "in a nosedive," headed "down the tubes," reflects a vision of decline I heard widely repeated by white people in Cape Town. It emerges in the obsessive concern with the need to maintain "standards" expressed by many principals and parents of formerly white schools, it echoes the insistence that black rule inevitably means civilizational decline, it underlies the constant talk of crime and disorder and the argument that affirmative action programs are promoting incompetence by advancing the unskilled too quickly. The "nosedive" view of South Africa's future leaves many whites wondering about their future in Cape Town, where they feel increasingly marginalized and insecure.

Talking about standards helps white people articulate their fears about black majority rule in a way that comfortably sidesteps race and allows them to focus their fears on a seemingly factual matter. Responding to my observation about the expensive private all-white schools that seemed to be cropping up in post-apartheid Cape Town, one mother who also teaches at one of these schools explained: "It's not a choice motivated by racism but by wanting what's best academically for your child. The private school is internationally orientated; it maintains an international standard so its learners can attend university abroad, and that's where the future and income potential is." The principal of the school where she teaches acknowledged that the school body is entirely white, because of the high school fees and lack of financial aid, but defended the school's elitism: "In the early years we feel we need to make a statement about academic standards. We're proud of what we're doing—we don't feel guilty." The principal of another elite, expensive private school explained: "The important thing during transformation is to ensure that standards are strictly adhered to—standards of living, of education, of values, of medicine, etc. Otherwise we will go the way of Zimbabwe, where the rule of law and the rule of property was allowed to erode." He noted that while he didn't necessarily predict that such decline would happen in South Africa, his job is to ensure that at his school, standards "aren't compromised," specifically that his students can compete in an international arena.

Late in 2002, I sat in John Gilmour's office at the private alternative school where he was then principal. A warm, dynamic educator thrilled about the possibilities for education made possible by the political transformation, he was dejectedly describing a conference from which he had just returned, attended by five hundred South African educators from private schools. He had found the conference "chilling." According to him, the mood at the conference crystallized the sense—militant and desperate at the same time—of many white educators and parents that South Africa's apartheid-era standards for white schools were under siege and necessary to defend. All the discourse was on "holding on to what they had, taking an orientation of defining themselves in a context of less rather than more opportunity." Rather than expressing excitement about moving in new directions, the focus according to John was looking to external standards of evaluation (particularly from Australia) and rejecting South Africa's new post-apartheid curriculum.[10] It was all about rejecting the local, which was imagined as disintegrating and deteriorating, and insisting that in the midst of this decline, they will remain committed to maintaining their former standards, now obtained from abroad.

In fact, formerly white schools have found a number of ways to hold on to what they had. In anticipation of reduced state funding after 1994, some sold off portions of their property (in exclusive neighborhoods) to developers, the profit from which created private endowments for their schools. The creation of governing boards allowed to hire their own teachers is defended by wealthier schools as a way to maintain standards. Such boards have the right to set school fees and use the fees to hire teachers of their choice, in addition to state-funded teaching positions, enabling wealthier schools to maintain much lower student-to-teacher ratios (I found ratios in wealthier schools to be less than thirty to one and ratios in township schools to be more than fifty to one), to provide their teachers with more administrative (nonteaching) blocks of time for preparation, and to ensure some class uniformity in their student body. Because teachers in comparatively underresourced township schools tend to have far fewer free time blocks per day, they may teach as many as two times the number of learners in a day than their colleagues in wealthier schools. These differences are, of course, in addition to the preexisting infrastructural and resource differences, such as playing fields; laboratory, library, media, and computer facilities; sporting equipment; a school hall or indoor performance space; school square footage relative to the student body; and architectural design and construction materials. Formerly white schools are vastly better endowed in all these areas.

Although views about standards expressed by teachers, parents, and principals were rarely couched in overtly racist language, these concerns evidence broader racist assumptions about the inescapable trajectory of countries under black rule. These assumptions are tied to a belief in fundamental cultural differences between whites and blacks and to the certainty that white culture will be marginalized in the new South Africa, which will result in civilizational decline because of the inherent superiority of white ways of doing things. Descriptions of South Africa's deterioration evoke images of white South Africa as a civilizational outpost clinging to the tip of Africa, as made clear in one man's description of his wife's family's relocations in Africa in response to the advent of black rule: "When Kenya went wrong, they moved to Rhodesia; when Rhodesia went wrong, they came to South Africa." "Now Cape Town is the only place left in Africa with white people," another man remarked.

For white South Africans with a self-consciousness of belonging to a people under siege clinging to the tip of the continent, visions of impending chaos and disorder loom large. As *Cape Times* columnist Sandile Dikeni observed, "The sudden realization that one is a minority with, besides money, only a culture to protect, can get one into a frenzy."[11] One woman who lives in Newlands described life in Cape Town these days: "I feel like a great tide is rising to engulf us."

"A tide of what?" I asked.

She closed her eyes: "Of theft."

Her feeling of living under siege is almost palpable as she notes the pattern "all over Africa of blacks rising up and massacring the whites. . . . If people could emigrate freely, there would be no one left in

South Africa"—meaning, of course, no one white. "It's all chaos; there's no order. There are shacks everywhere, people selling on the streets. It never used to be like this." As she continues talking, it is clear that her imagined tide of theft is stealing her white way of life, characterized by order, security, stability, and residential segregation.[12]

While some white people sidestepped the issue of race when discussing their fear of falling standards, others who dwelled on South Africa's decline toward chaos claimed a racist worldview. "There was nothing wrong with apartheid," one man from Newlands explained. "Races are at different stages of their development, and separate policies are necessary. It is unfortunate that those in power [during apartheid] made some poor decisions, but the basic premise of apartheid makes perfect sense." A woman from Rondebosch, who proudly declared to me that she is racist, wanted to distinguish herself clearly from "those liberals who claimed to support the end of apartheid and then fled when it came, or who now sequester themselves in big mansions and have no contact with black people." The people she feels most sorry for are working-class Afrikaners—"those poor sods"—who now must live next door to black people, thereby endangering their cultural distinctiveness and physical security. Explaining her brand of racism, she commented (six times, in fact, in the course of one conversation): "We have a great love for the blacks. We just don't want them marrying our daughters."[13] She emphasized all the cultural differences between blacks and whites that make racial integration not only folly but dangerous. School integration is a disaster, she argued, because the coloured and African children have such different standards and abilities from the white children, and their presence in white schools was negatively transforming those schools and enabling the horror of cross-race dating, which "none of the parents want" and which is "a powder keg ready to explode." Muslim girls who attend her daughter's formerly white school and who do not participate in sports are compromising the school's sporting traditions and thus the school's reputation. She is deeply troubled by the rise of cross-race adoptions, a sentiment I heard many white people express, because black children are unsuitable candidates for white culture and will end up traumatized and the source of endless problems for their white families. She couldn't even imagine the possibility of black families adopting white children.

Stories of white couples who adopt black children seem to strike a particular nerve. Some stories emphasize the trauma for a black child being raised culturally white in South Africa, some describe the horror of white grandparents who cannot accept their new black grandchildren, and some detail the anguish of white parents when their black children (inevitably, in these stories) decide to reject white culture (and therefore their white parents). Clearly, the growing practice of cross-race adoptions is a topic of significance as South Africans try to piece together new understandings of the relationship between race and culture. I met one white woman living in Muizenberg who took in and raised an abandoned, sickly, premature black baby. The child, now a young woman at university, gets a lot of questions about her culturally white upbringing; she does not speak an African language or practice African cultural traditions. "That's hard," I say to the adoptive mother. "No, not at all," she responds matter-of-factly. "It's the way she was raised." Thinking anthropologically, I was referring to what I imagined might be the girl's fatigue with having to deal with assumptions her peers make about her "natural" cultural orientation. The mother, also thinking anthropologically, was clarifying that assumptions about a biological link between culture and race are bogus.

Apartheid-era lessons that blacks are culturally inferior and at a lower stage of cultural evolution are deeply entrenched in the minds of many white people, even those who claim a liberal identity. The journalist Allister Sparks observes that English-speaking South African whites see themselves connected to a global arena, rather than assuming a South African identity. Distressed by crime and affirmative action, they are afflicted with a "subliminal unease that black people can't really govern efficiently," a persistent negativism that ties in to global Afro-pessimism.[14] An inability to overcome this assumption undergirds the widely held certainty of civilizational decline shared by many white people. One woman from Newlands explained:

> The transition happened too fast, it was too sudden. Suddenly everything is supposed to be different, but the new people in charge don't know how to run anything. They're like underprivileged children in a candy store. They see goodies everywhere and want to take everything they can as fast as they can. They haven't been educated; they haven't been brought up properly. They don't know how to behave. It's just like if you take an underprivileged person and put them into an upper-class home—they have to learn how to conduct themselves, and South Africa needs time to do that.[15]

The theme of theft recurs in comments from many white people about the loss of their neighborhood exclusivity: "Before 1994 we could walk the streets without fear," writes a "concerned citizen" in a letter to the editor of a local newspaper. "Granted your government has given all citizens freedom of access to previously restricted areas, but at what cost?"[16] Sitting in her well-appointed living room in Claremont, a white woman angrily said to me, "I live in a prison; I don't go out anymore. The criminals control the streets now."

All the white people who expressed to me their overtly racist views emphasized that they spoke for all their friends and neighbors: "We all feel the same way"; "You won't find anyone who disagrees with me around here"; "All my friends agree with me, but they would be reluctant to tell you themselves because they know the 'right' things they are supposed to say now." Self-identified racists chastise their like-minded friends who hide their real views behind politically correct language or who avoid acknowledging their racist views in front of strangers. After one particularly painful luncheon, at which the men had indulged in viciously racist storytelling about black people's natural incompetence and stupidity, one of the wives who apparently had noticed my shock and discomfort took me aside and whispered, with visible embarrassment: "Don't take my husband's comments too seriously. He gets going sometimes. . . . Please don't worry about what he's saying."

.   .   .   .   .

A *Mail and Guardian* commentary harshly critiques white gatherings where guests assume collective agreement and shared perspectives:

> You've been invited over to meet new people. They turn out to be white, professional folk. At first they seem interesting and pleasant enough. Then—whoosh—the conversation lurches unpleasantly. Suddenly, you find yourself trapped in an old, unwanted conversation, like being sucked back into a sinister time warp of apartheid hell. . . . Over the past year, despite entering the 21st century, this had happened all too often. Frankly, meeting new white acquaintances proves more and more, I find, to represent an appalling social hazard. . . . From purely personal observation, I would say that many white South Africans are now simply reverting to type: that our historical pigmentocracy—after a brief period of modest silence—is simply lapsing back into old attitudes. Increasingly I hear white people voice attitudes that I don't believe they would have dared vent, say, two years ago. . . .
> God rot their lily-white souls.[17]

.   .   .   .   .

An Afrikaner friend recalled a recent experience at a nice restaurant in Durban. One table was occupied by four white Afrikaner men, drinking heavily and behaving badly. Two "lovely young ladies" entered, accompanied by two well-dressed, polite black men, who held the door and pulled out the chairs for their dates, quietly attentive. As my friend watched, he observed how natural and comfortable the couples were, at ease and obviously enjoying themselves. The moment made a huge impression on him; he realized that he'd much rather have that situation for his daughters than the drunken, obnoxious Afrikaners at the other table. After clarifying that the "lovely young ladies" were white, I asked him if there are white fathers who would choose the latter. He looked at me like I was an idiot and responded, "Yes. Most definitely."

.   .   .   .   .

The commonly heard expression that South Africa is "going down the tubes" packages together white South African fears of economic decline, slipping educational standards, rising crime rates, governmental corruption, and importantly, the loss of white cultural integrity. The belief in "civilizational decline" points to white fears that white culture and white standards will become increasingly marginalized in the new South Africa, even for white people who deny that their sentiments are motivated by racism and who insist that they never supported apartheid. Many white people are deeply threatened by affirmative action and black empowerment initiatives, which they take personally as an indication that they and their children are no longer welcome in the new South Africa. "The pendulum has swung too far," one hears time and time again. "Before the whites had all the power, and now the blacks do, and it's just as unfair. And as for the poor coloureds; it used to be they weren't white enough. Now they're not black enough."

Next to crime, fears about affirmative action took center stage in white dinner party talk. White people often claimed that huge numbers of white men were losing their jobs—a claim not even remotely borne out by statistics—and that South Africa offers no future to their children, particularly their male children.[18] One young white mother of two daughters from Rondebosch told me that she and her husband were thinking of leaving South Africa because they might want to have a third child. "But if it's a boy, what chances will he have? We can understand affirmative action for now, but the future is the problem. The uncertainty." Another older white man from Constantia with two unmarried daughters worried about the prospects for his daughters' future (presumably white) husbands: "For a young white man to stay in South Africa is suicidal."

Another white woman, who has committed herself to professional work in township community development, emphasized her decision to remain in Cape Town despite having a British passport and a husband with Australian citizenship. She feels passionately about her need to stay, but she also believes that South Africa does not offer a future for her children. She wants them to leave, not only because she wants them to see themselves as living in an international context and a global world, which South Africa's low salaries and isolated geographic location would hinder, but also because she believes that "Zimbabwe offers instructive lessons about the possible futures for white people in Africa, and the immediate future may be a limited one for whites." She added hopefully: "South Africa may be for my grandchildren, but not my children."

In fact, despite their pessimism about their economic future, the economic status of white South Africans remains strong—stronger than any other racial group. Karin Lombard of Cape Town's Institute for Justice and Reconciliation reports that, nationwide, whites continue to earn salaries eight times greater than those of blacks, continue to experience the lowest unemployment levels of all racial groups (9 percent compared with 46 percent of blacks), continue to be disproportionately promoted to senior and managerial positions (60 percent of which are held by whites, 6 percent by coloureds, and 27 percent by blacks), continue to hold the vast majority (80 percent) of senior management positions, and continue to have a much greater chance of finding employment after graduation (during 1995–99, 75 percent of those leaving white schools and entering the labor market for the first time found jobs, compared with 29 percent of those leaving black schools). Lombard acknowledges that while the job market was beginning to shift by 2004, white South Africans continue to experience vastly greater economic security than their fellow citizens.[19]

In addition to the belief that affirmative action will force white men into unemployment or dead-end jobs is the concern that affirmative action policies will contribute to a deteriorating work environment. A conversation one evening in 2002 at a neighbor's home in Newlands with four young white men, all enrolled at the university, predictably turned to the perils of affirmative action and the skills gap created by companies moving black people into positions for which they have not been properly trained or educated. All four of the young men had assured local professional jobs waiting for them after graduation, and two of them were even attending university on bursaries funded by their employers. Their concerns were not about losing job opportunities because of affirmative action, but rather about the quality of their coworkers hired through affirmative action initiatives. These concerns were significant enough to encourage each of them to seek work overseas, even though they all had promising careers in Cape Town.

Most older white couples I met in the southern suburbs have children living abroad. One parent suggested to me that the younger generation of white South Africans in England dislike it there but are "waiting it out to see where things are headed in South Africa before committing to return." I heard endless discussions about affirmative action at white dinner tables in the southern suburbs. Such conversations always turned to white flight and the need for the younger generation to leave South Africa, although someone would occasionally remark on the miserable experiences of some white South Africans abroad which caused them to return and build careers and families back in Cape Town. These conversations were often a poignant mix of observations: white South Africans have to leave to find success and security, white South Africans abroad are miserable and miss home terribly, sometimes interspersed with humorous comments about white South Africans abroad who spend all their time with other white South Africans complaining about South Africa and justifying their choice to leave. The typical consensus was that whites don't want to leave but, sadly, have no choice because of government policies that discriminate against white people.

Conversations with white people about the effects of affirmative action and "reverse racism" on white men's job prospects rarely included an acknowledgment that job prospects are tight for everyone—much tighter in fact for black people than for white people—because of the economy. White people aren't losing jobs to affirmative action as much as they are, like everyone else, losing jobs to a shifting economy. Johanna commented that white people cannot adjust to the fact that they no longer have guaranteed job security and now must compete for a job. In an interview, Mary Burton (formerly of the Black Sash) observed that it would have been terrific if the transition had happened when the economy was booming, but because it happened during a time of national and international recession, increased competition for jobs in the context of affirmative action "is making life real," in stark contrast to the apartheid-era unreality of assured job security for anyone white and male.[20] As with real estate, feelings of entitlement have been very difficult for many white people to relinquish.

. . . . .

A dirty, bedraggled, apparently homeless young white man appeared one day several years ago at the major intersection in my neighborhood holding a sign asking for assistance. In all my months of residence over the next few years, driving past him sometimes several times a day, I never saw anyone give him anything. Then one day, for the first time, I saw someone reach out of their car window to give him some change. That day he was holding a new sign that said, "RETRENCHED. Sickly family to support. Please help." Coincidence?

. . . . .

At a question-and-answer session of Parliament with Thabo Mbeki in 2002, Tony Leon and the other Democratic Alliance (DA) members of Parliament relentlessly hammered President Mbeki about his refusal to publicly and forcefully denounce the behavior of President Mugabe's regime in Zimbabwe.[21] President Mbeki responded eloquently in a firm, controlled diatribe against the Democratic Alliance's obsession with Zimbabwe. He noted South Africa's intervention in averting conflict potentially affecting millions in Cote d'Ivoire, "yet the DA only wants to talk about Zimbabwe." He noted South Africa's involvement in seeking a peaceful reconciliation in Rwanda and Burundi, war-torn countries in which millions were affected by violence, "and you say, let's talk about Zimbabwe." Mbeki said he wanted to talk about the Sudan, where millions are affected by political violence, and the DA only wanted to talk about Zimbabwe. He concluded by saying that he knew why they were obsessed with Zimbabwe: because they were afraid that if the South African government didn't ostracize Mugabe and cut diplomatic and personal ties, the ANC government would be sending a message that white South Africans are not secure. Briefly, wearily, Mbeki concluded by once again defending his position on Zimbabwe, while a white Democratic Alliance member of Parliament turned to her colleague and slowly ran her finger across her neck.[22]

. . . . .

Some white people justify their privileges by claiming a kinship with whites in Europe, Australia, and the United States that gives them the right to enjoy the same lifestyle and material wealth as middle-class whites on those continents. White South Africans who feel increasingly marginalized in South Africa talk of their deep connection to their European heritage and to Euro-American culture. One man from Constantia explained that white people's post-apartheid choice to leave South Africa for Europe was natural, like completing a historic cultural circle to rejoin white compatriots in former European homelands: "All of our ancestors left Europe because of unfavorable socioeconomic circumstances. Now some are returning for the same reason." When I met this man in

1999, he was so ebullient and full of hope about the new South Africa that he had retired from teaching in order to open a new business in the tourism sector. During our conversation two years later, I tried to capture how his attitude had shifted after he told me, "To be white here now is terrible. We are marginalized, insecure, and not wanted."

"But you're OK here?" I asked, trying to resurrect his optimism of 1999.

He covered his face with his hands and said somberly, "No, no. I'm not OK here. I'm not OK." With a tone bordering on despair, he described his growing feelings of insecurity, discomfort, and fear for his children's future. He is now hoping to save enough money to retire in England.

Embracing the theme of global white kinship, Lynette, from Newlands, commented:

> South Africa is the only country of any economic power where white people are discriminated against. The rest of the world—white South Africa's relatives—doesn't care. The world hasn't been kind to South Africa, even though white Americans share their English heritage with white South Africans. Sanctions destroyed the South African economy and made things very hard for white South Africans. Now emigration is very difficult and these countries seem unwilling to recognize their historic links to whites in South Africa. We've been forgotten and ignored. Whites in the other economic powers aren't taking care of white South Africans. It's terrible.

A letter to the editor in the local newspaper, responding to the Home for All Campaign,[23] pursues a similar logic: "What do I possess today that I would not have had, had my grandfathers established themselves in New Zealand, Australia, or Canada? I have had the opportunities that are taken for granted abroad, and I have worked for everything I now possess. Effort (not privilege) has been rewarded the way hard work is rewarded elsewhere. . . . Would the campaign be satisfied if we were dispossessed of what average folk abroad have, so producing the lowest common denominator among the population?"

This insistence that white South Africans share a fundamental cultural and biological connection to white people abroad heightens white South Africans' feelings of disconnection and dislocation at home. As Cape Town becomes blacker, as workplaces and schools integrate, as black empowerment initiatives grow, some of Cape Town's white residents cling to Anglo-Saxon traditions and insist on their right to maintain a white middle-class lifestyle and to expect to be surrounded with Euro-American cultural practices. In one conversation at a friend's home in

Claremont, an older white man observed that whites who choose to stay in South Africa will simply have to "become African and let what happens happen, take it as it comes." His wife gasped and argued that such a thing was impossible—one can't simply become African: "Changing to become African would be really hard, especially for middle-aged people. You have to be born into that way of thinking and being!"

. . . . .

On evening in 2002, some friends invited me and my husband to a Muizenberg Ratepayers Association fund-raiser for the Cape Town Symphony Orchestra at the Muizenberg pavilion. Although Muizenberg had become an unusually diverse community within the Cape Town metropolis, with not only a mixed South African population but a growing population of foreign African immigrants as well, the evening was an emphatic celebration of white culture. The orchestra, a Muizenberg dance school, and a local diva performed American and English pop music and songs from hit Broadway and West End musicals. Acknowledging Thabo Mbeki's efforts to promote the idea of an African Renaissance, the enthusiastic emcee proclaimed that there was no better way to kick off Muizenberg's renaissance than with this evening's lineup of classical and pop European and American music, which represented the very best of what the community had to offer. Sitting next to me, a top-level university administrator who lives in Muizenberg and was obviously chagrined by the evening's programming kept muttering, "I'm here for community building. I'm here for community building."

. . . . .

According to white educators and some parents, discourses of deterioration are having a profoundly detrimental effect on the younger white generation. White flight and constantly voiced fears about the future, about affirmative action and retrenchment, about crime, and about disintegration are producing, according to several middle-aged white men and women, growing racism among white youth. "They're reactionaries!" one father said about his daughters and their friends.

"What do you mean?" I asked.

"Racists! They're racists!" he responded (notably, however, placing the blame on the government's "anti-white" policies for driving his daughters to this extreme). In a separate conversation, another man confided that he can hardly stand to be around his daughter's friends because of their intolerance and racism. I reflected with many friends on this seeming irony that some in the younger white generation may be more racist than their parents. Middle-aged residents of the southern suburbs emerged from the traumatic final decade of apartheid with their wealth intact and can afford to feel relief and some degree of certainty that they won't lose their comforts or their lifestyle. They retain clear memories of the awful and tense final years of apartheid, when they were aware of their status as international pariahs and that change was inevitable. For them, materially, change turned out to be far less painful than many anticipated, because the post-apartheid government pursued neoliberal economic policies that favor the wealthy, rather than the much-feared communist or socialist redistributive initiatives, and emphasized the need for reconciliation rather than revenge. Their children's generation never witnessed the worst of apartheid but is constantly reminded that their comfortable lifestyle is not guaranteed. Because they receive virtually no education about why white people accumulated wealth under apartheid and black people accumulated poverty, they lack any kind of systemic understanding of apartheid's unequal legacies and take personally discussions about redistribution or black empowerment. Over and over one hears young white adolescents argue that they were not responsible for apartheid's sins, so why do they have to pay the price? Why should they be held accountable for policies made during their parents' youth? Why should they lose out on jobs to black candidates? Why should they lose school bursaries to black students? Why should they be made to feel guilty for their material comforts? Those who credit black empowerment and affirmative action policies with increasing racial tensions, white flight, and producing racism among South Africa's white youth never acknowledge the effects on racial tensions of enduring apartheid legacies of inequality and white assumptions of privilege and entitlement.

In addition to those who observe a growing racism in the younger generation, teachers often commented about their white high school students' levels of apathy, hopelessness, and depression. One educator, reflecting on his students' parents' views of the country ("it's going to the dogs," "it's down the tubes," "it's falling apart"), their emphasis on the lack of opportunity for white people, and their pessimism about their children's job prospects, imitated a parent talking to his son: "You'd better work really hard and be better than anyone else, because that's your only chance, and even then it's not a good one. You'll end up a waiter in London because there's nothing here." Absorbed into their parents' pessimism, many of the kids he teaches feel completely hopeless about their future. He believes heroin use is skyrocketing (an observation I heard from several other teachers about their white students), which he sees as evidence of growing depression and desperation.[24] These educators blame white parents' unyieldingly pessimistic attitudes for the depressed mental state of their students, rather than the black empowerment initiatives supported by the government.

. . . . .

A pervasive negativity about South Africa's future. An obsessive and myopic focus on problems, especially crime and changes in the educational curriculum and school demographics. A certainty that affirmative action and black empowerment, as well as changes in the tax code and school integration, are anti-white initiatives that are unfair and unjust and will result in economic decline. A belief—whether overtly stated or not—in black inferiority. At its nasty edges—or is it at the nasty core?—an assumption that anything locally produced by South African black people (whether artistic productions or economic and political policy) is inferior. A refusal to acknowledge how apartheid structured the economy to create white wealth and entrench black poverty. A belief that "whites built this country," that "we deserve everything we have because we worked hard for it" and because "we don't have anything different from what whites in Europe, North America, and Australia have." "We have nothing to apologize for, and now we're being discriminated against." This constellation of attitudes around the nosedive view of South Africa is familiar to anyone who spends much time in white company.

Cape Times columnist Sandile Dikeni wrote of his frustrations with such commentary prior to the 1994 elections:

> It is a slap in the face when people, civilized white people, go out of their way to express their fear of a black government. . . . Should we as Africans in South Africa look at the history of the world and conclude that white people crucified Jesus Christ? Should we look at the two world wars caused by white Europeans and conclude that whites are murderous? Should we reflect again on the USSR experience as another example of white cruelty? Should I blame the pain of diaspora in America and the annihilation of native Americans to white hands? If I do, will anyone understand me? No they won't. They will call me a racist or an angry black man.
>
> Tell me, Table Mountain, what should I say when they say that the reason for this fear is because Idi Amin committed atrocities in Uganda and therefore I am also going to kill them here in South Africa?[25]

South Africans of color, as well as progressive white South Africans, offer a strong set of popular responses to the nosedive view. Some do so by pointing out that complaints about falling standards are poorly veiled attacks on school and workplace integration, some attempt to talk back in public and private forums to racist visions of South Africa's decline, and some work to promote local talent. Wendy's husband, Peter, tells me that he can hardly stand to attend parent functions at his children's school or evening social gatherings at his church anymore because of the barrage of complaints about the negatives associated with transformation. Black student athletes attending formerly white schools joke that the reason these schools are afraid to start soccer teams is because no one would play rugby anymore and the culture of white manhood would be compromised.

At a small party, Johanna overindulged in champagne in disgust at the endless grumblings of a group of wealthy young white women. Emboldened by the champagne, she told them, to their extreme discomfort, to stop their whining and acknowledge their privileged lifestyles. (She phoned the next day with an apology.) The Baxter Theater staged a play called *The Great Outdoors,* identified in one review as South Africa's first post-apartheid play, which features a white female protagonist who leaves her husband and comfortable, exclusive, protected, white middle-class lifestyle to run off with an unpredictable policeman who lives deeply and dangerously within the tensions of a transforming South Africa. Musicians of color stage musical festivals to celebrate and promote local artists, encouraging their audiences to celebrate homegrown musicians rather than importing music from overseas. The Artscape Theatre's invitation-only 2002 Roots Festival featured performers of color in one of the small theaters in the complex, prefaced with lots of speeches about making Artscape a venue that embraces a broad range of heritages and appeals to a broad range of audiences. At another downtown festival in 2003 featuring local groups such as Freshly Ground and Godessa, the emcee exhorted the audience to be proud of homegrown talent and stop running down local artists. Mentioning local groups that have received international recognition, such as MoodPhase 5 and Godessa, she shouted into the microphone, "Just because a group is from Cape Town doesn't mean they're inferior! We need to start supporting our local artists and recognizing their worth and stop thinking that things from away are by definition better!"

Stories about how companies try to avoid having to meet affirmative action targets circulate among professionals of color, who have seen some of these tactics in their own offices.[26] Repeatedly I heard township residents and middle-class black professionals remark that white people now care about crime only because white neighborhoods are no longer isolated; they never cared about the high levels of crime in black communities under apartheid. People of color mock white flight, derisively known as "the chicken run." In the words of a Black Noise member, "Go! Go! What good are you doing sitting here with your millions! Like Mandela said, if you're not going to contribute, then leave!" Al Witten, the primary school principal in Lavender Hill who did not receive a single response to the dozens of letters he sent to privileged white schools inviting partnerships, summarizes the viewpoint held by many engaged in community-building activism: "*Where* is this reconciliation? I don't see it. White people have no interest in reconciliation. They are only interested in keeping what they have." A secondary school teacher in Langa exclaimed about white people's inability to acknowledge the past and embrace reconciliation and redistribution initiatives: "They can't clear the cobwebs out of their heads!" I asked him, "What about whites' comments that they want to do the right thing but feel they need to be invited, to be told what to do in order not to be patronizing?" "That's just making excuses for inaction," he responded dismissively.

Small backlashes against white flight appear: in 2002 a book called *Reasons to Stay,* and another later that year called *South Africa: The Good News* (which became a best seller and was updated a year later as *South Africa: More Good News*), a magazine article about returning emigrants who are happy to be back home in South Africa ("The Boomerang Brigade"), dinner party stories about the misery of South Africans abroad, the Proudly South African public relations campaign and the Positively South African Web site.[27] Most of these interventions are public relations efforts oriented toward whites and South African emigrants. At home, Capetonians disgusted with the nosedive view of South Africa seek support from one another, write editorials and hold conferences, use comedy and satire, and express their critique of pessimism through personal and professional community-building work. One can only hope that these efforts will further isolate and eventually overwhelm white pessimism.

On the other hand, the culture of civility and the ongoing white cultural dominance ensure that expressions of outrage remain constrained and understated. Political elites may engage in public name-calling and exchange charges of racism, but I rarely encountered bold accusations of racism in mixed private settings. Merle tells me that "underneath the civility and silences people are seething"; it seems that many Capetonians silence their views about racist assumptions and behavior in mixed company. Perhaps such self-monitoring stems from standards of politeness and civil discourse inherited from English Victorian sensibilities; certainly many of my interlocutors acknowledge that Capetonians are very uncomfortable talking about race. Even some progressive Capetonians I interviewed feel the need to apologize to me for expressing their exasperation with white economic and cultural intransigence. Following my meeting with Al Witten during which he challenged white people's commitment to reconciliation, one of his colleagues apologized for his sharp remarks, explaining that the school administrators were "frustrated" about their failed efforts to create partnerships. Hip-hop artists say they refrain from fully articulating their grievances because to do so would be so shocking; they suggest that the local fascination with American rap reflects the recognition that local Capetonian artists could "never produce a rap album that says what they really want to say." Because of limited alternative media outlets, if they wrote a song called "If You're Going to Leave, Fuck Off," no one would play it. "Eminem can do it, but not us; not people here," explains one well-known hip-hop artist.

Another artist expressed his frustration that a biased media normalizes assumptions of white supremacy and black inferiority that few are willing to challenge, but when he puts out a CD that interrogates privileged whiteness, the newspaper review claims *he* is biased. In one meeting we talked for more than an hour about his uncertainty regarding the extent to which he can speak his truths during public performances. Testing how far he can go in different venues, he was pleasantly surprised that a supervisor at the V & A Waterfront had not criticized him for talking openly and forcefully about white privilege during a show there in 2004. Yet at the end of our conversation, he felt compelled to warn me that his newest CD contains some profanity. I responded that I've heard it before, but I couldn't help musing on his need to caution me.

The power of white supremacy and the culture of civility contribute to people's reluctance to voice their outrage at a system that continues to oppress them, to people's tendency to blame blacks rather than whites for Cape Town's problems, and to see their current problems as due to black incompetence rather than the apartheid legacy of white supremacy. One sees this tendency most blatantly—and tragically—in the calls for the reinstatement of the death penalty by those living in impoverished townships, urging capital punishment against criminals from their neighborhoods rather than challenging the injustices of a system that entrenches poverty and makes crime a more accessible option than employment.

Editorials and research undertaken by the Institute for Justice and Reconciliation consistently remark on the unwillingness of South

Africans to confront problems of race. "Beyond the few euphoric moments, we have very little to show after 10 years of nation-building. More aptly, we still don't trust each other fully, no matter the polite smiles we exchange at shopping malls. . . . The problem is that we are not willing to tackle race—the very premise of the apartheid ideology—head-on," writes Mondli Makhanya in a 2004 *Sunday Times* editorial.[28] Thabisi Hoeane echoes this view: "The most serious problem facing post-apartheid South Africa is the persistent failure to forge cross cutting relationships between races,"[29] in part because of the unwillingness to confront racial problems and talk about race, and in part because of racially marked economic inequality. These commentators and my interlocutors alike observe that the subject of race is taboo; it makes people uncomfortable, particularly those who want to imagine South Africa as achieving rainbow nonracialism through the means of democratic elections. Those who speak about inequality and racism are admonished for fostering racial tensions and promoting racial disharmony; Mbeki's image of South Africa's two nations—one white and wealthy and the other black and impoverished—and the government's affirmative action programs are criticized as somehow fanning the flames of racial tension.

How has this discourse been allowed to develop? How is it that those who speak of South Africa's racialized inequality can be described as uncivil, even irresponsible? The answer has as much to do with the historical burden of whiteness (not only white supremacy, but the Victorian inclination to avoid uncomfortable truths and to affirm the status quo), as with the lack of a critical global discourse on poverty in the current reign of neoliberalism.

.   .   .   .   .

"Apartheid was terrible for everyone. We never supported it."

"We were all damaged by apartheid."

"I didn't know. I had no idea what was really happening."

These statements—parodied by comedians and ridiculed in op-ed pieces—are characteristic of a segment of Cape Town's English-speaking white population who pride themselves on having opposed apartheid, even though they often claim to have been ignorant of its abuses, yet who aren't at all sure that they are comfortable with black majority rule. Opposition to apartheid among white voters did not necessarily mean support for black majority rule, for the ANC, or for outlawed anti-apartheid movements. For many in this category, the end of apartheid came as a huge relief, accompanied by the desire to move forward, forget the past, and *have everything be fine now*. The fact that things are very far from fine, that they are being blamed for their wealth, their exclusivity, and their veiled racism is distressing and shocking to many white self-identified liberals who feel that their opposition to apartheid, in whatever form it took, is not adequately recognized and who feel hurt when challenged as beneficiaries of a system they claim to have opposed.

White people who were deeply involved in anti-apartheid activism are among those who express the most disgust with white people who now deny that they were complicit with apartheid or that they unfairly benefited from apartheid policies. One former activist who now runs workshops for people who wish to pursue a process of personal political transformation mentions that many of his white participants begin their work with him by denying knowledge of apartheid's abuses. He seems bemused by the contradictions that these clients have managed to live with: for example, people who had family members who fled the country rather than completing compulsory military service in the South African Defense Forces, or who knew they had to hide their maids and nannies from the authorities because their domestic servants lacked the required passes. How such knowledge can translate into the broader insistence that "we didn't know" both mystifies and angers those who are clear that they did, in fact, "know" and that those who "didn't know" *chose* ignorance in order to reap the benefits of apartheid.

Cross-dressing satirist Pieter-Dirk Uys's alter ego Evita Bezuidenhout, "the most famous white woman in South Africa" and fictitious apartheid-era South African ambassador to the fictitious black republic of Bopetikosweti, remarks in her "Symbols of Sex and State" show: "I didn't know blacks had no rights! If I'd known I'd have done something, made some calls!"[30]

. . . . .

The argument that "we were all damaged by apartheid" infuriates those who point to the post-apartheid white retention of wealth and privilege. While this statement glosses over the vastly different damages wrought by apartheid policies and trivializes the state-sanctioned suffering of most black people, it is true that white people did not emerge from the apartheid years unscarred. Some white women point to patriarchal abuses fostered under apartheid, arguing that apartheid benefited white men at the expense of white women and protected a culture of domestic violence. Others comment on the psychological damages suffered by white men conscripted into the military as youngsters, particularly those sent to the border areas where terrible atrocities occurred. In the South African National Gallery, looking at the pacifier in the mouth of artist Willie Bester's figure of a soldier created out of bits and pieces of refuse and junk, my friend murmurs, "They were just babies. . . . They hardly knew what they were doing." Her close family member who was sent to Namibia as a commando at the age of seventeen has never recovered from the trauma of his involvement in that secret war, and three decades later he continues to suffer from recurring nightmares and deep depression.[31]

Other white friends speak with great sadness about how apartheid policies tore apart not just black families but white families as well. Several white women spoke to me about the culture of white manhood nurtured under apartheid that, in their view, produced emotionally damaged men whose autocratic patriarchal upbringing and mandatory military service left them unable to meet the challenges of transformation. Having, in effect, lost the war, white men have "shut down," as one friend put it. Noting the high divorce rate among white couples, she continued: "White men say, 'It's their country now. *They* won the election; *they* took over. They can do what they want; it doesn't have anything to do with me. It's not my business, not my concern, not my problem.' When you develop that attitude and put up barriers around yourself, it spills over into your attitude toward everything. White men just have closed down, and apartheid did that."

.   .   .   .   .

During a lighthearted conversation in which Richard, who lives in Constantia, poked fun at the New National Party and the Democratic Alliance, I ventured an observation about liberal whites who claimed to have opposed apartheid but who now continue to live racially segregated lives characterized by material comfort while complaining about feeling marginalized. Richard's demeanor immediately changed as he explained in a serious tone that there is nothing wrong with the fact that "whites just want to do what they've always done." He mentioned afternoons at exclusive clubs and dinners at expensive restaurants in the southern suburbs, arguing that these environments remain entirely white because of their neighborhoods and because people have maintained the same social circles as before. All-white social environments are a result of geography and wealth, he insisted, not white exclusivity. "Cape Town seems to have more exclusivity because it's the only place left in Africa with white people, and blacks are antagonistic about this," he explained. Richard's comments reflect a strong sentiment among some of Cape

Town's white population: the desire to go on as they always have, only now with no guilt, since apartheid is over. They don't see any need to change their lifestyle, their circles of association, or their leisure activities, and they don't understand why they should be judged for their lifestyle, since they never supported apartheid anyhow.

John Gilmour calls this the "aren't we all fine now?" attitude held by self-identified white liberals who cling to the rainbow image as iconic of the new South Africa but who cannot acknowledge the great gulf between this dream and Cape Town's reality. Pollyannaish comments about public spaces or school classrooms like "There are more blacks than there used to be" suggest to John the desire to believe that such tiny signs of change are hugely meaningful indications of transformation.

Elated after the 1994 election, many white people imagined they could wipe the slate clean and move on without having to dwell any longer on the unfortunate past. Mary Burton commented on this desire during her talk at our study abroad center: "I wanted to throw a slate at them! They wanted their own slates wiped clean!"[32] Father Michael Lapsley observed that, generally, many English-speaking whites in Cape Town don't think the concept of reconciliation applies to them because they weren't responsible for apartheid. "What do we have to be forgiven for?" one woman from Rondebosch asked me. "It wasn't our government then, and it's not our government now." The "I never did anything wrong" defense is earnestly claimed by many. Mary Burton comments that white people remain very concerned about how to protect what they've got and don't see the need for reallocation, because "now the blacks have everything; they have the government and they are in control." Consequently, she says, white people need an explanation of how the state paid for things that benefited whites and not blacks, because many genuinely do not see how they are implicated in the history of apartheid's injustices and vast racially based inequalities.[33] The feeling that "apartheid is finally over, we can all breathe a sigh of relief, not feel guilty anymore, things are fine now, *they* can't complain because they now control the country, so let's just get on with our lives" does not, for many people, include the understanding that transformation must be accompanied by structural socioeconomic change and not just the right to vote.

For some, behind this desire to move forward by forgetting the past and imagining a happy rainbow nation is a lingering sense of guilt over the past and the suspicion that one should have done more, or should now be doing more. One friend mentioned the hurt experienced by white liberal teachers who with the transition expected gratitude for having had the guts and thoughtfulness to state their disapproval of apartheid. Faced with the challenge that they had not, in fact, done much, and that the important question was "What are you going to do now?" many retreated into a space of cynicism and guilt at the recognition that they really weren't prepared to do more. Intertwined feelings of relief and guilt are further complicated by emotions of uncertainty, of not really knowing where one fits any longer or what one *should* be doing. For these white people, their identity is suspended in a place of existential discomfort, of not knowing how to be South African any longer, or of not knowing what it means for them to be South African.

Commenting on her Home to All Campaign initiative, Mary Burton explained that she hoped the campaign could provide a way for white people to overcome their guilt and feel engaged in transformation: "White people are sitting there with their skills certain of being rejected. It's extraordinary to me that so many white people feel so insecure and unloved. . . . The gist is whitey is insecure. We want to be told we're wanted here." Noting white feelings of marginalization and social uncertainty, my friend and sometime roommate Merle observed that white people "have a need to be invited. . . . They need to feel their presence is requested." Such attitudes reflect an unstated awareness of white guilt and the knowledge that one should not take one's status for granted, but they can also lean perilously close to self-pity when such hand-wringing becomes a reason to disengage and remain entrenched in a white world.

. . . . .

When he spoke to my class at the study abroad center, Ciraj Rassool, professor of history at University of the Western Cape, noted that "the interesting thing about a democratic society is that you do not have to think of yourself in the same ways that you were forced to think in before."[34] In contrast to those white Capetonians whose response to transformation has been a retreat into whiteness, some white residents have actively embraced the liberating possibilities of apartheid's dismantlement by exploring alternative identities and forming new kinds of families, communities, and networks of association. In place of the discourses discussed above that reaffirm white ideologies of supremacy and cultural integrity and disavow white responsibility or guilt for apartheid's injustices, those whites who have found personal liberation with the end of apartheid speak of the future with vision, creativity, and commitment to a new lifestyle. Personal liberation for white people has taken many forms: apolitical for some, intensely political for others.

Fozia claims the former when explaining her decision to reject her conservative, Dutch Reformed, National Party Afrikaans background in order to marry a Muslim man from the Bo-Kaap classified under apartheid as Cape Coloured: "I made no political stand when I married Ibrahim—he was just somebody I loved." Their attraction began when her firm hired him as an intern under a diversity program in the mid-1980s. Fozia—then called Marike—hid their courtship from her family. When they decided to marry in 1991, she converted to Islam, took a Muslim name, and moved into the Bo-Kaap with his family. Her family was utterly shocked. Her mother, giving the marriage three years, kept the union a secret from her neighbors and demanded that Fozia promise not to have children so she could abandon the marriage more easily. "Coming from her era, it was something big and huge to drop on her," Fozia observed. After six months of silence following the wedding, Fozia's mother eventually began visiting the young couple in the Bo-Kaap, where "there was no way in hell her friends would ever see her." Later, Fozia "threw a spanner in the works" when she became pregnant, because her mother had to acknowledge to her neighbors that her daughter was married. Fozia reports that upon learning the secret, they called up and down the street: "Hannah's daughter has gone and married a hotnot!"[35]

Fozia's brothers' outrage stemmed from their racism and their patriarchal views of her proper role in the family, which was to live at home, never marry, and care for their mother. Fozia recalls that her brothers responded nastily to the news of her marriage: "Oh, you leave the shit behind and we have to clean it up," referring to her marriage as "the terrible thing she did," to which one friend responded, "She's either a lesbian or she married a Hotnot." Fozia jokes half seriously that after she revealed to her family the nature of her relationship with Ibrahim, the mother started asking after Fozia's one lesbian friend: "Why don't you see her anymore? She hasn't been around in such a while!" Fozia heard that her other brother arrived at his office on the day she was married, white as a ghost, looking terrible, and simply said, "she did it!" Fozia muses, "My life was defined by my family as "before she did it" and "after she did it."

After her marriage, Fozia found her social world narrowing as even her liberal white friends found her marriage and religious conversion difficult to accept. "Sweet-talking whites put on this friendly happy-to-see-you face but say vicious things behind your back. They're such hypocrites! Friends from the past are so aware of being politically correct, but when you scratch the surface, the true feelings are there and they're not so nice as they'd like it to be." Fozia and Ibrahim created a small circle of like-minded friends, although they became status symbols to some, invited to dinner parties as an example of the host's with-it-ness: "Here's my friend Fozia and her Muslim husband."

Fozia describes her move into the Bo-Kaap as a relief which allowed her to move away from the racist environment of her natal community, where "everything is hotnot and kaffir" (both are ethnic racial slurs). Although some in her husband's community grumbled quietly that by marrying Fozia, "he's forgetting the struggle—sleeping with the enemy," in general she found a warm and welcoming family environment in the Bo-Kaap. In contrast, she felt unable to bring Ibrahim to her family's functions, because "they're not used to monitoring themselves. I felt guilt that my family was so wrapped up in their racist talking. That's when the compartmentalization started. . . . My life is compartmentalized. With his family it's fine. With my family, it's me and my daughter."

After learning she was pregnant, Fozia nervously informed her mother, who responded: "Well, we'll have to see what is going to come out of there." Fozia was so hurt and upset she stopped communicating with her mother for several months. "After the terrible birthday *braai* [barbecue, described below], it was the other thing I bawled my eyes out over." Although her brothers did not acknowledge the birth of her daughter until she left the country two years later, the granddaughter became a bridge that helped the grandmother reconcile her daughter's choice.

Three years after her marriage, she tried to attend a family *braai* to celebrate her mother's birthday, which ended disastrously after her brothers cruelly mocked her desire to eat halaal (meat prepared according to Muslim dietary laws) and her material lifestyle. "As we were leaving, my brother got into his fancy BMW and I got into my little car, and my brother said, 'Are you still driving that rust bucket?' I looked at him and said, 'Fuck off.' My brother was shocked! I could still see his stunned face as I turned the corner at the end of the street." She told her mother she couldn't come again to family events, because of her brothers' unrepentantly racist attitudes: "They all have shitty marriages and carry their Bible around under their arms and are such total hypocrites." After the *braai*, she recalled, "I mourned for my brothers. I cried for my family, but I have to put it behind me."

During the several years that Fozia and her husband spent in Ireland, her negative experiences with white South Africans there helped her come to terms with her new identity: "I don't know what Ibrahim and his family went through under apartheid. I'm aware of the struggle, and

I know they bear scars. I'm past the guilt point, but in Ireland I went through the anger point, because the South Africans are still stuck in the old world. They lament their loss. They're scared. The world they know, grew up in, is gone. They—or we—as whites are not equipped to fight and struggle like blacks did all those years. We don't have the armor to fight for a job—to be at the bottom and work hard for a job. Because of the privileged way we grew up, we didn't know how to struggle. . . . I experienced a lot of anger in Ireland about the whiteness of my fellow South Africans." She became disgusted with what she felt was the hypocrisy of white South Africans in Ireland, whose initial overtures of friendship and compliments on her daughter's attractiveness would disappear the moment they saw her husband: "Do they want me to wear a little plaque: 'Hi, I'm Fozia. I'm married to a coloured man'? They're thinking, 'Oh! I don't see them fitting into our little circle. And they eat halaal—we don't know what to feed them.' "

Fozia's feelings of isolation and hostility from immigrant white South Africans in Ireland encouraged her to return to South Africa, where she feels she has been able to create a new, comfortable identity for herself. "We see ourselves as the new South Africa in a certain sense. I'm secure in myself with my choices, so I don't have to belong to a group. We're in the in-between world. Ibrahim and I have our little world we move in. . . . I feel now I'm an African, and I love the diversity of our people. It was bloody boring back then—not being comfortable with people of another race."

Fozia's experience of transformation has been a fundamental redefinition of her self, her spirituality, her identity, her family, her community. It has been liberating and joyful—she has found love and started a family—but also a trajectory of sorrow as she came to understand that the break with her natal family would be complete, especially after her mother's death. What complicates her story is the intersecting experience of living in a globalized environment. She felt she could not escape the negativity she associated with the whiteness of her fellow South Africans in Ireland. But her brothers, with whom she cannot interact in Cape Town, felt able to visit her in Ireland, enjoy her family, embrace her husband and daughter, and share what to her felt like a strong sense of sibling connection. Since her return to Cape Town, however, that sibling connection has evaporated. An extended family that crosses racial, cultural, and religious boundaries was possible for this set of siblings only when it went global, when it crossed the national boundary as well. Yet Fozia ultimately felt she had to return to Cape Town to be able to embrace her new identity and escape the hypocritical burden of whiteness that suffocated her in Ireland.

While some white South Africans like Fozia have been able to move out of the confines of whiteness by marrying outside the laager and creating families that transcend apartheid's old categories, others have embraced alternative lifestyles that they see as artistic, spiritual, nonracial and nonpolitical, such as becoming sangomas (African traditional healers), joining African drumming circles, or participating in New Age healing and spiritual movements. South Africa's opening to the world has introduced a wealth of media images, an awareness of spiritual, sexual, and artistic alternatives, a mélange of choices from which to compile a personal identity. But some white South Africans who see their liberation as requiring political engagement wonder if the move to create new identities based in alternative spiritualities or aesthetics facilitates a retreat from the burden of the past. Does it constitute sidestepping the core issues that must be faced by white people? Is it a way to play with identity in the absence of political accountability and responsibility? Is it a narcissistic response to the hard questions of transformation—questions that demand white action initiated in response to a recognition of the particular burdens of whiteness?

Fanie du Toit of the Institute for Justice and Reconciliation responds bluntly:

> How does one engage black suffering without communicating paternalism? How does one prevent good intentions from slipping into condescending charity?
>
> ... Whites "who do dare to be white" stand a better chance of engaging in this country's dynamics constructively, than those who deny their whiteness. ... To be white in this country is a decision, yes, but it [is] also an unavoidable reality given our context and the perceptions of our fellow country-folk. And the crucial point is this: this context and these perceptions are of our own making. We dare not walk away from that now, not as individuals and not as a group. Blacks do not need, nor do they want charity from whites. Any white involvement needs therefore to bear the hallmark of acknowledgment. This acknowledgment comes through asking the "Who am I" question. Many whites have recently allowed [themselves] to disintegrate safely into the post-modern culture of deconstructed identity. "Do not impose a group identity on me," is the constant retort. That is a luxury South African whites cannot afford at present; perhaps one day, but not now. We need to dare to ask the identity question in an era in which it has become very unfashionable for the rich and the powerful to do so.[36]

So what options exist for white people who choose not to walk away? What does it mean to "dare to be white" in order to contribute to constructing a promising future in Cape Town? "What is liberation for white people?" Johanna asks reflectively. She struggles with how to speak about the past, such as in her (unsuccessful) efforts to talk with the contractor who had been evicted under Group Areas from (what is now) her home. She struggles with finding appropriate language to acknowledge the past, to recognize the legitimacy of grievance, to honor the damage and pain, and to find some common pathway forward. Is liberation, for white people, being able to participate in acknowledging the inequities of the past? Do white people have the right to share in these stories and experiences? And what are the terms of their participation? Johanna struggles with the complacency, denial, and racism of white acquaintances. Is liberation the right—indeed, the *requirement*—that one speak against racism and injustice at every opportunity? John Gilmour suggests that "those of us who understand [the reality of poverty, inequality, and racism in South Africa] must articulate it as often and as widely as possible." Is this the voice of liberation for white people, the freedom to gain such understanding and the right—the responsibility—to speak of it at every opportunity?

Johanna, her friend Lisa, and I pursued this question of what it means to be white and to be engaged in transformation in South Africa in an intense conversation one day. Lisa, who works as a teacher and counselor, reflected that before she can partner, build a relationship, and grow a friendship across old boundaries, she feels that she "must be forgiven for being white," for the privileges she has gained because of being white. For her, the initiative has to come from the one subjugated by apartheid, who can choose to indicate to her a forgiveness for "the unforgivability of being white, of being privileged."

I asked, "But don't you feel it's your place to ask for forgiveness?"

"That would be presumptuous," she replied, explaining that she "can't go marching in somewhere" and ask forgiveness or presume there's an interest in her friendship; rather, she must wait for an acknowledgment that her whiteness is forgiven before a relationship can be built.

"But," I asked, "how does one (a white one, that is) put oneself in a position to let others know one wants forgiveness? Who makes the first move? How is the slow walk toward friendship or partnership initiated?" Lisa responded with a story of a woman who lives in Khayelitsha with whom she had been working to start a preschool there. One day on the phone the woman said, "Lisa, you're my first white friend." Taking this comment as forgiveness, Lisa now feels she can hope for a deepening of the partnership into a friendship of equality and mutual trust.

In a follow-up conversation six months later, Lisa reflected that the unforgivability of whiteness has a subtitle of awareness: one must always be aware in relationships of one's whiteness, what that means in South Africa, and how that fact is present in each and every relationship.[37] As an example of how she lives her awareness of whiteness she mentions her acceptance of invitations to tea, to a meal, or for a visit from parents of the children she counsels at school and her practice of giving out her home phone number to parents; these are all things that might not be considered professional by her colleagues but that she considers to be necessary in the context of building a multiracial school community. In other words, in a different kind of professional context in a different place and time, she imagines that she would maintain a boundary between her professional role at the school and her social activities outside of school. In the post-apartheid context of South Africa, where she teaches at an integrating school that is working hard at embracing diversity and challenging hierarchy, she feels this boundary must be suspended in order to build trust.

For Johanna, one aspect of the way forward is quite clear. "I will not leave this country while there are so many people here who can't," she said emphatically one day. "I will never counsel my children to leave, because look at all the black children growing up here who are surviving in really bad circumstances. If they can survive and manage, then the white kids can buckle down and manage here too." Her stance directly challenges the nosedive view of South Africa that justifies white flight as a necessary survival strategy.

Looking toward the future, whites in Cape Town have many choices about how to locate and define themselves in a transforming South Africa. It seems to me that the choices fall into three broad categories that carry profoundly different visions: burrowing into a socially exclusive and protected life while waiting for things to fall apart; seeking an alternative spiritual or aesthetic lifestyle based on a new ahistorical and apolitical identity; and affirming a commitment to South Africa's future while acknowledging the historical significance of whiteness. The first is the choice of fear and pessimism; the second is the choice of utopianism; and the third is the challenging choice of transformative engagement.

CHAPTER 6

Dodging Bullets

As I write these chapters, I am consistently struck by the similarity of themes between Cape Town and the United States. As I record the voices of white Capetonians, I hear the voices of American colleagues; as I listen to critiques of Cape Town's white liberals, I think of the ways in which white liberalism at home simultaneously promotes elitism and narcissism. Critically documenting the efforts of Cape Town's schools to embrace multiculturalism, I see the same approaches as those chosen at home. My college's institutional rhetoric for the past several years has been about promoting multiculturalism and diversity. All staff members are required to attend diversity workshops; the attendance of faculty is requested. We hire staff to supervise multicultural programming and support "diversity students." Our discourse of multiculturalism focuses on our immediate environment—making it more accommodating, inclusive, welcoming: How can we, an elite, white-dominated institution in a white-dominated state, make "them" (our "minority" students and faculty) feel more at home? This is a good journey to take—to reflect on how one's culture, community, and social environment might be exclusive, elitist, and unwelcoming (although it is clear that we want to continue to be exclusive and elite but also welcoming). But while the whole "multicultural" impulse may be a good one, we are only willing to take the discussion so far. As at Cape Town's major performance halls, our musical programming is overwhelmingly classical Euro-American. Our humanities subjects—art, music, literature—overwhelmingly feature Euro-Americans. Our social sciences—history, economics, government—emphasize Euro-American traditions and experiences. Our architecture, our use of the chapel for performances, lectures, and college rituals screams traditional New England. Despite our rhetoric of inclusivity and internationalism, our appearance and our curriculum clarify whose traditions are most valued.

Trying to sort through my thoughts on white liberalism and anti-racism, I skim through dozens of books on dismantling white privilege. The books offer a uniform chorus of advice: that concerned white people should educate themselves about white racism and supremacy, develop empathy through imagining the experiences of those targeted by racist practices and structures, and denounce racism at every opportunity. But I feel frustrated by this common wisdom, which seems to require little of white people. How hard, really, is it to challenge racist comments, especially in an academic climate of political correctness, where such challenges are a badge of belonging? It is easy for white people to decry white supremacy and exclusivity from within an elite white-dominated space. Much more daunting is the challenge of leaving that space altogether and putting oneself in situations where one is profoundly uncomfortable (materially or culturally). That's what middle-class liberals don't seem to want to have to do—to learn to accommodate by fitting in to other people's environments, where one doesn't really know the rules, the interactive styles, the aesthetic.

The historian Noel Ignatiev and his colleagues suggest that one route to dismantling white privilege is to become a race traitor—to refuse to identify as white and to refuse the privileges that accrue on the basis of white skin.[1] The sociologist Michael Brown and his colleagues list the political and material possibilities available to those wishing to participate in dismantling white privilege (for example, living and educating one's children in mixed neighborhoods; actively campaigning for redistributive legislation).[2] The sociologists Vron Ware and Les Back propose studying such efforts historically and globally in order to create a documentary and comparative record of effective challenges to racism in different eras and cultural/sociopolitical contexts. Resurrecting stories about those who have removed themselves from the comforts of whiteness, they caution:

> There is nothing in the literature that we have read that ever implies that the destination of a nonracial and nonracist world can be reached other than by taking a tortuous, dangerous, and unpopular route in that direction. What we have tried to show is, first, that this route is well trodden and, second, that the project demands a readiness to travel in hope, con-

stantly on the alert for creatively subversive opportunities. . . . A commitment to do away with all manifestations of white supremacy requires an intolerance of the way things are and an oppositional consciousness that can counteract Jonah-style resignation [from the character in *Moby-Dick*] in the face of overwhelming difficulties.[3]

Whiteness studies in the United States, to some extent, address a different context than South Africa's. In the United States, a primary issue has been the nonracing of whiteness—the presumed normalcy of whiteness, its unremarkability, its invisibility as a marker (indicated in confusion about what whiteness is and the oft-heard claim that "there is no white culture"). Scholars in psychology, education, and media studies began interrogating the construction of whiteness in order to "make whiteness strange,"[4] to surface the material and political benefits hidden by the invisibility of structures that produce and support white privilege.[5] In South Africa, the issue of white denial of white privilege is also present and seems even more incongruous in that context of the recent dismantlement of apartheid, but whiteness is raced in South Africa. South African whites definitely "feel" their whiteness. As the South African scholar Melissa Steyn writes in her contribution to a book on whiteness, "I cannot remember a time when I was not aware of the fact that I was white, that it was the single most important fact about my existence, that it determined every aspect of my life."[6] The question of what it means to be white and uncertainties about what the future holds for whites are much more present in South Africa, and thus that context would seem to offer even more opportunities for dialogue.

Conjoining the two strategies—analytically surfacing whiteness (as a set of privileges) and viscerally exploring discomfort—is an agenda for which anthropology is particularly well suited. At its best, anthropology demands discomfort—a stepping out of one's comfort zone to enter another space, bodily, emotionally, and intellectually; a stepping out of one's social location "to occupy the subject position of the other."[7] Recognizing this ability as one of anthropology's signature strengths and obligations, the anthropologist Philippe Bourgois chastises the post-modernist orientation toward texts and images that allows some anthropologists to avoid "direct and uncomfortable contact with human beings experiencing social misery across the violent, apartheid-like divides of the United States." Bourgois urges anthropologists studying inequality to refuse to give up the demanding and rigorous methodology of participant observation, even when—*especially* when—it is dangerous, unpleasant, or horrible.[8]

John Gilmour suggests that anthropology's embrace of discomfort as a path toward understanding and self-reflection offers a model for people in Cape Town: perhaps everyone should take an anthropological approach to learning about their neighbors and their city. John's one hesitation is anthropology's lack of an explicit activist agenda—after six years of conversations with me about anthropology, he still struggles with the discipline's lack of a clearly articulated goal of social transformation. Anthropologists narrate the stories of others, translate experience, acknowledge unrecognized or marginalized truths, and provide witness to people's struggles, hardships, and joys. Some anthropologists research and publish books in order to make a living and get tenure, and some (probably most) do so from a position of empathy and genuine humanism. But this isn't good enough for John: he wants an anthropology with explicit transformative goals, an anthropology committed to a better future. What good is it to place oneself in a space of social discomfort if the experience does not lead one to a different consciousness and a different life path? Otherwise, John implies, but is too kind to say, anthropology is more like long-term tourism.

. . . . .

Over coffee in 2002, hip-hop artist Emile YX? of Black Noise listens as I describe my decision to focus my research on whiteness and the legacy of white domination in Cape Town. Over the previous several years, I had spent dozens of hours talking with Emile and watching his group perform at different venues around Cape Town and the Cape Flats, spreading their message of self-empowerment, community involvement, and Cape Flats pride. When I finish, he fixes me with his critical stare and says, "Well, that may be interesting to a few intellectuals at UCT [the University of Cape Town], but no one on the Cape Flats will benefit from it or read it, probably myself included." He challenges me to define my project beyond white experience and the domination of white cultural practices and values.

But what do people on the Cape Flats want to read? Emile argues that a focus on whiteness fixes an emphasis on the already dominant. I argue that a focus on the legacy of whiteness fixes the emphasis on cultural ideologies and practices that perpetuate white domination and thus can reveal effective ways to challenge white privilege. Emile is unconvinced, wondering why I must call it whiteness rather than defining my focus as the legacy of apartheid. He has me there—the term *whiteness,* he notes, references white people, keeping the experiences and expectations of white people firmly at the center of the analysis. I describe the growing field of whiteness studies in academia and the importance of subjecting whiteness to deconstructive scrutiny. This sort of deconstruction has not been thoroughly explored in South Africa, where the category of "white" gains its power in part from its naturalization. A study that carefully historicizes the construction of the "White" race category would delegitimize the biological basis of this category and contribute to a deconstruction of the cultural power it wields.

But my inclination to focus on whiteness grows not just out of intellectual desires: I must also acknowledge that I remained hobbled by an uncertainty about my ability to effectively express the sentiments and experiences of black people in the South African context. Wendy and others challenge me on this point. "It's a privilege that you get to come here," Wendy remarks one afternoon while we are talking about my ambivalence about starting a research project. "What are you going to do with this privilege?" Having the luxury to travel repeatedly to Cape Town, to move around the city talking with scores of people about their life experiences is a privilege my interlocutors never let me forget. Wendy tells me it's my responsibility to write a book, but with this caveat: "Don't just take our stories. It has to be clear how this makes a difference to us."

My interlocutors acknowledge to me the post-apartheid awkwardness of a white person writing about how aspects of transformation are being experienced by black people. But many meet these protests with consternation: If that's my attitude, then what's the point? Have I really come to Cape Town to focus on white issues? I begin to realize that in the context of white domination, focusing on white attitudes and values is something of an evasion—if I am unable to recognize and define the issues related to my status as a white person in this context, then I am a poor anthropologist. One of anthropology's great strengths is its insistence on the simultaneity of reflexivity and empathy, of deconstruction and evenhandedness, of subjective involvement and rigorous analysis. Our weakness is our turn-of-the-millennium reluctance to claim authoritative knowledge about the experiences of others. In 1992, the anthropologist Brett Williams chastised anthropologists for our reluctance to speak out with authority on poor people's experiences in American inner cities: "Anthropologists anguish over how, or even if they can claim ethnographic authority, how to make complicated stories one's own story, and how to grapple with the politics of selection and representation."[9] She concludes that our hand-wringing over such concerns has become isolating, leaving us on the sidelines reflecting on our hard-won, detailed, intimate knowledge while policy debates rage without us.

My interlocutors of color whose life stories I have listened to and life changes I have witnessed during these years of transformation are unsurprised when I ask if I can include their stories and experiences in my book. Many had shared their stories with the expectation that I would. Several years after meeting a group of young men from different townships and following their progress through high schools in Langa and Khayelitsha, I ask if they would be interested in a series of focus group meetings to talk about their lives and understandings of South Africa's changing social and economic landscape. Of course they're interested, they reply; can we start this weekend? My previous reluctance to move outside the idea of whiteness now feels like white neurosis.

. . . . .

In a focus group discussion in December 2003, the seven young men—Michael, Ayzo, Kaydo, Frank, Warra, Anele, and Siyabonga—are discussing why crime is so rampant in their township communities. Michael suggests that crime results from poverty and unemployment: "I do have a solution for crime. If the government can provide black people with jobs, they will immediately decrease the number of crimes, because, if you notice, black unemployment leads to poverty." Anele adds that apartheid's violence habituated people to violence more broadly: "You know, if you are fighting for education under apartheid, you will be taken to jail. You are beaten. And then you have a different mind-set." Ayzo argues that people steal because media images encourage people to desire more than they can afford: "There are some guys, they are really rich but they do crime. In Cape Town it is easy to do crime. . . . In Cape Town, you may want to wear this Reebok, this Nike, something like that. So if your mom doesn't provide you with that money to go buy Nikes, you are going to just go to be a criminal, and if you find that money, you can go and buy yourself some Nikes or a nice outfit. In townships, you're the boss and the girls will like you."

After debating the relative merits of these explanations of criminality, all agree that white people control more wealth and set standards of consumption that township people aspire to and some try to obtain through crime. They agree that township crime has exploded because Cape youth culture has become obsessed with consumption, as opposed to the rural areas, where people don't have the same kind of competitive consumption desires. I interject some questions:

C. B.: You're saying people come to be defined by their environment, whether it's poverty, or style, or the impact of the media, and they just give in to it?

Anele: Yeah.

C. B.: But why? Because they can't see alternatives? Because South Africa is not transforming fast enough?

Michael: [Laughing] Maybe. [He talks about blacks copying whites because they have a lot of money, including asking whites for jobs and for material things.] We are still living in the past. Because whites have the money, blacks think they must defer, copy, sell out. Because the whites have a lot of money, we have to follow them. But blacks need to find our own path.

C. B.: But it's true. The white people here *do* have a lot of money.

Ayzo: It's true.

C. B.: So how do you get around that? It's a double bind. A lot of the wealth in South Africa is still controlled by white people. And you're saying you have to aspire to follow your own path in life and not follow after a white person, so how do you do that if most of the wealth is in white hands?

Anele: That's what I want to know from you.

.   .   .   .   .

The acting principal of a primary school in Lavender Hill invites me to be their national Women's Day assembly speaker. Shocked, I accept and immediately feel inadequate. What on earth do I know about these boys' and girls' lives that I can effectively speak to them? I know the horrific rates of domestic and sexual violence in the community; I have heard stories of the appalling situations within which some children at the school manage; my interviews with the principal and deputy principal, the school psychologist, and the teacher support team have revealed many occasions where teachers had to intervene with authorities to protect children from harm; the essays on their community I collect from the grade-seven students share stories of rape, assault, gang violence, and the trauma of children orphaned by AIDS. Furthermore, school assemblies tend to be conducted in Afrikaans and make liberal use of Christian themes and biblical passages; I am fluent in neither. The acting principal suggests I talk about gender violence: that the boys mustn't hit and abuse the girls, and that the girls mustn't accept abuse from the boys. (Later, I learn that the school has called in a psychologist to intervene with a group of children who have devised a new playground game called "rape me.") I phone another teacher for suggestions; she remarks that she just counseled a mother that morning who had been badly beaten by her husband the night before. She suggests that I should emphasize that God is against abuse, and, mindful of the high rates of teenage pregnancy and single mothers, I should also emphasize that God is against divorce and single parents. Wendy suggests that I was invited because Americans are perceived to be further along the road to gender equity and combating patriarchy, so perhaps I am seen as a kind of role model. With each conversation my panic grows: I feel utterly incompetent to speak about the reality of domestic violence and rape in their community, I can't speak to what God does and does not want, and I can't envision myself as a realistic role model. I phone Johanna, who is finishing her degree in counseling and who works at a neighboring school, and because she is the person I often go to to sort out difficult issues. She suggests I talk about respectful practices.

At the assembly, the speaker immediately before me reads a passage from the Bible about a vessel of perfumed oil that breaks and fills the room with perfume when Mary is washing Jesus's feet. The lesson seems to be that when a woman's jar breaks, she must fill the room with perfume. Then it's my turn to speak to the hundreds of assembled children and adults, and I feel like I should be wearing a sign that says, "Godless Feminist! Fight Abuse!" I decide, feeling grateful to Johanna, to talk about respecting others and self-respect, and then ask the children for their views of Women's Day. Hands shoot up and children offer a multitude of comments about women's courage and the importance of equality. It seems incongruous (probably to a number of people at the assembly) that a foreign white woman is honored as the assembly speaker when local children have such wisdom.

. . . . .

At the New World Foundation, a nonprofit community center in Lavender Hill, I meet a local parish priest. Hearing that I am an anthropologist, he goes to war. "Anthropology is the study of man. Isn't that sexist?" he demands with hostility. As I begin to fashion a response, I am immediately cut off: "And it's the study of culture. Culture is artificial, like in gardening, according to the dictionary. What do you have to say about that?" Again, I try to respond with a quick explanation of the evolution of the concept of culture in anthropology and mention something about globalization. He leaps at this, challenging me: "Ah! So, you're interested in globalization? Don't you know about the Jubilee anti-debt organization? Aren't you involved? Don't you know Neville Alexander?" I struggle to respond that yes, I'm interested in globalization, no I haven't attended any Jubilee events, yes I know of Neville Alexander but have not met him, but I am interrupted again: "So what do you *do?* Do you protest? Have you joined the Marxist circles in Cape Town? I don't think there are any anthropologists involved. Who are the anthropologists that you know here?" Before I can offer any names, he concludes dismissively, "I've never heard of any of them. Don't they *do* anything?" His obvious contempt for my research and my profession leaves me silenced.

.   .   .   .   .

The insistence that I recognize my obligation to those who have taught me so much about Cape Town by writing their stories is counterbalanced with the utter lack of interest other interlocutors have about my book, which is clearly considered completely secondary to my relationship with and involvement in their projects. I witness this as well with Johanna's attempt to present her thesis to the women who are its subjects. After two years of work with a group of women and their children in one of Cape Town's poorer communities, Johanna has a party for the women to celebrate their years of work together and to thank them for welcoming her research. At the gathering she passes around the thesis. Although they seem pleased about her accomplishment, the thick sheaf of paper holds little interest for her guests. As they push it aside, they tell Johanna, "Oh, we have so much more to talk about. That's just the beginning!" For them, the book doesn't represent the culmination of the two-year relationship. Quite the contrary. It represents the introduction to the relationship. I realize how egotistical it is to imagine that all those about whom we write actually care what we say. Is our obsession with ethnographic authority and voice and representation motivated more by narcissism than engagement? By our need to make our writing vastly more important than it has any right to be? By our tendency to privilege the written word over the spoken, the text over the person, scholarship over the human networks of care and engagement?

Some of my interlocutors are patient with the importance I attach to my writing project—they recognize that in my profession the written product is the goal, and they are aware that some heightened consciousness may result for my readers. But they are also clear that the written product should be but one goal of the research they are giving their time and knowledge to support—and perhaps not the most important goal at that. What *else* will I be doing about all the stories I'm hearing, they want to know? Will I raise funds for their projects? Write grants to support local initiatives? Start a nonprofit myself? Will I be writing for a popular audience? For people who make policy decisions? What form of engagement will my anthropology take? Will I continue to care about them and invest in our relationship after my book is finished? Or will I be like other researchers with whom some have worked, drifting away after completing my book?

But my interlocutors also speak to me of the benefits they've received from our hours of conversations and interviews. Raymond, the community worker and project director at Zerilda Park Primary School, tells me that narrating his undertakings to me has helped him to take stock of his life decisions, to review his evolution as a community worker, and to reflect on his accomplishments and goals. Raymond grew up in Lavender Hill in a challenging family situation. Studious and serious, he attended university and found a job in the corporate world, but his religious faith brought him to a dramatic turning point. As a young father and husband, he decided to forgo the financial stability and potential for upward mobility available in the corporate world in order to reorient his life toward service to community and church in the townships of his childhood. When I first met him, his work with Zerilda Park Projects absorbed massive amounts of his time: he had responsibility for job, life, and parenting skills training, mentoring, counseling, and community outreach. As projects manager he ran endless errands and solved endless problems; he sourced materials for Zerilda's building projects, sold their products, and worked on placing his trained workers in permanent jobs. In addition, he worked on a number of other church and community projects, such as a housing construction project in the informal settlement of Vrygrond, with prisoners in the nearby Pollsmoor prison and with ex-gangsters in the community, and in countless ways he provided assistance to struggling families on a daily basis with everything from groceries to medical care. Raymond's phone rang constantly with requests for help from community members, community social workers, church members, and staff from local and city NGOs, and he typically spent his days in a whirlwind of activity moving between meetings downtown, housing construction in Vrygrond, his tasks at Zerilda Park, and home visits to Lavender Hill and Vrygrond families in need of help. I could hardly keep up with him.

Finally I managed to get Raymond to sit for several hours to recount his life history. Despite his initial reluctance because of time constraints and humility, Raymond found that narrating his development as a full-time community worker affirmed his choices and helped him understand their coherence. Later, after sitting in on some interviews with community workers in the informal settlement of Vrygrond that he arranged for me, he told me he was amazed at what he heard about their life histories, their struggles to work against the rage, anger, and hurt that life in the squatter community has brought. Raymond was deeply moved by these stories and thanked me for initiating these opportunities to sit and talk and share experiences—something he and his colleagues have little opportunity to do in the daily triage of managing the constant crises that afflict poor communities.

John Gilmour, who has given me hours of his time, remarks on the importance of our conversations to his sense of where he has come from, to his ability to understand his trajectory. Despite his misgivings about anthropology's goals, he suggests that the ethnographic practice of deep hanging out is exactly the model that people in Cape Town must learn to follow in their daily lives: to listen, to converse, to strive for mutual understanding and vulnerability, to take time to develop relationships that grow out of setbacks and uncertainties. The opportunity that anthropological research offers to people to reflect on their lives, to develop a narrative explaining or interrogating their life choices, and to receive affirmation that their accomplishments are valued, their hardships noted, and their desires appreciated is perhaps unique in the social sciences. I hear repeatedly from community workers how affirming it is that "somebody" from the outside cares what they are doing.[10]

. . . . .

"Are you surprised to have made such good friends here?" asks Johanna. I don't know how to answer this question—I'd never thought of it before. Anthropologists seldom talk about the friendships we form during field research. We set ourselves up to listen, deeply, to people's life stories, to their intimacies, to their pain and their joys. But we do so primarily on *their* terms, not ours. In this, anthropology deviates from other listening professions such as psychology or medicine, whose meetings take place in clinical contexts defined by the therapist/doctor. But the point of anthropology is immersion in the contexts of those whose lives we are studying. Professional boundaries are fuzzy, defined primarily by the adage that our research cannot be used to harm those we study. Given the consuming nature of anthropological engagement, how can one not become bound to those to whom we listen? How can one not feel affection, loyalty, care, and attachment to those in whose lives we become immersed? After years of listening to intimacies, watching family dynamics unfold and children grow, following the personal and professional trajectories of my interviewees, sharing moments of elation as well as despair, defining some of my relationships as friendships seemed obvious. But friendship implies reciprocity. How do anthropologists appropriately reciprocate?

One night, after five years of fieldwork visits, my sometime roommate and frequent companion Merle remarked on the close friendship we'd forged as roommates, often up talking until two or three in the morning, yet she didn't know me as a wife and mother. She'd never even met my children! Anthropologists rarely talk about the extent to which they begin to reveal personal details about themselves to their interlocutors in the field, to expect reciprocity in friendships formed out of associations born in research. Some write of how they were absorbed into a family structure as an adoptive child;[11] a few talk about loneliness, discomfort, fear, frustration, anger;[12] rarely does the anthropologist acknowledge involvement in romantic love or sex. Some write about their personal transformations or realizations about their character as a result of their fieldwork—the anthropological turn to reflexivity ensured we have many such accounts available. But rarely do ethnographies provide a sense of the texture of friendships. What expectations do anthropologists and their close interlocutors have of each other? What loyalties? Frustrations?

I first met Bonisile in 2002, when John Gilmour arranged for me to meet with some promising students who might be interested in pursuing an undergraduate degree in the United States. Bonisile, already two years into a bachelor of arts program in anthropology and psychology, was watchful and quiet during the meeting. At the conclusion of the meeting, he said he needed to "use me" to get past the secretary to see John, since he'd overheard John tell me to stop into his office after our meeting. I asked why he needed to use me; won't the secretary let him in to see John? He replied that since John is so busy, his secretary is very protective and has in the past made Bonisile wait for as long as an hour. "This time," he says, "I'll use you as my weapon." I retort that I'm not a weapon and don't like the suggestion of being used. Although we're both joking, we have missed each other's humor, and later Bonisile phones to clarify that we were, in fact, joking with each other.

Over the next two years Bonisile and I build on this first encounter toward friendship and collegiality, sharing many conversations about anthropology and its value in understanding cultural transformation in Langa, where Bonisile was raised. Just before my family was to join me in December 2003, I asked if he'd like to stop by my apartment after their arrival. But my uncertain, dangling invitation ("My family is coming tomorrow. I don't know if you'd like to meet them?") insulted him. His sharp rebuke was like a slap in the face: "What do you mean, [imitating me]: 'I don't know if you'd like to meet my family'? You can be a very rude person sometimes!"

"What?" I responded, hurt. "What do you mean?"

He repeated his imitation: " 'I don't know if you'd want to meet my family.' How can you say that? I feel comfortable with you, phoning you, being with you, talking to you. Don't watch yourself all the time with me! Please take liberties with me. Allow me to say no to you sometimes."

"OK, let me start over again. My family arrives tomorrow and I'd like you to meet them. Would you like to come by and meet them?"

"I would love to come meet your family," he answered.

In this short telephone exchange, Bonisile reminded me that part of growing a friendship is allowing oneself to be vulnerable, to take risks, to make mistakes. He caught me out by calling me on always watching myself around him, demanding that I let down my guard and take equal responsibility for the friendship. Up until that point, Bonisile had taken responsibility for defining the terms of our friendship: initiating meetings at local cafés, visits to his mother's home or to his quarters at the University of the Western Cape, or phone conversations. His annoyance at my uncertain invitation to meet my family made it clear that I also had the right to make requests of him, because this is what friends do.

. . . . .

I cook one night for an assemblage of friends, each of whom I had separately spent a great deal of time with over the preceding month: Johanna and Adrian; Raymond and his wife, Pat; John Gilmour; Merle. They have all met previously through me but live in far-flung areas of the city, and most have no interaction outside of their involvement with me. Over dinner my guests joke about getting nervous when my "little black book" (my research notes) comes out. The table erupts laughing as everyone has a story about their experience of my little black book. Adrian says, "We've learned to be very careful! You mention something conversationally one day and three days later she comes with her book, saying, 'Three days ago you said such and such. I have a few questions about that.' You have to be on your guard!" Raymond recounts how, during one of our intense conversations, "there I was pouring my heart out to her and she starts writing in that black book!" Adrian wonders if I could blackmail anyone there with what I know about them after our years of interaction. Jokes are made about the book falling into the wrong hands, about how the book records things they've long forgotten, about how nervous they are about things they might have once said that are now forever caught in its pages.

The tension and discomfort of being a friend and observer is acutely acknowledged at moments like these. While the teasing is good-natured and the conversation quickly moves on to other topics, it is clear how significant my note-taking is as a component of my relationships with each of my dinner guests. It is a dimension of friendship with me that they all share and about which they each feel uncertainty. And what an odd dimension of friendship it is, indeed. There are things about my friends in my little black book that I would never repeat, that I am uncomfortable having recorded, even, in some cases, that I wish to forget. Anthropologists do not acknowledge what we leave out; we keep secrets (although not always), we do not tell entire truths, we pick and choose our information. And we often do so on the basis of friendship and feelings of loyalty. The South African journalist Terry Bell tells me that I must report *everything*: the contradictions I witness between what people say they believe and how they actually conduct themselves, the compromised choices I see people making when faced with difficult situations. "Report it all!" he says, embracing the role of the investigative reporter who can afford to piss people off and always speak the truth. Will I speak the truth if it costs me friendships I value? No, I probably will not. I might speak in generalities, but certainly not specifics.

But what are these friendships I have come to value so much? Nancy Scheper-Hughes lists the multiple (and competing) roles played by the anthropologist in the field: a keeper of records, a recognizer of the invisible and marginalized, a field of knowledge, a field of action (a "force field") or resistance, a moral reflector, a political commentator, an activist.[13] She does not list friend, caregiver, or mediator, although these are roles she also clearly plays. What about confidante and keeper of secrets? Sometimes my friends speak truths to me that they cannot speak to one another, using me as an information dispenser or a mediator. Some of the community workers I work with have drinking problems. Is this relevant? Some of the men I work with are sexist. Some of the activists I interview seem unaware of their elitism toward the impoverished communities they work within. I remain attentive to Rhoda Kadalie's admonition not to come to Cape Town to romanticize; yet must everyone's less stellar qualities be presented? Alcoholism is relevant when it hinders the progress of community planning; sexism is relevant when women's concerns are marginalized; the elitism of activists is relevant when it constrains successful working partnerships. So those dimensions of Cape Town's reality are woven throughout my stories, just not with names attached.

. . . . .

In an interview, a prominent former activist tells me that she thinks the Institute for Justice and Reconciliation's large-scale statistical survey offers a more informative approach about the progress of reconciliation than ethnography. I'm stung by her comments and realize I need to think through why I disagree with her in order to claim ascendancy for the anthropological approach. The ethnographic technique—intense, lengthy conversations; focus group discussions; documentation of conversations that take place in classrooms, around dinner tables, at project sites, at public events, in NGO meetings, at church services, at backyard *braais*—can reveal a depth and breadth of emotion and experience left unexplored in large scale surveys. A 2001 survey conducted by the Institute for Democracy in South Africa indicated that a high percentage of white people "rejected the value of the Truth and Reconciliation Commission." The journalist Bryan Rostron remarked: "The statistics, while scientifically more respectable, cannot convey the breathtaking nastiness nonchalantly expressed in everyday attitudes. Most whites take no responsibility whatsoever for apartheid and now—having, as it were, got away with murder—have regained an unpleasant swagger about their complicity in that terrible crime, and are positively offhand about it."[14]

The anthropologist Richard Wilson, in his sharply written book assessing the Truth and Reconciliation Commission (TRC), similarly argues that the quantitative approach to truth gathering mandated by the TRC's "Infocomm" approach left the TRC unable to incorporate into its final report a meaningful analysis of violence. He notes, for example, that the report usefully demonstrates that violence and torture peaked at certain moments and indicates which population category tended to be victims of violence and which political party perpetrated the most killings and the most torture.[15] But such a positivist approach does not address the most fundamental questions about *why* violence occurred. Wilson suggests that truth commissions in the future must utilize the expertise of social and oral historians, who can create nuanced, subjectively informed theoretical assessments of the social, political, economic, and ideological factors that motivated and inspired violence. I echo Wilson but urge a less modest assessment of the value of anthropological expertise in social analysis that incorporates an understanding of people's subjective experiences and interpretations of the world they inhabit.

Anthropologists try to access emotion and intellect; we try to map the contexts within which people work out their passions and their beliefs. Anthropologists specialize in anecdotes and case studies; in observations and conversations; in grasping people's explanations of their social world and how they constantly readjust their explanations in dialogue with the rumors, gossip, and stories that filter through their social circles and family networks. How are emotions successfully conveyed in statistics? How are the emotional contexts within which people's thoughts form described by statistical summaries of what people say they think?

The statistical approach emphasizes the individual, but only insofar as individuals are generalized into categories: so many people say this, so many people report that. Anthropology listens to individual voices but also focuses on how those voices talk to one another and how people create and consolidate collectively held truths, offer challenges to such truths, express uncertainties about common understandings, and suggest alternative visions of the future. The anthropological approach offers a way to place individual voices in the context of the social collective and to explore the contradictions and discrepancies that emerge between individuals and their social networks.[16] As such, anthropology is, as Fiona Ross observed, about hope, about identifying new ways of imagining community and identity, about newly emerging forms of cultural creativity, and about affirming to our interlocutors that others are interested in their hopeful visions.

.   .   .   .   .

In a 2005 commencement address at U.C. Berkeley, Nancy Scheper-Hughes observed: "Anthropology . . . requires strength, valor, and courage. Pierre Bourdieu famously called anthropology a combat sport. It is an extreme sport of sorts—a tough and rigorous discipline. Anthropologists are the Green Berets of the social sciences. Like the old Peace Corps recruiting poster, anthropology asks: 'How much can you give? How much can you take?' "[17]

Anthropology's development during the first decade of the twenty-first century has moved the discipline closer to John Gilmour's desire for an anthropology of active engagement (and closer to the anthropology of our progenitors like Franz Boas and Margaret Mead). Its potential for facilitating social change through intellectual engagement is certainly the most promising in the social sciences. Among its promises is that it provides a way to educate for tolerance while offering a voice of critique. It denaturalizes reality and shows alternatives. Moving away from the production of holistic portraits of culture and culture change, contemporary anthropologists see anthropology as more of a dialogue and sometimes an argument. Anthropology's increasingly public orientation offers an authoritative and much-needed critical perspective on how to fix the wreckage wrought by the racisms, wars, and neoliberal economic policies of the twentieth century. Its great, unique strength is that it does so by wedding intellectually rigorous research with deep humanism and personal engagement.

CHAPTER 7

Identity Issues

It is not surprising that a significant proportion of black
people began to believe that they were inferior. How else does
one explain to one's children that you fail to provide them
with the most basic needs? That you are unable to stand up to
white people abusing you and assaulting your dignity? That
you are not knowledgeable about the most basic issues fundamental to everyday life in a modern society?

Mamphela Ramphele, 2001

In 2002, South Africans tuned in to the televised national search for the
South African "Coca-Cola Popstars." Three judges traveled around
South Africa auditioning young hopefuls, who sang one song chosen for
them and one of their choice. Five would be chosen as the Coca-Cola
Popstars, receiving fabulous prizes, traveling to Europe, and nationally
releasing a CD of songs selected for them to sing. About midway
through the audition period, two young women performed stunning
African songs for their solos and blew away the audience—they were
the first, out of hundreds, to avoid American pop music in their audition. The sole African judge, clearly moved by their performance, remarked that they made her reconsider her understanding of an African
pop star. Another judge, however, worried that the two candidates
might have "an attitude" that would keep them from being "team players." Would they sing what they were told, or would they challenge their
trainers and handlers? Despite their awesome talent, they were not chosen as finalists.

A hugely popular South African reality television show, the *Survivor*-
style *Big Brother*, featured a multiracial, multicultural group of house-
mates, one of whom was voted off the show each week by viewers. The
victor in 2001? Ferdinand Rabe, a rude white Afrikaner who entertained
audiences with his racist and sexist condescension. Nick Shepherd and

Kathryn Mathers explain this odd post-apartheid outcome by noting the ongoing salience of white power in South Africa: "Ferdi struck a chord with a racial cross-section of viewers, who voted for him as a reward for his brashness and arrogance." Noting that Ferdi's victory depended upon a significant show of support from viewers of color, they quote Njabulo Ndebele's observation about cultural power in post-apartheid South Africa: "Is it possible that South Africa's . . . black citizens [are] like people who awake in an enormous vacation house which is now supposed to be theirs but which they do not quite recognize," and around which they tiptoe for fear of offending the rightful owners"?[1]

. . . . .

Transforming the material legacy of apartheid offers a particular set of challenges in this era of neoliberal hegemony and the retreat of the welfare state. If white people do not accept that they have financial responsibilities to post-apartheid South Africa as apartheid's beneficiaries, the government has the option to enforce a redistributive budget and to devise an educational curriculum and public awareness campaign that makes clear the necessity of such redistribution. But in addition to poverty and inequality, one of the major effects of colonialism and apartheid in Cape Town was the imposition of a cultural and social system that valorized whiteness: white superiority, white ways of doing things, and white standards of success. The ideological legacy of white hegemony is harder to target and transform. Not only do many white people in Cape Town feel the desire and the right to inhabit a world characterized by Euro-American culture and norms, but, more significantly, assumptions about the desirability of such norms have shaped the lives of Capetonians of color. The South African media continue to transform, as new television and radio shows are introduced and the portrayal of African lifestyles and languages grow in prominence. Yet at the conclusion of the first post-apartheid decade, one was hard pressed to find original African music or dance prominently and regularly featured in the main theaters around Cape Town. The musical lineup at Cape Town's major theaters was disproportionately and overwhelmingly Euro-American, as were most of the plays performed in theaters from the Atlantic seaboard to Muizenberg. In the media, in Cape Town's major performance venues, and in schools, African originality was continually subverted in favor of things seen as white-associated or foreign-derived.[2]

Subtle assessments of status within white-linked prestige hierarchies appear in countless guises, and adherence to white norms, practices, and values is read as an indication of class. Coloured friends describe the emphasis in mixed-race settings and in institutional settings on one's professional credentials and the pressure they feel professionally to conform to white lifestyles and white evaluations of competence.[3] Emile YX?, the widely known and respected hip-hop artist who is deeply involved in community activism in Cape Flats communities, understands that people outside hip-hop circles cannot recognize him as a legitimate thinker when they see him as "just a rapper." He regularly meets with business and government leaders who wish to work with his group to reach the youth demographic. He says when they learn he was a teacher, he can see their opinions change. He is angered that potential sponsors, backers, and politicians seem to require this kind of stamp of legitimacy before being willing to listen to him and realize, as he puts it, "I've got a brain."

I watched the transformation on the faces of a wealthy white couple when they learned that Wendy's husband, Peter, holds a professional position as rector of a local college with strong international connections. Later, Peter mentioned that although he had known the couple for years, their attitude toward him shifted radically once they could place him in a prestigious professional context. At a meeting where three community service supervisors were being introduced to a new group of volunteers, the one white man, who is a high-level school administrator, was introduced by his full name, complete with the honorific "Mr." and professional title. The colored and black community workers were introduced by only their first names: no honorific, no surname, no professional title. The young black township men with whom I work describe how frustrating it is to see their jack-of-all-trades elders categorized as "unskilled labor" because they lack educational certification.

Merle's half-sister Val describes how, with her entry into the corporate world (in a management position with a major department store chain), she had no choice but to adopt a white ideology, "because in that system that was the only way I was going to win, and I was gonna win, boy!" Adopting a white ideology meant changing her speech at work (no Cape Coloured accents), socializing at cocktail and drinks parties (which, her husband observed, she had to do to "be corporate"), "needing to have a nanny at home—That was a very white thing to do!" and moving into a white neighborhood (which Val refused to do). "There was a lot I had to deal with because I had to acknowledge that I—in order to survive in that system for so many years—had subconsciously taken on what was definitely a strong white ideology. That was the only way to navigate your way around a system like that and stay whole and succeed." Val attributes to her family her ability to retain an independent sense of self and connection to her coloured community; her husband worked in education in the Cape Flats and ensured that she did not fully remake herself in the image of corporate whiteness, and her brothers-in-law lose no opportunity to teasingly scold her when her speech slips into corporate whitespeak.

The subversion of African originality to imported (non-African) aesthetics is perhaps most evident in coloured teen musical culture. Students I talked with in Lavender Hill regularly mentioned Britney Spears, J-Lo, Slim Shady, *Nsync, and the Backstreet Boys as their favorite music. Don't they listen to any local musicians? The students look around at one another and snicker. I took my students to a performance of a group from Bonteheuvel (an apartheid-created township for coloured residents) described to me by others in their community as musically cutting-edge. Group members performed American boy band music with breathtaking harmony and fabulous synchronized dancing (including one number in which they dressed as American cowboys). When my students asked whether they ever perform any songs of their own, they sang two original ballads about life in Cape Town—one about a homeless child, the other about hope—that are hauntingly beautiful and evocative. But no one in Cape Town wants to listen to it, they explain: they are hired to perform at nightclubs, fund-raisers, parties, and proms, where everyone wants the music they hear on the radio. Their challenge is to prove they are the best at copying the American hits, because this is the basis on which they will make a name for themselves locally.

I went with friends to the Joseph Stone Theater in Athlone (built by the apartheid government as the coloured performance space in Cape Town) to see a locally renowned dance school that teaches dance in coloured communities. The wonderfully talented dancers gyrate their way through songs by Madonna, Britney Spears, and other American pop stars, incorporating the stars' dance moves into their numbers while mouthing the lyrics. They perform numbers copied from *The Sound of Music* and *Mary Poppins* and conclude with a number from the film *Chicago*. After the show, city luminaries and national politicians take the stage to commend the young dancers, repeatedly remarking that they are as good as the originals, that they have proved they can match the best. My friends loved the performance and chided me for my naïveté in imagining we might see something original and unique to Cape Town or emblematic of a novel aesthetic; to my mind, evaluating the skill of these enthusiastic young performers on the basis of how well they copy the American original seems tragic. "Perhaps our enjoyment of the perfor-

mance just shows how fucked up we are!" a friend responded after I explained the reason for my discomfort. The next day, Evaron (the emcee,
comedian, and graffiti artist) explained to me the sturdy tradition among
coloured performers of perfecting cover acts: performances that ap-
proximate the (foreign) original as closely as possible. Evaron began his
career as a young emcee by copying American rappers word for word;
other pioneers in Cape Town's hip-hop scene recall how practicing their
New York accents marked their early days as hip-hoppers before they
began to feel they could express themselves in more original ways.

Cover acts and the desire for Western products are evidence that the cultural landscape is shifting; class status is beginning to trump racial identities. Young black people aspiring to consume material goods and media
images formerly available primarily to white people are not trying to be
white; they are trying to be modern, global, "new South Africans." Aspiring to consumption is more about class than race. But it remains significant that many of the desired images and goods come from outside of
Africa, and it is sometimes hard to see how a pride in African heritage is
supported by aspirations to consume non-African media and products.[4]

Siyabonga and Frank addressed this theme in one of our weekly discussions in 2003, placing part of the blame on the media for emphasizing only the negative aspects of life in South Africa. Siyabonga observed:

> That's how it is portrayed to us. Everything good comes from the West. So
> you grow up as a kid, watching TV which is Westernized, listening to music
> which comes from the West, you know, everything that you do, we did not
> think it was worth anything. That's what we were made to believe. And
> whatever you do now, you have to match the guy from the West so you will
> be seen as someone who's good. So now, half the people will feel that South
> Africa is not close to being the best. America is the best. Because that's what
> they've been given all along.

Frank breaks in:

> Just to add to what he said. It's true. In my family we used to listen to the
> radio news. That's what we knew. We'd listen to the radio, sit down with
> the parents, do your homework, listen to the news. This is what they told
> you. Someone is being robbed, someone is being killed, around Cape Town,
> Jo'burg, whatever. So I grew up not believing South Africa is a good coun-
> try at all. I was mad to find myself in this place where everything happens,
> like crime, everything is too bad. I never knew there were things that were
> happening that were good in the country 'cause the radio, the TV, all you
> ever heard: there's a rape somewhere, there's a killing, there's a car crash.
> It's true. It's the media that's at fault in making us believe that our country
> is not nearly as good as it is. But as you grow, you realize no, there's a curtain

behind everything. Once you move that curtain, you can see what's good about our country. And when I go in there, I can see there are a lot of good things happening around the country. And I can see, what a country, what a beautiful country we have here. But it will take some time for people to realize what treasures we do have in this country. As long as the media's there doing its thing, making money, there will be people who hate the country and think it's not doing its best. But it is doing its best. The constitution is really great. It's so great. Nobody knows about it. All we hear is, "This is great! It's from England. This is amazing! They have it in France! In the states." So you grow up thinking that's the place to be. You want to go overseas because you think, "God! This is the worst country!"[5]

The pattern of lauding white Euro-American cultural practices has created, as Father Peter John Pearson of Cape Town's Catholic diocese observed, "an enduring legacy that white is better."[6] How did the tradition of valorizing whiteness develop? How is it that here, at the tip of Africa, things original to Africa or Africans are devalued in favor of things identified as white or from outside of Africa? Is it simply that the fist of apartheid so effectively circumscribed popular culture through media control and white domination? The ongoing vitality of African cultural traditions and aesthetics in African townships—even if devalued or ignored by most in the white and coloured population (as well as by some in the townships themselves)—complicates this explanation. The force of the legacy that white is better seems to sit most heavily on the shoulders of Cape Town's coloured population.

Analyzing the political and cultural consciousness of Cape Town's coloured population has bedeviled many researchers, intellectuals, and activists. A glance at Cape Town's history shows a story of entanglements and disentanglements of color. From the arrival of Dutch settlers, who fought and cohabited with the local Khoi people until the abolition of slavery in the 1830s, a spectrum of complexions emerged in Cape Town, although social and legal guidelines made certain that whiteness remained a dimension of status.

Following abolition in the 1830s, hierarchies of color became entrenched through processes described in detail by scholars of colonial Cape Town such as Robert Ross, Vivian Bickford-Smith, and Cheryl Hendricks.[7] Ross writes of the power in the colony of British-derived social norms of "respectability" in the early nineteenth century. Respectability—measured by possessions, education, and behavior (comportment, clothing, hygiene)—provided guidelines that all could aspire to and implied that all should want to. Christian definitions of civilized behavior augmented the understanding of respectability, especially in the Christian mission stations that educated so many coloured people in the Western Cape. The heightened Anglicization of Cape Town in the late nineteenth century further emphasized English virtues of "thrift, the sanctity of property, deference to superiors, belief in the moralizing efficacy of hard work and cleanliness."[8] Over the course of the nineteenth century, according to Ross and Bickford-Smith, the somewhat flexible color hierarchies of the early part of the century hardened into white racism as whiteness and not just Anglo-derived cultural practices affirmed another measure of respectability, one that excluded people of color from joining Cape Town's upper classes. (In response, "Malay"—a categorical label applied to Muslim people of color—emerged as an alternative religious and cultural identity for those whose complexion denied them English-linked "respectability.")[9]

Late-nineteenth-century African immigration to Cape Town, imported theories of hygiene and segregation from the metropole, and economic changes began consolidating exclusionary white racism. By the end of the century, elites fostered stereotypes of Malays, Africans, and coloureds as dirty and degenerate, leading to early calls for segregation. Bickford-Smith argues that government and popular discussions of segregation "promoted the emergence of a coloured ethnicity in Cape Town," as self-identified coloureds sought to distinguish themselves from African natives.[10] The Cape government's differential treatment of Africans from the 1890s on (through, for example, liquor laws, the Morality Act of 1902, and the resettlement of Africans into segregated locations) further consolidated these ethnic categories. As the twentieth century began, the Cape government began enforcing coloured and white segregation in schools, government institutions (prisons, asylums), and hospitals, and Capetonians formed racially delineated sports leagues, political organizations (such as the African Political Organization, which promoted the concerns of coloured elites), and community groups. Metropolitan concerns about race degeneracy arrived in Cape Town, spreading fear that lower-class racial mixing would be harmful to poor whites, thus making white poverty—rather than poverty—a government concern. Theories of race degeneracy supported calls for segregation and contributed to the efforts of coloured elites to distinguish themselves from native Africans. "Despite some rhetoric about the need to cultivate 'race pride' among Coloureds, the aspirations of the Coloured petty bourgeoisie were almost entirely assimilationist," writes historian Mohamed Adhikari. "They wanted little more than to be judged on merit, to exercise citizenship rights, and to win social acceptance within white middle-class society."[11] Early coloured political organizations focused on upliftment through civilizing interventions like education, which, in the words of Denis-Constant Martin, rewarded coloured Capetonians with "points on the civilization scale determined according to the canons of white South African Society." Aspiring to whiteness, and thus the class position it signified, was affirmed by the leaders of these organizations, as well as by whites who were involved in promoting Malay/coloured cultural organizations, which nurtured class hierarchy within the coloured population.[12]

Apartheid policies continued the consolidation of racist exclusion and class hierarchies developed during the previous centuries. Forced removals shredded networks of support and mutual care that ran through coloured and mixed neighborhoods as families were torn apart and sent to different coloured locations. Extended households were split into isolated nuclear family units; those who could pass for white removed themselves from their darker siblings and started lives in white neighborhoods. John Western's account of the history of Mowbray describes how Mowbray's racial fuzziness was cleaved by forced removals, which irrevocably split coloured and white relatives. He notes that forced removals also made visible class differences within the coloured community, which had been muted by proximity and support networks within Mowbray. Some who were removed could afford to relocate to coloured home ownership locations (such as Fairways, Walmer Estate, and lower Wynberg), whereas others were forced into council flats in coloured ghettos. Class divisions grew over the next few decades, as those families in wealthier coloured neighborhoods broke contact with Cape Flats public housing communities.[13]

Thinking over the history of coloured class divisions, Merle remarked that middle-class coloured people are still busy escaping from any association with stigmatized working-class and impoverished places like Manenberg. Following the "white is right" dictate, they remain uninterested in (re)connecting with impoverished coloured communities. As an example of coloured class snobbery, Merle recounted a story about her neighbor who moved to Muizenberg from Mitchell's Plain. He played loud music, had big outdoor family parties, and let his kids play boisterously in the street. Another coloured neighbor (who is a professional realtor) in their small cul-de-sac was disturbed by his lifestyle and approached Merle with a plan to force him out of the neighborhood and back to Mitchell's Plain "where he belongs." The realtor neighbor thought the noisy neighbor was bringing down their quality of life, behaving inappropriately for a middle-class, respectable environment, and affecting the value of their real estate. Merle rebuffed the realtor's scheme, responding that her neighbor's lifestyle is the lifestyle of her childhood in the Bo-Kaap: "I have no problem with his lifestyle. I grew up with noise, with children in the street, activity outside. That's my background."

. . . . .

It seems that everyone I interviewed has a story about the family hurts created by apartheid's privileging of "white" people over their darker siblings and cousins. One hears poignant stories of siblings who passed for white ignoring their coloured siblings when they happened to meet in public, of cousins who grew up separated and unknown to one another because of differences in family skin tones, of the constant commentary that runs through coloured families about degrees of "fairness" worn skin-deep by different family members, of the psychological pain still plaguing those who worked so hard to achieve white acceptance. Merle describes her life as "practicing to be white"; her appearance allowed her to "pass" in particular contexts, depending upon her assessment of the context. She recalls, for example, riding the bus to work every day from Green Point with a white colleague, where they sat together in the white section despite her constant fear of public discovery and humiliation. One day her colleague was ill, and Merle, wracked with uncertainty, boarded the bus alone and began climbing the stairs to the coloured section. The bus conductor reprimanded her, telling her that the upstairs section was only for coloureds. With a mixture of relief and self-loathing she followed his directive to sit in the white section. Merle's stories mirror the stories told time and again in novels, autobiographies, and poetry of the psychological damage of constantly negotiating the color line, of orienting one's life to hiding one's heritage, of the ongoing fear of discovery, of the self-disgust generated from denying part of one's heritage and the self-hatred of having a heritage demeaned by the society within which one is passing.[14]

Other memories focus on the favoritism within coloured families offered to fairer family members and the efforts on the part of parents to push fairer children into white networks. In a conversation with a coloured couple who now live in an elite neighborhood, Pauline talked about her very fair cousin who occasionally spent a weekend, together with her, at their grandmother's in Parkwood, a coloured ghetto to which the coloured members of her family had been relocated from Constantia. The granny insisted that the fairest grandchild receive priority because of his whiteness, feeding him first and fussing over him. On Mondays, all the cousins would walk together to the train, where he would get on the white compartment and the others would climb into the coloured compart-ments. Pauline went on to note that she had recently met this cousin again after several decades of separation and discovered that he was struggling with deep psychological wounds created by a childhood of striving to pass for white. She had had no idea how much he suffered during his child-hood as a result of the pressure to deny a coloured identity.

Pauline's husband, Basil, recounted the story of his friend who en-rolled his fair-skinned son in a white school. Basil claims the son now suffers from psychological problems because he can't self-identify as white, but he has been distanced from any association with a coloured peer group. Ironically, Basil followed this story with a comment about how he himself always tries to stay out of the sun because he's on the darker end of the spectrum. Recalling his family's challenges to accom-modate its white and coloured members, Basil concluded our conversa-tion by remarking, "You'll find this in every family." Pauline wondered aloud, "Why did our parents accept this?"

Reflecting on their parents' generation, my middle-aged coloured in-terlocutors offered a thoughtful set of reflections on their parents' ori-entations and responses to the dictates of apartheid. "The coloured pop-ulation was probably the most damaged by apartheid, because blacks retained a collectivity, sense of rootedness, of belonging, of having an origin, but coloured people didn't have this because everything about being coloured was oriented to whiteness," a writer explained to me. "Being coloured was about aspiring to be white. . . . It was about for-getting your past and embracing white culture."

Trying to achieve success in white-defined hierarchies where people of color would always be second-best ensured that for most of the twenti-eth century coloured families were encouraged to value whiteness and reject the African strands of their heritage. My coloured interlocutors recalled that their parents rarely talked about their past but gave promi-nent acknowledgment to white ancestors. "Our parents cut themselves off from parts of their heritage," one woman observed. "We're Dutch or German, or English, or Afrikaans, but never Khoi or African." Historian Sean Field similarly notes the "repeated exaggeration of white ancestry by most of the interviewees" and their silence about black ancestry in the oral histories he collected from former and current coloured residents of Windemere.[15]

The history of colonial and early to mid-twentieth-century coloured education and experience in Cape Town was characterized by practices that promoted whiteness and demeaned or ignored African indigenous-ness: coloured children learned European and American music and musical instruments but never African music or dance; white ancestry on the family tree was promoted and displayed in family photographs; coloured children learned to value white aesthetics, white fashions, and white ideas of beauty; they learned to denigrate African aesthetics while straightening their hair and staying out of the sun; coloured families understood (and yet were pained by) the choices made by those who could pass for white who, after the imposition of Group Areas, cut themselves off from those who could not.[16] To this day, Cape Town does not yet have a citywide acceptance of African culture as city culture, and one often hears the proud comment that Cape Town is a European city in Africa.

Commenting on their parents' submissive attitude toward apartheid's status quo, many coloured friends emphasized the effectiveness of the Cape's Coloured Labor Preference Policy in orienting their parents to white standards and the white world by, as my friend Val explained to me, "granting them more benefits because of the white part of their ancestry. So everyone wanted to be white and get the benefits." The privileges over black Africans offered to coloured people by the Coloured Labor Preference Policy gave a clear class dimension to aspiring to whiteness, a pattern rooted in the colonial emphasis on British definitions of respectability and nurtured by pre-apartheid political and professional organizations headed by coloured elites advocating for the citizenship rights of the coloured community on the basis of their "civilized" status achievements. The Coloured Labor Preference Policy also emplaced a deep and suspicious competitiveness toward black Africans. Wendy's husband, Peter, suggested it was the most damaging apartheid-era policy for the coloured community, because it so effectively turned on a vision of black African hordes poised to engulf Cape Town.

Although the Coloured Labor Preference Policy might have indicated a white preference for coloured employees (and white support for coloured "advancement"), Group Areas laws ensured a minimal mixing of coloured and white families. Forced removals divided coloured people from white people, driving the former into mostly isolated enclaves spread over the Cape Flats. Many scholars and removees have written about how forced removals destroyed coloured community and solidarity, breaking up extended families into nuclear families, replacing traditions of community involvement and membership with isolation and fear, assaulting coloured aspirations of respectability and entrenching poverty. According to sociologist Don Pinnock:

By the end of the 1960s, the working class in Cape Town were like a routed, scattered army, dotted in confusion about the land of their birth. . . . In the lonely crowd of satellite clusters, with no control of communication networks, life tended to become reduced to what came through official channels and the ghetto grapevine. And with rising rates of violence in these areas, the townships became increasingly difficult places to meet people after work—forming what Paulo Freire calls a culture of silence and not of rebellion (rebellion was to come much later). The ultimate losers in this type of urban atmosphere were the working-class families, torn out of the areas they knew and scattered across the Cape Flats.[17]

Thus apartheid policies constructed coloured identity as a racial category, supervised its fragmentation by class, and promoted coloured mistrust of black Africans. The realities of coloured township life hindered the development of a coloured working-class consciousness that was not co-opted by whiteness, and valorizing whiteness, in turn, was about aspiring to middle-class status. The implications of status hierarchies linking class and race permeated coloured communities throughout Cape Town, and still do.

Coloured friends who grew up in middle- and working-class Athlone, lower Wynberg, Grassy Park, Retreat, and Lavender Hill recalled sheltered childhoods embedded in conservative family- and church-oriented social worlds. "We didn't venture outside those confines, we didn't question, we pursued success within the avenues open to us," explained a middle-class teacher from Athlone. Many of my interlocutors commented on the force of conservative Christian attitudes in keeping their parents and communities nonpolitical and submissive during the apartheid years. The form of evangelical Christianity practiced by many in coloured communities urged adherents to look beyond their present world and focus on the afterlife. A middle-class pastor from lower Wynberg observed to me that "in the South African context, coloureds really took this on, especially in the Western Cape." He noted how evangelical religious practice met the need for expression by encouraging strong involvement by the laity, while simultaneously denouncing political involvement. For him, a defining moment came after the Sharpeville massacre in 1960, when the Council of Churches discussed the role of churches regarding the government's dehumanization of blacks, and evangelical churches withdrew from the ecumenical movement to become, in his words, "a little holy huddle" by themselves.

A social worker and daughter of an evangelical pastor echoed this description, recalling her working-class upbringing in Lavender Hill as narrow, closed, and hostile to other orientations. She grew up in an atmosphere that emphasized authority, close family ties, patriarchy, knowing one's place, and, most importantly, following the rules: parents' rules, government rules, God's rules. Looking back, she sees how the church's orientation was on saving souls to bring them into the Kingdom of God while ignoring worldly material and political needs. Her adolescence was characterized by deep church involvement and a rejection of politics: "It simply would not have been acceptable to be involved with student politics. Challenging the government or authority was unacceptable! Rather, you prayed for things."

The journalist Terry Bell observed to me that the effect of this ideology was to make people afraid of change and of those in their communities who broke the rules. His friend Hennie, a man from Retreat who served time in prison and in jail for his political involvement in workers' union activism, soberly recalled his family's experience. He and his wife were very involved in their community's Catholic church—their seven children attended Catholic schools, and his wife was a catechism teacher—but after his first arrest, his wife's church community and their neighbors pulled away from her and offered her little in the way of support during the long periods of her husband's incarceration. To this day, Hennie remains resentful of their response. His union brethren offered her their support, which encouraged Hennie's involvement following his release from prison in support groups for families of those serving prison time. His family's abandonment by their church community helped push Hennie outside of his community to greater political engagement. He recognized government practices that indoctrinated fear of political involvement among his neighbors and church congregation. For example, he described the huge display of power that accompanied the police's attempt to arrest his son-in-law (then a student at the University of the Western Cape) for political activities; they surrounded the house with cars, tanks, and guns in order to make a big show and demonstrate to the neighborhood "what happens when one becomes involved in politics. . . . The work done by the security branch has created this [fear of political activity]. [Coloured] families that were involved during the liberation struggle were very isolated within their own communities."

In 2003 I accompanied Salomie, the woman from Lavender Hill whose struggle to buy a home I recounted in chapter 2, to a service at the popular Church of Power in Retreat and found disturbing echoes of the messages of the 1960s and 1970s described by my interlocutors. For over an hour, the (white) minister thundered about the necessity of submission, knowing one's place, and deferring to the authority of one's parents, leaders, and church. Never challenge those in positions of authority, the minister counseled, but rather submit and strive for excellence in your assigned role, even within an "evil" context. Submission will be recognized by God; betrayal will be punished. The sermon to the large coloured congregation seemed to replicate the closed, narrow, submissive upbringing described in the biographies recounted by coloured acquaintances of mine who grew up in this part of Cape Town.

. . . . .

Confirming the memories of my interlocutors, scholars write of the "silent '60s" and "the '60s quiescence," noting in particular the force of government repression during that decade.[18] The apartheid government invested in the embourgeoisement of the coloured and Indian working class, a strategy that deflected interest in anti-apartheid militancy.[19] But by the late 1970s student and union activism had exploded in Cape Town. Many of my middle-class, middle-aged coloured interlocutors found their way out of conservative and submissive homes oriented toward white-linked respectability through student activism. Those privileged to attend one of the prominent coloured high schools in Cape Town (Harold Cressy and Trafalgar in District Six, and Livingstone in Claremont) recall the powerful influence of Black Consciousness and the Unity Movement, nurtured by their teachers. Those who attended high schools in Cape Flats communities recall the marches, the boycotts, and the exhilaration of protest. As youth activism took over the Cape Flats communities, parents began joining the struggle as well, producing, according to the historian Colin Bundy, "a decentralized, localized, radicalized community-based politics."[20] Scholars and my interlocutors alike are quick to explain that such activism, which spread from students and teachers to parents, did not necessarily mean loyalty to the African National Congress (ANC), which many in the coloured communities viewed with distrust or skepticism because of its portrayal in the media as a communist organization of terrorists.[21] Fighting for their citizenship rights or for changes in policies specific to their immediate neighborhoods did not, for many, mean fighting for black majority rule or an acceptance of black African identity.

  With the dismantlement of apartheid laws and policies and the preparation for democratic elections in 1994, coloured voters in Cape Town wrestled with questions about their political identities and concerns about the future. Those most animated during the activism of the 1980s by Black Consciousness ideology easily gave their votes to the ANC. The majority of coloured voters, however, could not reconcile their sense of their political and cultural identities and their hopes about the future with a political party they saw as black African or communist. Many of my younger coloured friends who supported the ANC describe family arguments around the dinner table with their older relatives, who were appalled at the possibility of being ruled by a black communist organization. The coloured vote gave the Western Cape to the National Party in the 1994 elections, an outcome that horrified and dismayed coloured elites, intellectuals, and activists. One distraught man said to me, holding his head in his hands, "We voted for the Nats! It's humiliating!"

Political and social commentators have produced thousands of pages analyzing the coloured vote in this election, revealing confusion and disappointment among elites and intellectuals that coloured anti-apartheid activism did not produce mass coloured support for the ANC. But coloured acquaintances candidly voice their fears of a black government and of the growing African population in Cape Town, which tripled between 1982 and 1992. A history of articulations with whiteness and a media- and church-nurtured fear of blackness have been hard to overcome. Hennie echoed some of his neighbors in Retreat, who, even after all they suffered under the National Party, including losing the right to vote, defended their support in 1994 for the National Party by arguing, "I was born a Nationalist!" Hennie mused on post-apartheid political consciousness:

> Why the coloured people are so distinct is that they are very dependent.
> They all believe that they are not from this continent—their heritage is located in some other, European continent—and they are definitely not black.
> They like anything that is not black. They do not like black people. Even now. Even now. And even though we were part of the broad black liberation struggle during that period of time, shortly after the unbanning of the ANC you could see the clear lines starting to come through again, clear lines of separation: white, so-called coloureds, who would rather become closer to the white people and not to the black people.

Coloured racism against black Africans is an uncomfortable truth. Many coloured acquaintances shared their fears of an African takeover of Cape Town. I witnessed the cruelty toward African children who live in squatter camps by their coloured classmates in a coloured township school that borders an informal settlement. I was told repeatedly that "things were better under the Nats" because apartheid instilled order. I heard painful stories recounted by white activists and community workers who are expected to be complicitous with anti-African racist jokes told by coloured Capetonians. A white friend, for example, found herself positioned as the sympathetic customer by the coloured checkout clerk at her local convenience store. Barbara was in line behind an elderly African customer, who, after carefully counting out coins for his purchase, came up short. Rolling her eyes, the clerk said to Barbara in Afrikaans: "You can take them out of the bush, but you can't take the bush out of them." Barbara responded by slamming her groceries on the counter and walking out, declaring she would take her business elsewhere in the future. Coloured support for the National Party rested on the same set of stereotypes and suspicions about black African competence and ability to govern that one hears in white circles. Coloured complicity with anti-black racism is a sensitive topic for activists and intellectuals, who argue that coloured voters loyal to the National Party have not yet thrown off the weight of oppression and subjugation and continue to look to white culture for their future.

But while it may seem simple to explain the political choices of coloured voters by pointing to a history of internalized submission to white domination, coloured identity is about much more than an aversion to blackness and an orientation to whiteness as a marker of class status and a strategy of upward mobility.[22] Coloured identities carry shared cultural themes rooted in histories of slavery and forced removals, in religion and respectability, in creativity and creolization. The contradiction between the intense involvement of Cape Town's coloured schools in the political struggles of the 1980s and the force of the coloured vote in returning to power the architects of apartheid in the 1994 elections in the Western Cape demonstrates the unique complexity of coloured identity politics and the fallacy of defining post-apartheid Cape Town in racially dichotomous terms. The sociologist Zimitri Erasmus writes: "Living with these contradictions is part of the pain of being coloured."[23] And, as she recognizes, it is also part of the liberating possibilities of being coloured.

. . . . .

Emile YX? cuts a solo CD called *Who Am I?* that challenges the stereotypes of coloured identity and claims an African identity. Merle, who describes her life history as "practicing to be white," enrolls in therapeutic workshops to recapture a personal identity that makes her whole. Hennie, the ardent socialist union organizer from Retreat, finds himself moved by efforts to link contemporary coloured identity with indigenous Khoi culture (although he recognizes that his socialist colleagues "are not very impressed" by this interest). Al Witten, the primary school principal in

Lavender Hill, teaches his coloured students to embrace their identities as Africans. Hussein, a former anti-apartheid fighter who now runs an NGO for anti-apartheid veterans, rejects the coloured label as an apartheid invention, preferring to identify as "Arab-African." In myriad ways, the end of apartheid has liberated coloured Capetonians to assert their understandings and preferences about their identities. Such identity explorations—intellectual or political projects for some, personal journeys of emotional discovery for others—produce conclusions that are sometimes contradictory and discordant. Because Cape Town's coloured population is cleaved by class, by language, by religion, and by generation, post-apartheid coloured identities are a multifaceted, creative spectrum.

The end of apartheid destabilized the color hierarchy and introduced challenges to the superiority of whiteness, opening a space for complex conversations about the interweaving of whiteness and colouredness. Many in the coloured population are caught in the grip of white norms— if they reject "white culture," what are they left with? One hears over and over about feelings of being "in-between": "We don't know who we are." "We don't know our ancestors, our history." "We have no culture of our own. We are defined by what we are not. Blacks have initiation, they have cultural traditions and rituals. What are our rituals and traditions?"[24] The oft-repeated mantra "It used to be we weren't white enough; now we're not black enough" summarizes the feeling of dislocation and marginality felt by many coloured Capetonians. Such *mestiza* categories are recognized throughout the world for their ambiguity and creativity; as elsewhere, coloured Capetonians have fashioned within their political buffer role a rich and cosmopolitan cultural world.

In her seminal essay about post-apartheid coloured identity, the sociologist Zimitri Erasmus describes coloured identity as a creolization: an identity creatively woven from cultural practices drawn from the dominant and subaltern in a context of racial hierarchy. Over my years of research in Cape Town, it was apparent that those who shared with me their uncertainties about their cultural integrity and cultural content nevertheless shared a collective of cultural markers: food; jokes and styles of humor; notions of respectability, propriety, and appropriate gender roles; domestic and fashion aesthetics; and shared sentiments of holding an ambiguous identity. Despite the fact that some are heavily invested in white definitions of respectability and submission to authority while others actively oppose but remain in dialogue with such a construction of community and self, a shared set of cultural markers and sensibilities is easily discernible.

Erasmus argues that discussions about the future of coloured identity politics must acknowledge coloured racism and the circumstances under which coloured culture developed—a context of white domination and coloured complicity in racist practices. For Erasmus, the way forward is clear: "With the construction of whiteness having been a colonial project, discriminatory and racist, the ethical imperative—necessary participation in a liberatory project—is that of affiliation with Africa."[25] Such an affiliation does not mean, however, a fixation on blackness or Africanness as the only authentic or moral identity available to coloured people, she insists. Rather, liberated identities—identity constructions that break free of predetermined racial boundaries—are the future. Erasmus urges her coloured readers to move beyond the limitations set by aspiring to whiteness or by embracing a notion of authentic blackness, to move beyond attempts to reduce coloured identity to cultural performances of coons and carnivals, or to indigenize coloured identity (as Khoisan), thus stripping it of its creolized heart. "Mestiza means that which does not obey or even see boundaries: that which blurs sharp distinctions in favor of what is best or most appropriate; that which thrives in ambiguity because ambiguity means survival, creation, movement," writes Deborah Miranda in a passage that captures the liberatory possibilities of mestiza identities.[26] Or, as the political activist Rhoda Kadalie says to me, with a satisfied smile: "I can be anything."

In the words of Gloria Anzaldúa:

> The new *mestiza* copes by developing a tolerance for contradictions, a tolerance for ambiguity. She learns to be an Indian in Mexican culture, to be Mexican from an Anglo point of view. She learns to juggle cultures. She has a plural personality, she operates in a pluralistic mode—nothing is thrust out, the good, the bad and the ugly, nothing rejected, nothing abandoned. Not only does she sustain contradictions, she turns the ambivalence into something else. . . . That focal point or fulcrum, that juncture where the *mestiza* stands, is where phenomena tend to collide. It is where the possibility of uniting all that is separate occurs. This assembly is not one where severed or separated pieces merely come together. Nor is it a balancing of opposing power. In attempting to work out a synthesis, the self has added a third element which is greater than the sum of its severed parts. That third element is a new consciousness—a *mestiza* consciousness—and though it is a source of intense pain, its energy comes from a continual creative motion that keeps breaking down the unitary aspect of each new paradigm.[27]

If these writers—intellectuals and activists at the forefront of defining new social and political locations for those of "mixed" heritage or ambiguous and in-between identities—are correct, the same contradictions that afflict people's sense of their identity as coloured Capetonians offer liberatory potential. The transition to democracy inaugurated in 1994 freed coloured identities from the dictates of whiteness, even though whiteness remains part of the dialogue of identity politics in Cape Town. It is inaccurate to claim that coloured identity is still about aspiring to be white; coloured dialogues with whiteness carry a critique of whiteness as often as an embrace. Coloured identities also contain the pride of black consciousness, which continues to nurture an engagement with blackness. Language politics inflects debates about coloured identity as Afrikaans is claimed and promoted by many as the language of the Cape Flats rather than of apartheid. Class status continues to play a critical and increasingly complex role in the negotiation of coloured identity, particularly since the move to incorporate blackness as central to coloured identity seems to emanate more from coloured elites than from the poor. Tracking how class status markers continue to mirror markers of white culture and how new markers of class status are unlinked from racial identity will provide a fascinating window through which to assess post-apartheid transformation. Coloured identities, as profoundly Cape Town identities, are foundational for Cape Town's future.[28]

Cognizant of this fact, cultural workers in Cape Town are at the forefront of exploring and imagining how coloured identities have taken shape and in what directions they might evolve. Some have formed cultural organizations to promote coloured identity as an indigenous identity linked to Khoisan ancestry or to promote a focus on slave heritage as the cornerstone of coloured identity. But, as Hendricks observes, "The collapsing of these identities with coloured identity has not taken root in the broader community," whose members do not necessarily feel their identity is problematic or inauthentic.[29] Nevertheless, from 2000 to 2004, an acknowledgment of Khoisan and slave contributions to their identity—so long subverted in favor of white ancestry—begins to appear in the family histories I record with my interviewees. Reflecting on his emotional reaction to the use of Khoisan rituals in the reburial of an anti-apartheid activist, Hennie explains that despite his commitment to socialist ideals and politics, recapturing an ethnic history is vital for him and his comrades: "We must know who we are! We must know where we came from!" Casual references to "our Khoisan ancestors" crop up with increasing frequency in conversations as friends begin to shift their autobiographical narratives.

While some Capetonians now embrace a Khoisan or slave heritage as the full definition of who they are, many cast their ancestral net more

broadly to encompass a variety of heritages. Some refuse a racial or ethnic category altogether, rejecting the label *coloured* (or always prefacing
it with *so-called,* a practice that became popular with the younger generation after 1994). The ideology of nonracialism sometimes collides
with bureaucratic realities of redistribution. Peter, for example, discov-
ers that his son has left blank the identity boxes on his application forms
for university in protest against being forced to categorize himself—Peter
must intervene because the boxes are used to distribute bursary funds.
Peter's son and his friends argue that being forced to check an identity
box runs counter to their understanding of the possibilities for nonracialism offered by the new South Africa.

   An emerging orientation among many cultural workers is the emphasis on bodily and culturally embracing a rootedness in Africa. Culture is far more meaningful to explore than race, and Cape Town's dynamic cultural history offers Capetonians the ability to reject race as
salient to identity. Cape Town's most original and vibrant cultural producers, for example, explore identity questions by playing with and in-
tertwining many strands of Cape Town's history in their plays, novels,
poems, music, comedy performances, and art, often while embracing the
distinctly urban Cape Flats culture.

.   .   .   .   .

It's 2001, and Cape Town's hip-hop group Black Noise is performing at
a high school in Grassy Park. Like most schools on the Cape Flats there
is no auditorium, just a couple of two-story, prison barracks–style buildings set parallel to each other across a small paved open area. The group
is performing outside on the broken concrete that surrounds the school,
which is surrounded, in turn, by barbed wire. Perhaps two hundred students are gathered in a semicircle, ten deep, straining to watch the bboy
skills and to giggle at their classmates willing to join in. Emile punctu-
ates the performance with commentary on community pride and self-
motivation. At the conclusion of the presentation, Emile asks, "Who
here is African?" Two students and all the Black Noise members raise
their hands, while everyone else looks around in obvious confusion and
uncertainty. Then he asks, "Who here lives in Africa?" All the hands go
up. Emile reminds them they live in Africa; they are African, and they
must claim this identity with pride.

   Emile uses hip-hop to entice Cape Flats youth to listen to his message
of self-empowerment and pride in an African heritage. His philosophy,
promoted in school demonstrations and public performances, links hip-

hop to indigenous African art forms, drawing connections between graffiti and San rock paintings, rap and griots (West African praise singers), break dancing and African traditional dancing. When hip-hop first hit Cape Town in the 1980s—brought on airwaves and through films like *Wild Style, Style Wars,* and *Beat Street*—young adherents copied all the American stuff. Denver, a well-known Cape musician laughs as he remembers the "Yo, wazup man?" style of his youth. Media controls enforced a government-determined cultural isolation and an emphasis on white pop music. With the school uprisings in the 1980s, new music such as reggae and hip-hop came in underground, and local youths began seeing parallels between U.S. rappers' experience and Cape Town township experience. Emile recalled the sensation created by Public Enemy's tapes when they appeared underground: Shocking! "Most hip-hoppers didn't like it at first. They were shocked at the audacity to say it out loud, even though everyone was thinking what they were saying."

Hip-hop offered a way for township youth to connect with a transnational urban and ghetto youth culture, but it also provided an art form for exploring local realities and identities. "To find an identity for a specific so-called coloured person was hard because there were no records—not everyone can really trace his or her ancestry," Emile says. "Coloureds came from all over the place. So each individual must locate himself and develop his identity for himself out of such a huge diversity." As another Black Noise member noted, because "hip-hop is a potpourri," it resonated with coloured youths who could identify with the political, economic, and historical position of urban African-Americans and Hispanics. Gradually Emile and a few others began asserting connections between hip-hop and indigenous African art forms, finding in hip-hop a path to reconnect with their Africanness, a heritage rejected and obscured in coloured communities.

In her excellent research on South African hip-hop, Rosemary Lombard notes how a logic of self-empowerment and a consciousness of resistance inform hip-hop, which is about self-awareness, subversion, and inversion: emcees sing rather than talk; bboys dance on their heads, not their feet; graffiti goes up on public walls, not private canvases; disc jockeys never play a record beginning to end. Within adherence to the four core practices, there is a lot of room for choice, play, and invention.[30] In addition to such creative possibilities, hip-hop offers the opportunity to tell truths, to be confrontational and angry, and to express rage. An obvious reason why hip-hop became so popular in the Cape Flats is its subversiveness and its fame-seeking orientation. For example, what could be more challenging to an established order that denigrates your existence than insisting on recognition by tagging graffiti—emblazoning your name in a public space?

Not all local hip-hop groups share Black Noise's emphasis on African roots, but embracing an urban, ghettoized, black aesthetic enabled hip-hop pioneers to localize hip-hop, using it to comment on Cape Town ghetto realities while promoting transnational connections.[31]

. . . . .

At a birthday party in 2000, the assembled group of young coloured professionals and graduate students argues about the ongoing importance of politicizing a black identity that encompasses Africans and coloureds, in opposition to whiteness. The hostess shares her sense of discomfort with such politicized identity categories, which demand that she categorize herself in opposition to her mother, who is white. Several guests tell the hostess she has to give up her white mother because her mother's white society oppressed people like her. How, they ask, can she feel an affinity for that culture?

The Black Consciousness movement influenced a generation of coloured high school students in Cape Town, particularly at leading coloured high schools such as Harold Cressey, Livingston, and Trafalgar. Graduates of those schools talk of their political awakening through their teachers, of deciding to challenge their parents' complicity with apartheid by defining themselves as black. Merle's half-sister Val, the political "black sheep" in her family, recalls the dramatic moment when she proclaimed her black identity against her parents' wishes. Her father and mother had worked hard to achieve a white lifestyle and aspired to have their children classified as white. From the Bo-Kaap, where Merle was born, the family relocated to Athlone and then to racially ambiguous Rondebosch East. The moment of identity reckoning came for Val when, as a teenager, she asked her mother for her birth certificate in order to obtain her first driver's license.

> My mother said to me, "Well, you don't have one." And of course I thought this was ridiculous. "What do you mean I don't have a birth certificate?" "No, you don't have a birth certificate." "I don't have a birth certificate? Why don't I have a birth certificate?" And I remember my mom going into this whole explanation: "Well you know, your dad thought this would be better for you so that you could have choices about this, and he is quite happy to help all of you get white IDs." And I went berserk. I went absolutely berserk. And my mother was like, "You know, this is only for your own good. Your father only wants the best for you." I was hysterical. . . . They

just chose not to register us! [so that we could try for white IDs as adults]. . . .

This caused huge drama in our family. And then my brothers and sisters were all against me: "Why are you doing this? This is so unnecessary." I was like this outcast that I wanted to make such a big deal about being a coloured or black and they were angry at me, and once again, I was the only person in the family that was making a big deal about my identity. But you know my identity became so important to me then because I realized that all of this was going on and that many coloured kids at that stage who weren't exposed and talked about what was happening and going on sometimes weren't sure who they really were, and I didn't want to grow up like that. You know: "Am I this? Am I that? Where do I belong? How do I define who I am?" I already had that sense, that I want to know who I am. Of course, this was all compounded with all the demonstrations that then followed and the UDF [United Democratic Front] that then became very militant and I was involved. So I went and registered myself [as coloured] and they were *furious* with me. I felt I was the only black person in that family, officially, with official black papers!

Val enrolled under a special permit for coloured students at the University of Cape Town, where she and other black students decided to boycott their graduation in protest of the university's exclusion of students of color.[32] She describes the impact of this decision:

Well! My parents were *livid!* That was the last straw! To be graduating from a white university and not giving them the pleasure of sitting there as proud parents and seeing their first child being capped was like a sin never to be forgiven. Oh . . . to this day, Catherine, that will be mentioned. The topic will come up and they'll say, "You robbed us of going to your graduation because you were such a smarty pants." To this day they resent me. You can imagine, that was such a big deal! And I was so proud of myself! I was not doing this, not for anybody! For me! I was not going to this graduation! And so we all boycotted, and I think that was the final blow. My family has never forgiven me. The funniest part was that this dumb, rebel, black sheep of the family was [at that time] the only one who ever graduated from university!

For Val, continuing to validate herself as a black woman is critically important. She recalls her struggles in the corporate world to achieve the acknowledgment and respect she deserved. In the interview excerpted below, she describes how her history orients her identity:

I got the job at [a major retail corporation] and worked my way up the system, and I went through all the issues of being an oppressed black person in this corporate world and always having to prove that I was a *thousand* times better than my white counterparts. . . . It wasn't always easy, and I still left that business with a lot of wounds. I never felt that I was good enough. I had huge confidence issues, even though when people saw me and spoke to me they would say, "Are you kidding? I mean, you're a confident, outgoing, wonderful person. You can do whatever you like." I would say, "no I can't," because of all those years it was so internalized and I had so believed because of all the messages I got that I was just never going to be good enough. Even when I started my own business, people kept on saying to me, you do this so well, you're the best person I've seen doing this kind of work, and it took a long time for me to actually believe that. I was good, and I still find it difficult to accept when people say, you're good at what you do. I have to sometimes consciously say "thank you" and just, and just kind of let it go, and [she is openly weeping now] it's so hard.

Val *is* a very successful woman whose consultancy services are much in demand by organizations trying to address issues of racism and transformation. Her ebullient personality and tactful yet penetrating approach to pursuing post-apartheid change in the workplace has won her many admirers. She and her husband have a wide group of white and coloured friends and colleagues. I asked if she still feels the importance of defining herself racially in the post-apartheid context.

I still have a strong connection about being a black woman and about having found my place in a new society in Cape Town, but I still believe, as a black woman. . . . It's our time now and there's a real place for me legitimately in this new world, and I think I've found my place in that new world and feel very confidently that I have a contribution to make. . . . And that's why a lot of my work in the race and gender stuff and in working with these senior magistrates and judges was really affirming for me, because I kind of felt like wow! The tables are really turned today, and now it's about you [e.g., white people] having to prove that you can do it in this new dispensation. I don't have to do that anymore! [laughing]. . . . And I think that what's also been amazing for me is that I've found other white colleagues that I work with, and now today they have those issues about, "so am I going to be accepted as being genuine?" It's been an interesting turn of things, and so now I'm the one to say, "Yeah, we talk the same language, we have the same values." But there's that today, of white women having to prove that they still have a place in this new South Africa. And I feel like I can help them along that journey because I've been there. Those tables have been completely turned. It's quite interesting.

Val's half-sister Merle has been following her own journey to connect with an identity authentic to her sense of self. Her path first took the form of therapeutic workshops and retreats, which she hoped would facilitate a spiritual and psychological self-affirmation and help her realize a self-identity that felt authentic. One day while swimming near

Muizenberg, she encountered a group of fellow swimmers, women her own age from Retreat. As they struck up a conversation, she realized that she felt a visceral connection to these women—to their mannerisms and their speech. After decades of "practicing to be white," she discovered that she feels a profound comfort in these women's companionship, an easy familiarity that takes her back to her childhood days living in the Bo-Kaap. Her search for her roots takes her to the language of her childhood and to a political self-assertion she feels she was denied by her compliant, upwardly mobile family. I asked her what got her started on her journey of self-recovery. She responded:

> The same question would always come up, of "who are you?" [I was] quite unconscious about the fact that I was denying my roots. And then when these women started swimming with me, and listening to the way they spoke to each other, using their Cape dialect, it triggered excitement in me, and I thought, what is it I find so exciting? I thought it was a feeling of being . . . at home. And when I got that feeling, it was an awakening. Yes, this is real. I am at home, and they are my roots. And I was made to believe that I was unaccepted because I was not white, and the roots were rooted in slaves and negativity and poverty, and I didn't want to know that, and that was my escape. Making the effort to practice to be white. I mean, you know that side of me. Practicing to be white. Learning to cook like white people. . . . Because to be who I truly was, was unacceptable, and I didn't want to be not accepted.

Where did her understanding of unacceptability came from, I asked. From her parents?

> Yeah! Not only my parents, my grandparents. My whole family spoke of it, when they would speak about people and their friends, they would say, "You know, so-and-so's daughter, she is very fair." It was always, she wasn't black, she is very fair, so she was the right color, you know. This is what was thrown around in our home; you were acceptable when you were fair. You know, [my uncle], he battled! He and his brother, they would go travel to the same jobs together, get on the same train, stand on the same platform, but when the train came, the brother got in the white coach and Uncle got into the black coach because he was too dark to, you know. . . . He couldn't play white. And I think because I could pass, [it] made it worse for me, because it made me deny who I was even more. You know, if you're black, you're black; there's nothing you could do about it. But if you're in-between, you could swing between both worlds.

Merle concluded by talking about her recent realization that all along she's been looking for acceptance in the wrong places. But Val's embrace of her black identity and Merle's embrace of the dialect she recalls from her Bo-Kaap childhood continue to distinguish these two half-sisters from their other siblings and from their parents. Val's parents still cannot bring themselves to include photographs of Val's beautiful and darker-skinned children among the array of family photos on display in their home.

. . . . .

Raymond, the projects coordinator from Lavender Hill, and I are sitting in my family room in Maine during Raymond's whirlwind trip to the United States in 2003. For Raymond, this trip is a rare break from his consuming round-the-clock community work in coloured townships. Exhausted from a hectic schedule of meetings and talks, we're sprawled across the furniture chatting about odds and ends before he has to catch his bus to New York. Raymond remarks that he had come to understand something profound about himself during the past several weeks in the United States. After mentioning to my husband that he was missing home, he realized he felt a visceral understanding of my husband's description of his sentiments of longing for the country of his birth. Listening to Jorge talk of his emotional bond to Colombia, Raymond says he realized that his feelings meant he had acknowledged South Africa as his home, and that he was missing the place and the culture to which he belongs. The revelation was that he was forming, for the first time in his life, a sense of self-identity and belonging.[33]

Such sentiments had first come to him just a few weeks earlier, as he was departing a meeting with his service club and had a few spare moments of reflection as he looked out over Cape Town's harbor. Thinking about the years he had committed to serving the community of his birth, he recalled how his upbringing had been pervaded by feelings of anger, resentment, and frustration, as his teenage years were spent in the midst of boycotts, violence, and throwing rocks at white-driven cars on Prince George's Drive. "We never focused on the good things: feelings of pride, ownership. We focused on negative emotions, and now we don't see the positive emotions of belonging. We haven't emphasized restoring those emotions. . . . Now I'm discovering it, at the age of forty! It took until I was forty years old to learn these feelings." Raymond realizes he has begun to gently weep, and I realize with shock how deeply meaningful this admission is for him.

After he recovers his composure, Raymond describes how his new-found pride in his community is a product of his association with Al Witten, the school principal with whom he has been partnering in community development projects. "Al taught me about national pride and pride in the community. Our song, flying our school flag alongside the country's flag"—the symbolic association of the local with the nation. "Many of us walked in shame, ashamed to say 'I'm from Lavender Hill.' Al tried to restore that pride." Raymond recalls that he learned Al's lesson intellectually, but only now was he experiencing the emotion of cultural belonging. Driving home from Cape Town's harbor after discovering this feeling, Raymond says he realized the enormity of the cultural injustices experienced by the coloured population. "I thought of all my insecurities, all my problems during my life, of not belonging. It could have all been avoided." Being able to embrace who he is "took intensive involvement for four years and a commitment to really get involved in the community. It took loving people in the community. Now I can look people in the eye and say with pride, 'I'm from Lavender Hill.' " Raymond observes that "some might desire to suppress the acknowledgment of what was taken from us because they're afraid of a surge of anger. Our leaders need to help people work through their anger to pride and ownership and responsibility." He concludes, as we're gathering his suitcases, "Whites don't understand. They don't realize what was taken, the depth of the emotional trauma."

.   .   .   .   .

All over Cape Town, coloured educators, cultural producers, writers, and scholars are exploring the language of belonging—to a past, to a country, to a continent. Coloured identities are being forged from a creolized culture that developed in a psychological and material context of white supremacy. With the dismantling of white supremacy, the creolized/*mestiza* center of coloured community culture can flourish and offer new models for South Africa identities, models that reject the narrow oppressiveness of white domination, the rigid confines of black authenticity, and the class elitism nurtured by early coloured political associations and the Coloured Labor Preference policy. Zimitri Erasmus has the final word:

> The decision to acknowledge the act of living with complicity means that all black South Africans have to forgo certain claims, for example, the moral authority based on blackness, Africanness, or indigenous-ness. It calls for a new kind of politics premised not on "who we are" but on what we do with "who we are." . . . For me it is a "truth" which defies the safe prison of the dominant ideology; that I ought to identify only as black and not coloured; that coloured identity is an illusion from which I need to be saved

by my black sisters who promise to put me on the right road and confer my "true" blackness upon me; that the former aspect of my identity is best discarded as a relic of the past. I refuse the safety of identifying only as "black," because it allows me to forget or deny the "truth" of racial hierarchies between coloured and African and of present privilege, and their significance in the formation of my own identities. The safety of identifying only as "black" denies the "better than black" element of coloured identity formation. It denies complicity. It denies the privileges of being coloured.[34]

CHAPTER 8

Transformers

While the struggle against racism and poverty is of course central to modern South African experience, in many ways the post-apartheid democratic arena lacks the urgency and sense of moral responsibility that galvanized social activism prior to 1990. After 1994, the choice to orient one's life toward social transformation is a choice to reject and fight against the status quo, but a status quo that typifies much of the world, where racism and inequality are norms rather than exceptions. For those whose moral compass tells them that inequality is wrong, the struggle against apartheid has been replaced by a struggle against the assumptions and political economic structures that maintain poverty.

Although fighting against poverty, racism, and segregation after 1994 may be physically less risky than in the past, we should not underestimate the significance of such a life choice. This chapter explores the hopeful visions and determined activism of a small group of Capetonians who have entered zones of significant social discomfort to dismantle white privilege, to challenge relationships built on unequal power and dependency, and to work toward transformation, within themselves, their community, or their city. Previous chapters described the mental and material barriers to integration and transformation that continue to have force in contemporary Cape Town, but as I have suggested, the city is also home to a broad range of projects and initiatives to change the status quo. Everyone I know in Cape Town is involved in some kind of endeavor to help others, whether by supporting indigent family members, caring for the child of a relative, donating clothing or food to the poor, or contributing to a charitable organization. Many of these are "safe" undertakings that don't disrupt daily life or require a change in lifestyle, personal ideology, or social networks. In contrast, here I focus on those who have chosen to embark on projects with transformative agendas that demand lifestyle changes, ideological investment, and the creation of new social worlds.

Each of the six undertakings I profile here is small-scale and local in focus, created by people who hold a specifically transformative agenda for a particular community. Three are school-based undertakings: one focused on high school students, primarily from Langa; one in Lavender Hill based at Zerilda Park Primary School; and a third in another impoverished coloured community I will call Heatherton Primary School. One is an internal attempt at self-transformation by a primarily white church I will call Gardenview Baptist Church. Another is an initiative that I will call the Hope Project to build a community center for educational, nutritional, health, skills development, and psychological services for families devastated by HIV/AIDS in one of Cape Town's poorest African townships. One is an informal support group formed by a group of young African men (from different high schools and different townships) who feel they share a moral commitment to community work. One member calls it his "Circle of Courage," a name I adopt in this chapter.[1] All the projects demand self-transformation in their participants, and all require participants to create new kinds of partnerships across apartheid-era boundaries. I have chosen to profile these particular projects because I learned of them early in my fieldwork and followed their progress over several years, but it is important to note that they are like hundreds of others sustained by dedicated, hopeful people throughout the city.

The following descriptions outline the trajectory, context, and goals of each project. Each description concludes with a brief assessment of some of the innovations and major challenges that emerge from the projects' stories, as well as the frustrations and elations of people who are actively working to effect transformation.

THE LANGA EDUCATIONAL ASSISTANCE PROGRAMME

Pinelands High School is a lovely complex set back from the road along a circular drive bordered by flowers and surrounded by sports fields. The school's neighborhood in the garden suburb of Pinelands stands up to its name: pretty, spacious cottages set on well-tended green lawns with lavish flower beds. From the eastern edge of bucolic Pinelands, you climb over a concrete wall, dash across a major four-lane road, clamber across several sets of railroad tracks, scale another fence, and cut through an open field to enter Langa township.

Isilimela High School stands on the far edge of Langa, surrounded by barbed wire and an electric gate, its grounds concrete and dirt.[2] In contrast to the sweeping Pinelands high school facilities, Isilimela architecture reflects the township standard for apartheid-era schools: prisonlike two-story classroom blocks connect by covered passages and locking barred gates. The neighborhood surrounding the school outside the wire fence is the poorest section of Langa, home to thousands of squatters and informal shacks.

As the tumultuous decade of the 1980s moved toward democratic resolution, teachers and students at Pinelands High School began yearning for greater connections with their peers across the apartheid divide. Students in Langa's high schools, striving for an education in a deliberately impoverished school system, looked across the barriers at what Pinelands had to offer and wondered how to gain access to it. The Langa Educational Assistance Programme (LEAP) grew out of these yearnings for connection and broader educational opportunities.

Teachers involved in founding LEAP in 1990 credit their students with pushing them to create linkages between the communities separated by apartheid laws and physical barriers. Some Pinelands students had joined the black student organization in the late 1980s, pulling their teachers along to political meetings and protests (as student activists did throughout South Africa). In response to their students' commitment and desire to make connections with other students, some teachers formed LEAP to promote sports exchanges between Pinelands and Langa. At one such exchange, Langa students approached John Gilmour, then a teacher at Pinelands, to ask how they could attend his school. Remembering this moment fourteen years later, one of these students said: "John was enthusiastic and told me to phone him. I still remember the phone number!" Embracing this expression of interest, John created a program to bring Langa students to study at (and integrate for the first time) Pinelands High School. An additional component of LEAP offered after-school math and science tutorials at Pinelands for Langa students, initially funded by SA Breweries.

A statement in LEAP's 2001–2002 report articulates LEAP's goals for the previous decade: "We recognize the enormous needs of the community of

Langa and we attempt to assist in small, direct ways with a view to strengthening the schools and the community. We work hard to create a bridge across the traditional socio-economic barriers in this city with a view to furthering the process of reconciliation and nation building. LEAP serves as a small agency of empowerment working with a small budget but with a real shared vision for the young people of Langa."

John Gilmour describes his awakening to the realization of the vast inequalities in education between white schools and township schools that encouraged his vision of LEAP as a bridge between communities empowered and disempowered by apartheid:

> The starting point really is the recognition that the inequalities that are built into our social system—and economic and educational—are entrenched and are not going to change incrementally just by conduction; they're going to have to change by real specific action. So my own context was that having had contact through sport particularly with young people from the township of Langa, I began to have some of the scales lifted from my own eyes in terms of understanding the horror of living without opportunity or the horror of living without choice. My experience as an educator was that I was creating choice—I was contributing to the process of creating opportunity and choice for young people and that historically I had been doing that for privileged young people, for which there is a need, but I'd done it fairly blindly, recognizing all the historical realities of apartheid but not really understanding the living realities of apartheid. . . . We began to realize that these inequalities were certainly brutal, but they were not going to change by a change in government.

A central goal of LEAP was to improve the abysmal matric results for Langa students, particularly in math and science. After a few years, some teachers questioned the wisdom of holding after-school tutorials at Pinelands for Langa students, because of the implication that "our environment was superior," in the words of one LEAP teacher. The program shifted its focus to tutoring students in Langa but, after the corporate sponsor withdrew funding, became dependent on student volunteers from the University of Cape Town (UCT), the University of the Western Cape (UWC), and the Colby-Bates-Bowdoin (CBB) program.

Students who participated in LEAP during its early years agree that the project made progress toward the goal of encouraging barrier-crossing, but those who left Langa to enroll at Pinelands also recall the personal challenges of leaving the township environment to attend a white school. It was a rugged transition, in part because the academic standards were so drastically different. Eric, a top student in his Langa high school, struggled so mightily with the English-language medium that he decided to drop out after three months. John talked him into staying, and he moved in with his first white friend at Pinelands, whose mother was one of LEAP's founding teachers, so he could more intensively focus on his studies. Another of the extraordinarily motivated LEAP students spent afternoon after afternoon in John's office, weeping tears of rage at the system that provided him utterly inadequate preparation for secondary school and ensured a life of poverty for his struggling family. This student also recalls the social challenges: none of his white friends from Pinelands ever visited his home in Langa until the day he left for a semester abroad in the United States, when his best white friend met his mother for the first time. They recall feelings of academic insecurity as well as discovery and acknowledge the awkward multicultural space they came to occupy as township residents at a privileged white school.

Bringing students from neighboring Langa into staid, white Pinelands for sports exchanges and after-school tutorials produced some predictably stereotypical moments. In several instances of criminal mischief, Langa students were the first to be accused even when they were not the culprits. The buses from Langa were occasionally late for a sports exchange day, prompting angry Pinelands parents to complain about the lack of punctuality inherent to "African time," but as John points out, without bothering to ask the question of why; what does it take to get a bunch of kids from all over Langa to Pinelands? A number of students dropped out of the after-school tutorial program, prompting an assumption of disinterest and ingratitude, but the real reason was the students' inability to concentrate because of hunger—they had not eaten since early morning. Each of these instances could have been enough to cancel the entire initiative (justified by a view of Langa students as irresponsible, disorganized, or ungrateful) had it not been for the perseverance of the core group of LEAP educators and students, who consistently saw the larger context and approached such "problems" as things to understand and work through rather than signs of failure.

Two of Langa's high schools lost interest in actively participating in LEAP after the corporate sponsor withdrew and the focus became after-school tutorials. But the students and the new principal of Isilimela High School remained eager to participate. While LEAP tutorials had targeted grade twelve students, Isilimela's new principal, Pat Qokweni, urged LEAP to form a grade ten LEAP group in order to work with them through grade twelve. Beginning the tutorial process in grade twelve was belated, she suggested, and her group of grade tens that year included a particularly outgoing and motivated group of young men (some of whom later formed the "Circle of Courage" described below). These students recall their excitement about the opportunities provided by LEAP volunteers to practice their English, learn new skills, and form friendships with American students. The LEAP group that participated in after-school tutorials from grades ten through twelve were dedicated students determined to pursue all avenues open to them for academic improvement and social opportunities.

This was the final group of students to participate in the LEAP program. Unfortunately, after thirteen years, the participating teachers and principals had to acknowledge the devastating truth that LEAP tutoring was having no impact on matric results. Even the brightest and most promising of the grade-ten students who took advantage of LEAP tutorials through grade twelve, including Siyabonga, failed the matric exam. Such continually disappointing matric results made it clear that after-school tutorials run by volunteers were utterly inadequate in compensating for the massive educational disadvantages faced by township schools.

This recognition offered a point of reckoning for John Gilmour, who had left Pinelands to become a headmaster of an innovative private school called Abbotts. He recalls his early assumptions about what LEAP could accomplish: "There was a very idealistic view that as a support agency we could get in and upgrade schools quickly. Offer money, offer expertise, offer our own 'vast' experience [with an ironic smile], and that would all be fine within a couple of years, that we could do so much within a couple of years. And the reality is that from the period of first involvement in 1990 to—take a ten-year period—very little shifted because the issues were far deeper than just the superficial, visible inequalities."

Increasingly frustrated by the slow pace of transformation in education, and increasingly certain that transformation would happen only through radically new approaches to education (rather than add-ons, like after-school tutorials), John made the life-changing decision to quit his job in order to search for funding to create a new school focused on math and science specifically for African-language township students. After reviewing the appalling statistics of educational success for African-language students in the Western Cape,[3] John decided to take his background in experimental, individually focused education from the private school environment and turn it toward a transformative model of education for students from educationally impoverished backgrounds:

> Hopefully if we can create a model that will work—it will give strength to organizations like that of Abbotts to take risks. It became clear that I needed to look outside of existing structures to look for a way of helping

this process of transformation by creating something that uses the best of what exists—the best facilities that exist. A school like Bishops [the most elite school in Cape Town] has everything it possibly needs. . . . I could see there was need for somebody to look at a systematic way of creating access. And so I began to look at the option of taking learners from schools in Langa, or Guguletu, or wherever, and putting them in close proximity to a school like Bishops, and as a short-term way of dealing with the crisis, creating an Abbotts kind of model to help learners who, if they didn't have that opportunity, would be destined probably to failing matric at worst, or at best passing matric without maths and sciences. The real goal remains, in my head still remains, the fact that those schools in Langa need to be strengthened. The question that's often thrown at me is, "Well, why don't you just go and work there?" And the answer simply is that they won't have me and they can't have me. It's not their fault. There's no movement within the system. To go in and work as a teacher, endlessly there, would be to lose what I have to offer, which is, I now have some experience of organization, of time-table management, setting up systems that could really benefit, but I need to be in a position to actually implement them. And so working with a township school [helped me realize] that the schools were open to the idea that some of their students should be offered the opportunity to attend a school like the one we're envisaging.

I asked the principal of one of Langa's high schools about her views of John's new LEAP school. She explained why she supported his initiative, even if it meant losing some of her best learners:

How you answer that question depends on who you are who is answering that question. If you are a township teacher, they are taking away your cream. John says he is taking the township learners as they are, at whatever level of preparedness they come with. Our teachers should look and see what he is doing that *we* can do. They always say, "we don't have resources. Those schools have all the resources so we can't be like them." In fact we *do* have some of those resources too. We *do* have resources, but they don't use them. There is a lack of a culture of teaching. . . . Sometimes, that's the main difference between our schools. I know that some of the schools have better facilities, but there are schools with worse facilities, but because of a lot of commitment of the teachers, make a lot of difference. In any particular school, there are always people who do their best. But then the difference between school A and school B will be, how many of those teachers did their best, performed their best? And if in a school 80 percent of the teachers did their best, there will be a difference compared to the school where 50 percent of the teachers did their best, and the other 50 percent didn't. There tends to be a lot of that in our schools.

"What makes a difference with commitment?" I asked. "Why is it that one school might have 80 percent commitment from teachers and another school does not have that commitment?" The principal responded:

I really don't know. Really. You agree on how you are going to run the school, but then . . . some of them don't come to school. Or they are at school but they don't go to the classrooms. Some of them go to the classrooms, but once they're in the classrooms, but they're not doing anything! We've reached the stage where we can say, "OK, we keep telling the HOD [Head of Department] or the SMT [School Management Team] to go to the classes and see if everything is as it should be." Some of them are very clever, and they avoid being caught. They go to class so you can't say they aren't teaching, but they are just sitting in the chair, talking, but not teaching. So you do have those problems, and I suspect that the people who do those things are those who crash-landed into teaching. . . . Most of them are people who really don't care. You can see that they are tired. And now with all the changes in the curriculum, and with the increase in students' indiscipline, with all the riots and everything, it's not an easy task being a teacher, it's not the easiest thing. Even for those who love teaching. . . . [Many] are just overwhelmed.

After quitting his job to spend a year developing his proposal for a school and madly networking, John Gilmour received a major grant from the Shuttleworth Foundation to open and fund his school for three years. He hired teachers and counselors, located a building in Mowbray close to public transport, interviewed prospective students and their families, held preliminary math camps to assess and train students, and began classes in January 2004. He developed a partnership with Bishops, the elite private school, to allow LEAP students access to its facilities. The demanding LEAP school curriculum requires students to attend classes until late afternoon and offers Saturday morning sessions as well as significant outreach to students' families, life skills courses, and counseling services. The life skills courses are run by a stunningly direct and indomitable Muslim woman who creates a daily safe space for students to discuss the life-and-death issues that define their families and communities, a part of the curriculum that John feels is significantly responsible for the students' success. Furthermore, the students are required to give back to their communities through community service, such as offering evening and weekend tutorials to other students in Langa.

LEAP graduated its first class in 2005, achieving excellent matric results. In 2007 LEAP had over two hundred students, ran after-school tutorials for nine township schools, ran Saturday classes for about two thousand learners from all over Cape Town, and had gained the notice of provincial authorities and other private schools, who have asked John to replicate the model elsewhere.

.   .   .   .   .

LEAP's trajectory is a remarkably promising success story on a very small scale. Over the years of developing the LEAP program and vision, those involved have managed to make LEAP a true partnership effort, bringing in wisdom and expertise from all participants across class and race lines. The primary challenge for the first incarnation of LEAP was its inability to compensate for the structural shortcomings built into systems of education in African townships. But rather than give up, LEAP's founder forged ahead to create a whole new model to overcome these challenges. The new school curriculum ensures students receive theoretical and practical training as well as emotional and psychological support, and it helps the students to see themselves as community members and moral leaders. Its first location in a gray area made it a comfortable space for people from all backgrounds in Cape Town. Its successes are clearly visible in the students' self-confidence and matric pass rates, the interest in replication by the government, and the good will and trust that permeate the program. The primary challenge will be sustainability and replicability. Creating LEAP was possible only through John Gilmour's concerted and unrelenting effort and his willingness to make a potentially disastrous career move as a middle-aged man with a family to support.

The challenge for a visionary leader like John is empowering colleagues to take on the mantle of leadership and develop the strength to continue the struggle. Perhaps the success of charter schools in the United States gives reason for optimism, if the concept can be replicated in South Africa. Another challenge is exhaustion and the threat of burnout. The demands on teachers and counselors are so extraordinary in this type of school that opportunities for relief, reflection, and rest must be built in. For energetic transformers like John, that can be a difficult thing to recognize.

ZERILDA PARK PRIMARY SCHOOL

This letter is to tell you what the most important thing in my community is. There is too much violence and crime in my community. The most important reason is because most of the young girls are being raped. I would really like this to stop.

Here goes number 1. Try to stop crime, abuse, and rape, etc.

I ask this from the bottom of my heart. *No more Crime.*

I am writing this letter to tell you about the crime that is happening in our community. This is very bad for the small ones and people and children who are dying from guns, knives, and other sharp stuff. This is an escape for the people who do crime and people can't take it when there families get killed.

There is a lot of violence and crime happening in my community. I would like that all to come to an end. Because it is not nice to live in a violent place. I am one of the youngest people in the community and for our safety I would like it to stop. There are much more younger children who are being hurt and raped.

I want you must help Vrygrond must be no crime and . . . I want you must tell all the people must stop crime stop children abuse and rape women and children.

Letters written to President Thabo Mbeki by grade-seven
students at Zerilda Park Primary School, 2001, about the most
important thing in their community

. . . . .

Built in the late 1980s, Zerilda Park Primary School is the newest school in Lavender Hill, an apartheid community created in the 1960s far from the city center to house people evicted from District Six. By the 1980s, Lavender Hill had gained a reputation as one of Cape Town's most violent townships. Gangs dominated street life, many or most families had members in prison, and domestic and substance abuse had become frequent features of family life. Its isolating geographic location relative to business centers contributed to high levels of unemployment and poverty. Zerilda Park Primary School, like other apartheid township schools, is all concrete, bars, fences, and gates. Across from the school, the road is lined with overcrowded and decrepit council flats, and gangsters claim control of the street corners outside the school property. The sewage treatment plant across from the school contributes its particular aroma to the neighborhood. From its inception, the school's reputation was a dumping ground where other schools unloaded their problematic students and undesirable teachers. Built for eight hundred students, by 2000 the school had over twelve hundred learners and struggled to maintain a forty-five-to-one student-to-teacher ratio. Many of the students walk all the way from Vrygrond, a squatter settlement south of Lavender Hill.

When Al Witten arrived in 1993 as a teacher, the school—only two years old—was like a war zone, with an appalling regularity of assaults and rapes against students, gangsters roaming the school grounds, and burglaries (of windows, bars, furniture, and even light bulbs). The vice-principal remembers her horror at being reassigned to Zerilda Park, where the life circumstances of the children haunted her—"I wanted to bring food for everyone!" She began suffering from insomnia and faced every morning in tears as she drove to work. Other teachers I talked with echoed her words as they compared their coping strategies for the daily task of teaching children so traumatized by an inhumane living environment.

When Al became principal in 1996, he inherited a principal's office that, because of robberies, was bereft of equipment. "It was like a bombed out shell," he recalls. His early years as principal were tumultuous, as teachers and principals struggled with the implications of post-1994 educational reform and rationalization. Several township principals described the struggles they faced after 1994, as they lost their best teachers to better opportunities and felt they were left with teachers who were more interested in asserting their rights and unwilling to undertake reform in the classroom. Al's fellow principal at Heatherton explained to me:

> Teachers felt, "I don't need to do that. I don't need to do this. I don't need to prepare my lessons the way I did before," and so on and so on, which led to our children suffering at the end of the day. . . . I don't know if you remember '96, because that was the time when the [retirement incentive] package was offered to teachers, but it was also a time when teachers sort of just gave up everything. You know that burden that was placed—they saw it as a burden, preparing their lessons, the rules and so on. Principals before 1994 were autocratic, and dictators, and so on. . . . So teachers [after 1994] sort of fell back and said, "These are my rights." They concentrated more on their lunchtimes, how many hours they missed work. That noble thought, that noble profession, didn't exist.

Al determinedly took on recalcitrant teachers who missed work, came to class drunk, or avoided teaching responsibilities. Things came to a head when he fired a teacher for incompetence (unwittingly overlooking the new labor law) and provoked a major teachers' union march to his school against him. As the crisis mounted, he appealed for help to the Department of Education, which intervened and negotiated a resolution. But Al had established his position as a no-nonsense, demanding, challenging leader who refused to accept incompetence. His teaching staff split between those who supported his vision and those who preferred the status quo. One dedicated teacher explained: "Al's autocratic tendencies came from his impatience. He didn't want to stand around waiting—he was impatient to make things happen, to move forward. And he pushed us. In our school, some don't get onto the bus—they're always looking at the bus. [Thomas] and [Neville] and I want to be on every bus that goes through our school. . . . Those who stand looking at the bus—Al didn't have patience for that."

After surviving the initial teachers' revolt against his energetic assumption of principal's duties, Al set about creating new programs for students, teachers, and community members. He gathered enough teachers around him who shared his vision, commitment, and enthusiasm. One recalls: "He would say what he wanted to have happen and would ask for feedback and responses. Teachers could challenge him, argue, debate—he welcomed that. We fought to curb his authoritarian tendencies, and he would listen." As part of his commitment to transform the school, Al approached dozens of formerly white, and thus better-resourced, schools to forge partnerships. He understood transformation to mean reconciliation and believed that wealthier schools would be eager to partner with a school like his in order to confront and rectify the inequities of the past. He was sorely mistaken: not one single school responded to his invitation.

When he realized that transformation at Zerilda Park would not happen through partnerships, he turned to those teachers on his staff who were loyal to him because of his charisma and emphatic inclination to see the positive. One teacher described how in the face of complaint and collapse Al would redirect everyone's attention "to the one thing that was working, saying to us, "But look at this! This is going well!" He forced his staff to look at positives and, as one teacher explained, ignored those who didn't pitch or participate. Within a few years, he and his most committed teachers had transformed the status quo at the school. They developed extracurricular sports, art, and music programs. They created a school library, staffed by parent volunteers and a part-time staff person, built a computer lab with donated equipment (which offered training to community members as well as students), and began a greening project on school grounds. They created a school song, for which Al composed the score, and their music program cut its first CD of original songs. They developed a SafeSchools cluster in Lavender Hill; formed a parent volunteer group to help make and serve free lunches; created a teacher support team; formed a pupil support program that included after-school tutorials, psychological counseling, and life skills training components; and located a private psychologist to work with the teachers on crisis intervention. Al made sure the school participated in every local and state competition he could find—whether in poetry, music, ecology, or whatever—just for the opportunity and to foster pride and self-confidence within his learners.

Recalling the ambitious development of extracurricular activities at the school, one teacher laughs at Al's charming strategy to get teachers

committed to school projects: "If there was a sporting day on a Saturday, he'd get all the teachers there to support, not just those involved in
coaching. He was very good at identifying teachers' strengths and assigning them to different activities: [imitating Al talking to a teacher] 'I
think you'd be very good at organizing the library!' "

The teachers who joined with Al to transform Zerilda Park Primary
School viewed the recalcitrant or apathetic teachers with disdain. One of
the youngest teachers felt that many of the teachers who left the system
with the retirement package offered as part of the post-apartheid rationalization of education were among the innovative and dynamic
people who embraced the challenge of moving in new directions. Many
of those left in the system, in his words, "were either complacent, just
keeping on with the same old same old, or older folks who preferred continuing with the security of what they knew, even if they were bad at it
and didn't particularly like it." The younger teachers at Zerilda Park felt
their polarized teaching body reflected the national situation, with
schools characterized by a divide between younger, committed teachers
and older, disengaged teachers. In the absence of dynamic leadership, the
younger teachers understood that the latter could easily become a drag
on school reform and could inhibit change.

In 1998, the school started its most ambitious and innovative undertaking. Recognizing that pouring effort into nurturing and educating
young children ultimately would have little effect given the pressing realities of adult unemployment, violence, and substance abuse outside the
school fence, Al formed a partnership with Raymond Engelbrecht, the
local pastor born and raised in Lavender Hill, to create job skills and
training programs for parents, aftercare and preprimary care for children, and life skills assistance to families. Envisioning a school that empowered everyone in the community, not only the learners in grades one
through seven, the projects team called their approach "Community Development through Schools" and began writing project proposals and
press releases to articulate their model. Their literature describes the aims
of the Zerilda Park Projects: "Encourage greater interest in and participation in school related activities. Encourage ownership of the school as
a community asset. . . . Create a safe school and community environment that is free from gang-related activities and violence."[4]

Through this initiative, Zerilda Park added a preschool program
headed by Raymond's wife, Pat, to prepare children for entry into grade
one, and developed a brick- and block-making job-creation project for
unemployed parents and early school leavers. Both of these programs

In front of Zerilda Park's new preschool. Photo by the author.

provided family and life skills counseling intervention by Raymond, who became the project director for Zerilda Park Projects.

The "Community Development through Schools" model pioneered by the Zerilda Park Projects won national attention when Al and Raymond received the prestigious Impumelelo Award in 2000, the only recipients in the entire Western Cape. The annual award recognizes organizations throughout South Africa for innovative approaches to reducing poverty. Crime at the school had plummeted; the demand for places at the school, the preschool, and job training skyrocketed;[5] and school pride (on the part of learners, teachers, and parents alike) was palpable. The school's success received wide publicity in newspapers and radio broadcasts and was featured in an article written for an issue of the academic journal *Daedalus* devoted to South Africa by South Africa's minister of education.[6]

In contrast to the desolate feel of so many township schools I visited, on any given day Zerilda Park buzzed with activity. Volunteers and visitors from outside the community passed through the school weekly, from politicians looking for votes, to members of local and international service clubs interested in supporting the projects, to parent volunteers working in the library and kitchen, to volunteers from outside the community who run music, ecology, and sports programs, to corporate donors, to student teachers for UCT and UWC, who provide tutoring or are training in counseling, social work, psychology, and physical development. Al's strategy was to ensure that each visitor felt not only inspired by the school's successes but also participatory. His welcoming speeches to guests and donors as well as his orientation briefings to student teachers and tutors emphasized his vision that visitors would form sustained relationships with the school.

Al Witten left the school in 2001 to pursue an advanced degree in education on a full scholarship in the United States and was replaced by his vice-principal, another committed teacher who shared Al's vision. She continued his policy of building ties to donors and volunteers, ensuring that visitors are welcome at the school but are expected to form a commitment and not pass through as educational tourists. One of her primary jobs has become fund-raising, because school fees provide far less income than the school requires to maintain its programs. Although fees are very low (about fifty rand per year), entrenched poverty makes it difficult for many families to pay the fees, and under the current system the burden is on the principal to collect. Because the school receives only about half the fees it should, the principal spends a lot of time networking with donors. The list of regular contributors is long and impressive. Several corporate sponsors provide annual donations for programs and maintenance of school facilities. About a dozen NGOs offer programs to Zerilda Park students (in art, music, physical education, and sports teams), training and support for teachers (in crisis and trauma counseling), and support for end-of-year prizes to high-achieving students. A few volunteers come regularly to run greening and environmental programs for students. UCT and UWC students provide tutoring and counseling support. Visitors from around the world ask to visit the school's programs and often offer small donations. One of Cape Town's civic clubs adopted Zerilda Park as one of its charitable projects, and another civic service club adopted the preschool, raising funds to construct a new building and playground and to purchase school materials.

Zerilda Park's success has thus continued, although in the transition following Al's departure, the school lost Raymond as well as some of the most involved teachers, who felt they needed to move on for their own development and progress. But the process of active self-transformation at the school left a strong legacy. As one of the involved teachers told me in 2004, chuckling, about one of the recalcitrant teachers assigned by Al to supervise an extracurricular sports team, "She used to say, 'Mr. Witten forced me to be there.' But Mr. Witten has been gone two years and that teacher is still there, doing the job. She can step down but she doesn't."

. . . . .

Like with LEAP, Zerilda Park's success depended on a visionary leader willing to make tough decisions and face the consequences, and on a few inspired teachers willing to stand by the principal even if it cost them professional advancement. This core of educators saw as their target partners the entire community (parents, pastors, NGOs, and other school principals and teachers). They valued volunteerism and parental participation, encouraging people in the community to identify with the school and see it as a community resource.

In addition to their efforts with the local community, the principal and his committed teachers were willing to work hard to form partnerships with organizations outside the community, even though this meant significant time commitments outside of school. They shared a strategy of effectively binding outsiders to the school through event-oriented activities that brought outsiders into the school and enabled schoolchildren to join programs outside of the school.

Zerilda Park's major challenge, again like LEAP, is sustainability. The partnerships and programs were driven by Al Witten's energy and leadership. With his departure, the staff who had been so loyal struggled with decision making. Al's determination to offer programming meant he sometimes made decisions without consultation. His supporters chuckled that after making an authoritarian decision he would apologize for failing to consult with them by explaining, "I had to make a quick decision!" Several years later Al told me his working practice for making decisions quickly but undemocratically was, "Act now, apologize later." But the ability to act authoritatively and still maintain staff loyalty is a hard act to follow and depends on a rare blend of wisdom, charm, and charisma. After his departure conflicts became more difficult to solve, and several staff members left.

Another challenge is contextual: what does Zerilda Park's success mean in context of a failing high school? The drop-out rate at the local high school is extraordinary, making painfully clear the need to extend the Zerilda Park model through the next level of schooling.

HEATHERTON PRIMARY SCHOOL

John Gilmour's involvement in forming LEAP, first as an ensemble of tutorial programs and later as an independent school, and Al Witten's efforts to transform Zerilda Park Primary School by drawing on school and community strengths mark both men as effective and remarkable transformers in the Cape Town context. The story of Heatherton Primary School is far less dramatic in terms of its scope, but equally meaningful as a story about personal journeys of transformation. Heatherton is located in an impoverished coloured township with a high incidence of substance abuse and domestic violence. Due to declining school enrollments, the elementary school currently utilizes only half of its classrooms; the other half sit empty, some vandalized and filled with rubbish. As is typical with township schools that struggle with a lack of resources, the school grounds are barren and surrounded by a chain-link fence. The neighborhood surrounding the school is one of dilapidated buildings, backyard shacks, and unemployed men and early school leavers gathered on street corners. The principal, who was appointed to the position with no prior administrative experience, brings empathy and gentleness to the post, drawing from his experience as a pastor and his childhood in the neighborhood.

In the late 1990s, the school was struggling with ongoing staff conflict, and my friend Johanna was asked to offer conflict mediation workshops. Her workshop efforts had been frustrated by chronic teacher absenteeism, so after the initial training, Johanna suggested the principal should phone her when they were ready to move forward with the conflict resolution process. He never phoned, but Johanna decided to renew the contact four years later. As part of her journey to sort out what she stood for in moral and ethical terms and to identify a career she would find meaningful in South Africa's new context, Johanna had resigned her post at another school as a teacher and began a master's degree in narrative therapy and therapeutic development, which required a practicum. Feeling she had left things dangling at Heatherton, she phoned the principal to ask if she could volunteer as a counselor in order to fulfill the practicum requirement for her master's, and he welcomed her return.

Johanna's commitment grew over time as the needs of the school became apparent. From once a week her involvement grew to two days a week, and finally three days a week. Her practicum required her to complete fifty hours of practical narrative therapy counseling at the school and write a case study. However, as she explained, "The fifty hours were filled up very quickly, and then I realized I couldn't leave now because

I'd made a commitment to some of the children. And somehow, it just fitted for me."

Although Johanna had returned to Heatherton to write a case study for her master's degree, the principal understood her underlying motivation to contribute in a personal way to transformation as well as her devotion to children. He explained:

> When Johanna came here, I could see in her a desire to help, but more a passion for the little ones, you know. On many occasions when we would talk, tears would come into her eyes, when we talked about the struggle these children have, that the families have, the abuse, the dysfunctional families, that kind of thing. And she would sit there and just feel so sorry for these people. But what I found about her was that she didn't just feel sorry. She came here and said she wanted to do something, and she put her passion, her love for children, into action by wanting to help. . . . It has been helpful to the children, but more so to the parents. I've always sort of moaned to her in our conversations that we have, that the struggle is trying to get parents on board. . . . I feel that parents need to be empowered and enlightened, specifically with regard to parenting skills. So she's come together with a group of parents. And she hasn't told me this, but I hear from the parents as I've conversed with them that they're phoned regularly, they are taken out for breakfast or lunch sometimes, and she keeps a tab on how they are progressing. I know especially the one parent who is schizophrenic, and Johanna's really into the family, helping the family.

Johanna confirms the principal's observation about her emotional trajectory at the school, describing her transition from envisioning a "small, contained involvement" to her realization "that it never works like that," because the children's needs were so great:

> I think I was aware of the need of the community for support, but I was also very overwhelmed by how much there was that one could get involved in, that there didn't seem to be many structures. I phoned around for social workers, but there wasn't anything they could do, or they were very offhand, or they were overrun and just didn't get to things. And I think what made a huge difference for me—there was a young girl who was part of the case study that I wrote about, who had tried to commit suicide. And in trying to draw in her family, there was one or two days that I actually had gone and sat with them at the Victoria Hospital, just in the queues. In these long, long, long lines, waiting. And I realized this was the waiting. This waiting. This waiting for something to help. This waiting for something to make a difference. This need to stay hopeful somehow or other was so important in people's lives. And somehow if I could bring that, or bring a little bit of hope, a little bit of sustenance, to make people stick it out just one more day, then that is what I could offer. I think that, just sitting in that hospital, seeing *all* these people waiting to be helped, and waiting patiently,

and often being treated with such coldness, or aloofness, uninvolvement, no one's involved in their lives, no one remembers them, this whole system in the hospital where you go and they draw your chart, and it's any old body that sees you. No one builds up a history and is interested and asks you about your previous time that we're so used to in our medical care, in any kind of care. So for me I really started becoming aware of people's need just to know that someone is aware of them.

The principal describes his own journey of working with Johanna, accepting her ideas of appropriate teaching strategies and teacher-student interaction while tempering them to suit his assessment of his teachers:

> Sure she's got some ideas that need to be implemented, I feel, but not right now. She comes from a background where these things have been implemented, and have been taking place, but because of the past and how things have been developed in our schools—by our schools I'm talking about the township schools—the mind-set of teachers is different to the mind-set of the ex-Model C [formerly white] schools, for example. And so she comes with her ideas, and I know the mind-set of my teachers, so I try to balance the two. And I sort of try to convert my teachers to what she's saying, and also convert her to understand. It's a process and we need to take it one step at a time. It doesn't happen overnight. And she has come to understand that. What I appreciate about her is her openness, her honesty, her ability just to say something the way it is, and then after she's said it, she says, "Oh, I hope I haven't overstepped the line now." And then I would assure her, "I appreciate that because you are stepping on my toes with regard to certain aspects of the school and I need to see that. If I want to make a success and try and win the struggle here at the school, then I need to listen to all parties. I cannot do it on my own."

As an example, the principal described the annual beauty contest held for little girls at the school, which Johanna found deeply disturbing because of the objectification of the girls in front of the entire community. After she spoke to the principal about her discomfort, he brought the issue before his teachers and discovered that many agreed with Johanna. As a result, they replaced the beauty pageant with a different annual fundraiser.

Johanna and the principal worked hard to find a way to talk openly and honestly about their concerns and perceptions of each other. Johanna recalls:

> I was very, very, very depressed about the situation [at the school]. And I started understanding that this is just a small little picture of what is out there, I mean, I think that was also part of the depression. I was just one person going in, and I was a stranger; it was going to take a long time for me even to become part of the community, to be a support person to the

community. And then, a lot of my friends, when we were talking—I often spoke about my experiences there, and the conversations I had with the children, and how frustrated I was with the school—and so as I spoke to friends, well, many people would say, "Why do you go? Why don't you just chuck it? Go and find another place where it's easier." And then I'd kind of think, "Yeah! I'll go. That's right! I don't have to go there. I'm choosing to go. This is volunteer work—I don't have to do it anymore." And then I'd go back to the school with every intention of telling [the principal], "Listen, this is the last month that I'm coming." And then I would have the most phenomenal conversations with one of the children, or I would have a conversation with [the principal] where he speaks exactly to the stuff that I was upset about. And then I realized that somewhere along the line he's also moving. He's not moving in radical ways, but he's moving, because he's starting to understand things. And during last year, quite early on in the year, I just didn't know how to tell him in a caring way that somehow or other he's got to take the lead. I wanted him to know that that's how I felt about it, but I didn't want to sound like this outsider who comes and provides the way to do it. . . .

So I wrote him a letter at the beginning of last year where I just said to him, "These are the things that you give to people. You're one of the few people who gets in your car and drives to a child's home and says, 'Why aren't you in school?' Or will put a sick child in his car and drive the child home, and then say to the mom, 'Listen, you need to take your child to the hospital,' and put them both in his car and drive them to the hospital. He's a man who will see that a little boy doesn't have clean clothes or new clothes or whatever, and he will find the clothes in school and he dresses the children. He collects the clothes from the community and he dresses the children. He's the one that the people will come to to do their wills. . . . So there's a lot of real caring work that he does in that school and that community. So in that letter I wrote all these things that I'd noticed or heard about in the way he went along, and I said to him it sounds to me that this is quite a lonely place where you're in, because it doesn't sound that you get much support from the staff, but I just wanted to say to him that for me, that's where somebody has vision. For me, that was my interpretation of care and creating community. In a way, I almost see him as the custodian of the vision for the school, because of the things he says around giving the children an opportunity, of treating them with respect, and so on.

The principal read the letter privately, and when Johanna returned the next week, she asked for his reaction:

He said, well, it actually made him cry because it acknowledged—this is the thing—it acknowledged the things that he does. And somehow there I think he really invited me in—from the point of the letter, he really invited me in to the school. And so after this thing, I went and I told him about the depression and how it had taken over my life and that I was finding it difficult to come to the school. There was this one teacher who used to sit and scream and scream and scream at the children the whole day. I'd walk in in the morning; she'd be shouting at them in this high, piercing voice—and they were six-year-olds—and she would scream, and I'd leave in the afternoon, and she'd still be yelling at them. And this went on for weeks. And it used to kill me. And three of the children in the class I was seeing at the time, for conversations and things like that. And this one little boy resisted her treatment, and he threw tantrums in the class and he really was angry. . . . So then [the principal] stepped in—he started making a change, and he actually spoke to the teacher. And she's not doing this anymore.

The principal acknowledges that Johanna's comments have forced issues to the surface that might otherwise have gone unacknowledged or unresolved. Her insistence on respectful relationships and on listening to children resonated with him and provided him with support to intervene with problematic teachers. He knows she is frustrated with the slow pace of change, but he also knows that she will support his quiet efforts to transform troublesome aspects of the school. He describes how he feels situated between "where Johanna comes from and the teachers—when I say the teachers, I include myself, because I have a struggle myself. You see, Johanna came in with an idea, with this reality of hers, this world of hers, in how you treat children. You try to understand them, you listen to them. We have a tendency to want them to listen to us more than we listen to them. To me that was a challenge."

The transition away from corporal punishment, the historically autocratic approach to teaching, and the myriad problems the children bring to school from home contribute to a classroom environment of, in the principal's words,

. . . shouting at the children and hammering on the desk and on the board. To me that's more frustration than anything else. And the children reach a stage where they close their ears to those things, and they don't want hear anything else. So teachers are talking more to learners, trying to understand them, and they are allowing the learners to talk more to them so that they can hear what the children are saying. To me that's a *big* change, because when I started here seven years ago, it was, "You do what I say and that's it!" That's been real to me. I've seen it. And we're not there yet. We've got some time to go where that is concerned. . . . But I think Johanna has come to help. She's helping to hold up my arms so we can fight the battle and win the battle. I know we can.

Johanna's presence helped the principal work with teachers to develop the Teacher Support Team and implement a coherent structure for assessing and promoting students for the first time since the transition. He discusses Johanna's contribution:

I admire her greatly for her patience and her understanding with me. . . . I don't get a lot of feedback from parents, but what I do know is that parents do talk out there in the community as to what is happening in the school. In the main it's positive comments, and people have a lot of respect, and there's a lot of acceptance for Johanna. Not for who she is. It started off for who she is, because some parents would come in and say: "Mr. [X] (they would speak in Afrikaans), can I speak to the white lady that's here?" That mentality that existed. But that mentality is slowly being eroded. She's accepted for who she is and what she wants to do for our community and for the children. In fact, it's not our community, it's her community, she's part of the community, as such, because when she comes to school everybody knows her. She drives down the street, comes into the school; the little ones run to her, they know her. So I have great admiration for somebody who comes from a different sort of culture, background, and enters into another one. For me, I think it's a big sacrifice. I don't know if I would be able to do that.

He concludes: "You know, there are many schools, the [Education Department], all of them know about Johanna, and when we have principals' meetings, the circuit managers will talk about that, and the principals say, 'You know, you are lucky to have someone like that!' "

"Is it so unusual?" I ask.

He responds: "It's *unusual*. 'You are so lucky. Who is this woman?' . . . everybody in the school community is talking about the fact that [Heatherton] Primary School has a *volunteer* helping us with counseling and social problems. Because I can tell you one thing, that is a big concern and a big struggle in township schools, where teachers are yearning, really yearning for help in that area, where they can be relieved from listening to the problems and get on with the job of doing what they're supposed to be doing, and that's teaching the child."

. . . . .

In contrast to the vision that engendered LEAP and Zerilda Park Projects, the vision of transformation that guided Johanna's volunteer work in Heatherton was much more personal and modest. Johanna's achievement was to form a strong supportive relationship with the principal and with a few parents and students. The principal's achievement was to draw on Johanna's outside perspective to introduce new ways of thinking and interacting within his school community. They came to see each other as models of compassion and humanity. While it is hard to gauge what structural difference one volunteer makes, the personal relationships that grew from Johanna's years at the school offer an important

example of the possibilities of volunteerism in South Africa. Dedicated volunteerism, based on a principle of mutual respect rather than stereotypes
of dependency, may not produce the kind of visionary transformation
that took place at LEAP or Zerilda Park, but it begins to break down the
walls of ignorance and mistrust that still stand so firmly in place.

GARDENVIEW BAPTIST CHURCH

One day in 2002, Wendy excitedly told me about some new developments at her church. Wendy and Peter attend a church near their neighborhood, Gardenview Baptist Church, because their children joined the
church youth group with their friends from secondary school. The
church is clearly prosperous, located in a large, fully staffed complex that
includes an office building, a hall, gardens, and meeting spaces. Although
Wendy and Peter attended the church for their children and because they
agreed with its spiritual doctrine, they never formally became members,
because they were less convinced about the church's commitment to
transformation. As Wendy explained, the church felt multiracial but not
integrated: "And all the happenings up front were always white, so it
didn't fit into my understanding of integration. Knowing some other
people of color sitting around us with tremendous gifts in terms of music,
preaching, speaking, you name it, they were always sitting in the pews;
they were never up front doing anything." The overwhelmingly white
congregation (about 70 percent of the seven hundred or so members) and
the entirely white staff and clergy left an uncomfortable impression on
many members of color.

Wendy's news was that the church was embarking on a project of self-
transformation. The church leadership had become aware that members
of color in the congregation felt marginalized and unwelcome at church
functions. According to one of the associate pastors, whom I'll call Pastor Williams, "It was when we discovered from people in the church saying, 'Guys, we still feel that we are prejudiced against, that people look
at us funny, they don't want to talk to us, etc. etc.'—when we discovered
that, we thought, 'Wow, guys, we do have a problem. Let's look into this
further.'" The church embarked on a process of reconciliation and transformation, which Peter jokingly referred to as the "church TRC" (Truth
and Reconciliation Commission), because part of the agenda was con-
fessional. In several planned meetings, church participants were invited
to share their stories about their experiences and actions under apartheid
in order to work toward a community of trust and love. It sounded like

a remarkable undertaking for a prosperous, mostly white church. As the process got under way in 2002, I followed Wendy's guarded hopes for where the journey might lead. I returned to Cape Town the following year to find Wendy and Peter utterly alienated from the church, their hopes turned to disgust. What went wrong?

The church made reconciliation and transformation the topic of its 2002 annual church camp retreat weekend and invited several members and attending nonmembers, including Peter, to address the camp. One goal was to draft a church statement of apology for apartheid. Against his better judgment, Peter says he accepted the invitation,

> . . . because, I thought, here was a positive invitation coming from a community that I didn't quite expect would be up to it. . . . But I then said, as part of my closing remarks [that weekend], that this will probably be the biggest challenge that the church will ever face, because if they don't go the whole journey now, they will probably never ever have the credibility again to *ever* pick up the issue of transformation, to even talk about it again, because the suspicions that they are now beginning to slowly alleviate on our part—people of color—that suspicion will be multiplied beyond all these. . . . So we will never ever sit down again. So before you go the way of formulating the statement, taking it to the church, know that. You'd be wiser to stop the process now, but if you're feeling to go for it, then you cannot get a hiccup and say, well, no, we've made a mistake. You've got to keep going, whether you lose half your members or not. This is the cost you've got to accept. But we will not be around if you hiccup on this one.

To Peter's surprise, following the camp retreat, the church leadership pursued the issue in two sequential Wednesday evening meetings, in which people were asked to share their stories of apartheid, racism, and injustice. For Pastor Williams, hearing participants share their stories of humiliation and injustice from the apartheid years and from their experiences in the church was "an eye-opener, where we realized there were still a lot of things that had never been worked through." Inspired by his involvement in other church movements of the 1970s, Trevor, an active coloured church member, embraced the church's vision of transformation and encouraged other coloured churchgoers to participate: "It's a painful thing to go and expose yourself and reveal your story. It's a painful thing. You don't do it easily. But we said, 'Look, for the sake of unity, we're prepared to do it.' And I got a few people to come and tell their stories, and I could see and feel their pain. And those in the room could feel their pain." Trevor himself addressed the assembled leadership at the meetings, explaining why coloured churchgoers continued to feel the weight of apartheid injustices in their interactions with white churchgoers who remained ignorant about apartheid's abuses and their status as beneficiaries. Like Peter, he warned the leadership that "reconciliation is no cheap matter" and that pursuing a meaningful agenda of transformation would mean discomfort and brutal honesty because, as he explained to them, "we are supersensitive to hypocrisy." Wendy recalls that Peter spoke about trust in one of the meetings:

> We sit there today as a group and we are asked to be one with each other, but we can't because we are suspicious of the past, because when I look at some of you, I don't know where you've been. I don't know whether you've been part of the Security Branch, I don't know whether you've been part of the military, and I'm wondering just . . . about your actions. . . . You cannot start at this point and then just expect the person who's been oppressed all the years to accept you as a white person and without any questions, just to kind of forget the past and forge a very close friendship. There *are* those suspicions, and they must be worked through.

In response, the church leadership crafted a statement of reconciliation and apology, described by Pastor Williams as "a written statement to bring clarity to what we're talking about, to hopefully bring closure, to cause the issue to be put, so that we'd have to face the issue, talk about it, so that we could then move on, having, as the white people in the church, clearly made a statement: that this is where we stand on the whole race thing." The letter introducing the statement to the congregation opened as follows: "As you know, since the Church Camp we have been on a very significant and exciting journey, a painful and difficult journey, but a very necessary one. The objective of the journey is to bring about in our church a greater and deeper experience of reconciliation and unity than we have ever known before, particularly between our members who for decades suffered the hurts and injustices of the apartheid system and those who did not." The "statement regarding [Gardenview Baptist Church] becoming a racially integrated church" continued with strong language:

> Those of us at [Gardenview Baptist Church] who were not victimized by the Apartheid system wish to place on record our sincere sorrow and regret concerning the system of apartheid that was the political dispensation in our country for over four decades. . . .
> We believe that generally speaking, the Church of Jesus Christ in this country, should have done more to address the sin of apartheid. Similarly, during the days of apartheid, the so called white people, who formed the overwhelming majority of members of this church, could have and should have done more corporately to bring about the demise of the apartheid system. As a church we want to acknowledge that we should have done more

to work towards the ending of the apartheid system both individually and corporately.

Many of us took the road of least resistance relationally, socially and politically and either through willful ignorance, passivity, a choosing not to know or naiveté to propaganda sinned by not loving our neighbor as ourselves. . . . For this we wish to ask for forgiveness and repent.

The document democratically acknowledges that not all white people supported apartheid, and it concludes by rejecting "any form of racism, nationalism, xenophobia and prejudice."

The process begun at the weekend retreat and carried through subsequent evening meetings culminated in an open-mic service at the church on Youth Day (Soweto Day)—Sunday, 16 June—during which anyone could share their story and their response to the statement. Trevor, for example, spoke of his rage about the white desire to forget the past and move on:

I said, "Look. I've been here now for twenty-five years. You all know me. I've been in many of your homes, many are friends, my children's friends. But *nobody*"—my close friends are sitting there—"*none* of you have ever asked Mary and I, 'How did you survive apartheid?' " Now why didn't they ask? Wouldn't that be the first question? If I came to visit you, wouldn't you ask, "Trevor, how did you make it through the apartheid years?" And I said to them, "None of you have ever asked us, 'Mary and Trevor, how did you make it through apartheid? When now we see what happened, what did you do? How did you manage?' Nobody's ever asked us that."

But things began to go wrong at the Sunday open-mic service. Peter was appalled that the white woman charged with presenting the message of 16 June mixed up the significance of the day:

What offended me beyond all offenses was that they asked people on that particular day to participate in giving directions in what was to follow— mainly people telling their story. One presenter who was supposed to have spoken about what does Soweto Day mean in the context of our country, spoke about Sharpeville Day! . . . And she spent twenty minutes on why we should come together, why we should be remembering this day, because this and that happened, at Sharpeville all these young people got killed, totally messed it up! And went along as a white person, talking all this nonsense. Now I thought here's an opportunity for them to bring someone, at least of color, to say, here's how *we* feel about a day like Soweto Day. This was what we felt in 1976, in Cape Town, in the aftermath of Soweto. Of course, I walked out and I don't want to say anymore, but this has been a huge offense. Because a day that had so much deep painful memories for us—we saw the blood on our streets, post Soweto Day in Cape Town, and you don't even have the historical facts? That you can speak with such confusion about . . . it's just a painful thing to listen to. And that day, the sixteenth of June, was the last day I ever, ever heard the word *transformation, nonracialism, healing,* ever mentioned in that church. And what I'd said two or three weeks earlier, in terms of if you fail on this mission, this journey, then never ever pick it up again, because you have lost all credibility, the trust that you have creeped towards rebuilding will be drained. And that's my position. I have no desire, I will absolutely never participate in any forum of that kind again, and I have no expectation of the church at all, not at all.

Trevor was disgusted that some white church members spoke about *their* experiences of victimization under apartheid, refusing to acknowledge the racist basis of apartheid. Whereas members of color expected that the service would mark the beginning of the process of transformation, the church leadership viewed it as the culmination. Reflecting in 2003 on his perception of the success of the church's efforts at transformation, Pastor Williams told me: "I think there's been a huge amount of positive improvement. I think others probably think differently, but they're entitled to their view, of course. It gave me the freedom to say to certain individuals in the church, 'You know now that we've spoken about all of this, are we OK with each other? Has there ever been a problem between us?' . . . There's certainly a greater awareness in the church when it comes to voting in leadership, etc., etc., that we need to be more aware. There's a greater sensitivity."

Pastor Williams expanded on the issue of sensitivity, explaining that some white church members "were fed up with after ten, fifteen, twenty years of knowing coloured people and being close friends, that twenty years down the line they're suddenly accused of being racist. So some white people were really deeply fed up and offended. But [the process] also revealed, we grew up in different worlds, and many of us don't understand the implications of apartheid, and I think the apology in the statement is certainly sincere." His view was that the statement

in itself cleared the air, brought a measure of healing. Maybe some people who had felt they'd been prejudiced against realized it's not actually because I'm not white that people don't want to talk to me, but there's other reasons. So I think there are a lot . . . you know, the problem is, say a person's got a perception people don't like me because I'm black. Then you meet somebody and they don't immediately like you—it's just a normal human being, you know, we don't gel, but then the assumption is it's because I'm black. And then you tell your friend and they confirm yes, it's because you're black and before you know it you've bought the whole thing.

So I think there's a lot of that going on in the church. . . . So I think a lot of what we had to deal with at our church was untrue perceptions that people had, and because apartheid degraded people to such an extent, these things are deeply engrained in people, to assume that as soon as something goes wrong, or the pastor hasn't visited my child, you know, it's because the child is not white. Had the child been white, well, the pastor would have visited. I'm sure there are hundreds of white kids I never got around to visiting. You know, I didn't pick, now that kid's black, I won't visit; that one's white, I'll do that one. It's all sort of perceptions that people have. The statement served, not to solve all our problems, but it did highlight the issues and be informative. The statement served to put forward our church's official position.

For Wendy, Peter, Trevor, Mary, and others, however, the promise of the Sunday service dissipated and disappeared. To their dismay, the strong language in the letter was not reflected in church action. The next several staff appointments following the letter—a youth pastor, an office appointment—were white, as were all the invited speakers for the following year. In 2003 Wendy remarked on what she perceived to be a remarkable disconnect between rhetoric and action:

So we sit in there today, saying, "*What* was that all about?" Peter is saying, "Why did I waste my time?" You know. It just made, as far as we're concerned, no difference. Remember, since July, we've not seen *one* person of color as a preacher in that pulpit. There have only been white speakers. You know? So you ask yourself, "Did they mean it? What was it all about? Was it just a moment of weakness [laughing], being politically correct, seemingly progressive? What?" . . . Peter is a fantastic preacher, but he sits in a pew. It's just amazing! He sits in the pew. . . . You've got to somehow engineer and make it happen. But no one is thinking through these processes. No one is doing it, you see?

In addition to making affirmative action staffing choices, Peter offers thoughts on what else the church might have done:

Now, I realized—we realized—that you can't just start telling stories or get the church to revise its giving habits, or its staff selection criteria, that you needed to conscientize. God forbid they'd be expected to do that! But nevertheless, it's probably too late to do this, but sitting inside a number of evenings, or whatever times, really—for example, the church has house church meetings on Wednesday nights. So, now, from that Sunday onwards, they should have said, for the next month, what we try to do and listen to each other on a Sunday morning, now in a more intimate and less threatening environment, we're going to pose the following questions and ask a facilitator to guide you through a discussion on saying, "When we talk about Soweto, June the 16th, how do you feel about it? Talk about it." A clear program to be set for at least a month, where folks just focus on those issues. You know, going beyond that, the church should have been able to organize—someone had in fact suggested this—Let's go on a walk of healing memories. So let's go and walk through District Six and pause at key places and try and understand what happened there, and bow our heads in silence and commemoration and hopefully with some sense of repentance, as people of faith. Let's go to a Mosque that has been closed down, and ask forgiveness for this . . . you know, or whatever. But they never ever got to that kind of process and program. . . . I really don't know, Catherine, but it just died a hugely sudden death, and never picked up again.

When I visited the church in 2003, information about the church's impressive and ambitious planned expansion was on display. Visitors could peruse a wide variety of pamphlets and documents on the church's mission and broad array of projects and interest groups. Only when talking with Pastor Williams did I realize that nothing was on display about church efforts toward integration or transformation. He brought this up in our conversation:

Some people said why aren't we framing the statement and sticking it in the foyer. And the answer to that is that we don't want to look like we're showing off: "Look what we've done, we've done this nice apology, aren't we great" kind of story. So I think that was the motivation for not giving a public profile to the statement. But in other places the statement does feature, like in literature we're putting out about our church. It's not a secret. But we also don't want the statement to now go out into the media, our local area, and there's an article ten years after the rest of the country has decided apartheid's bad, "[Gardenview] Baptist Church also decided . . ." You know, that's also not quite accurate [laughs].

The statement was a spiritual thing, it was an important time line. Some people in the white community may have felt that there should have been a greater response from the nonwhite community. And maybe that too wasn't that helpful, but one can't criticize people that have been apologized for reacting in whatever way they do. That's their business. But as long as you get the bit that the statement needed to be there, but it's not like we just woke up to the fact that apartheid was wrong. (CB: *Yes, I understand that.*) There is a degree of genuine confession in there, should have done more, blahdy-blah . . . you know, it's very broad, but the idea is there, and hopefully we can point to that and say, guys, whatever you experience in this church, that's what we stand for as a church, and the church has accepted that statement and owned that. That's our position. If you experience prejudice, well, so do the people with red hair, or bumpy noses, or whatever.

So what failed? Pastor Williams is genuine about the church's desire to acknowledge and apologize for apartheid. He wants reconciliation so he can be right with his flock, and he wants coloured members to be able to overcome racially based sensitivity and realize that their perceptions of racist behavior within the church are often unfounded. He thinks the document makes this clear, and he is disappointed that some coloured members have not responded enthusiastically enough to the statement, although at the same time he doesn't want to make a big deal of it and the process through which it was produced, because it might look like the church had a problem. The coloured members also expressed enthusiasm for what they perceived would be a process of transformation toward integration. But for them, they needed more than a letter of apology. They wanted genuine interest and investment in their experiences and stories. To them, transformation meant a willingness to delve into the painful issues of the past, to confront and acknowledge the reality of apartheid-created inequalities, and to develop a clear plan for transforming the church staff, leadership, and programming. They knew such a program would likely cost the church membership and thus financial support, and they feel the church's ambitious expansion plans were viewed by the leadership as contradictory to and more important than pursuing a plan of ambitious transformation.

A year after the 16 June open-mic Sunday, Peter reflects:

> I think sadly it was probably one of the few churches that even attempted to think about starting a journey. And if they failed, having started that journey, failed fairly miserably I should say, others haven't even thought that there's a journey to embark upon. So I guess at the end, the writing on the wall as far as the church communities, and again I think it could be extended to most other institutions in our society, is that people generally don't want to know about the past. It's uncomfortable. And it's uncomfortable all around. I certainly don't gloat and enjoy trying to recall the '76 through '80 period in the city. No one feels comfortable speaking about it. Because as a society we place such a high value on reconciliation and peace building, we've learned to sweep things under the carpet very significantly.

.   .   .   .   .

Gardenview deserves commendation for recognizing that multicultural does not mean integrated and that internal dialogue about the past would be necessary to achieve integration in the fullest sense. Unfortunately, the lack of a practical outcome left the coloured churchgoers in disagreement with the leadership's view that their initiative was successful. The opposing views result from different understandings of the nature of the problem and its appropriate resolution. The church's white leadership wanted congregants of color to get over their sense of being prejudiced against, to be less sensitive, and to recognize the church's goodwill and nonracist attitude. They felt the problem was one of a perception of hostility. But congregants of color were not concerned about racist interactions; their concerns had to do with the utter whiteness of everything that happened in the church and with the ignorance about the past of their fellow white parishioners. They wanted acknowledgment of apartheid injustices on the part of individuals rather than the church as an institution, and they wanted real actual changes in the hierarchy, practice, and vision of the church. To them, anything less did not qualify as transformation.

THE HOPE PROJECT

Nyanga is one of the poorest areas of Cape Town, with one of the highest rates of HIV infection and unemployment. It is also home to a remarkable initiative to provide care for AIDS orphans and HIV-positive adults and children, which I will call the Hope Project. Joining together community-based groups formed around child care and employment concerns with NGOs and government offices that specialize in mental health, AIDS counseling, nutrition and health care, and skills development, the Hope Project ambitiously built a multifaceted, innovative program to meet the needs of Nyanga's poorest, sickest, and most vulnerable community members. Following the project's progress provides a lesson in the challenges of community building and bridging in post-apartheid South Africa.

The project's beginnings are rooted in a children's playgroup developed by a woman in Nyanga over twenty years ago. Beatrice (not her real name) used the vacant lot across the road from her home as a play area, and within a few years she was training women to care for more than a hundred children in different playgroups throughout the community. By the late 1990s, the Playgroup Mothers recognized a growing rate of illness in the community and had become alarmed at the rising number of orphans. In fact, health workers warn that AIDS orphans will become South Africa's greatest challenge in the next few decades, when perhaps hundreds of thousands of children will be left to care for themselves. The Playgroup Mothers, from their vantage point on the front lines of the AIDS crisis, realized they needed to find a way to provide intervention and care to support not only the orphans themselves, but their caregivers as well.

In 2000, an adviser to the mothers learned of a conference presentation made by a woman I'll call Madeleine, who lives in the southern

suburb of Newlands and used to head the AIDS counseling division of a
large NGO that provides crisis counseling services. Madeleine spoke of
the alarming implications of an expanding population of vulnerable children and pleaded for a community-based intervention to support AIDS
orphans, a place where health professionals could refer parents handicapped by AIDS to find support for their children:

> Well, I had realized that there was a real problem, not just from reading I'd
> done, but from my counselors' experience in Khayelitsha. I could see that
> one of the biggest pressures on them was their distress at mothers moving
> into the final stage of AIDS who had young children, and the mother saying
> to them, "Please look after my child; I want you to have my baby," and
> they did not know what to do about this. . . . I began to realize [AIDS coun-
> selors] needed somewhere to refer the mother before she died, where she
> would then be able to relax because she knew, "Ah, my child will be cared
> for by these other mothers." It's much easier for a Xhosa-speaking person
> to get that concept than for us [white people], because we so are attached to
> the idea of one individual mother. If there was a center, the child could be
> there during the day with the mother, and so when the mother died, the
> place would be familiar, would be a mothering place; the other mothers
> would be there. For a young preschool child, every day's routines would be
> the same, and the other specially trained mothers would provide a kind of
> mothering presence for the child. So attachment would be easy to transfer
> in a way.

Madeleine and Beatrice had first become acquainted years ago, when
Madeleine, a white woman, broke apartheid law to attend church in the
township (a manifestation of her faith that landed her in a jail cell in Manenberg). Madeleine's daughter had been a bridesmaid at the wedding of
Beatrice's daughter. Although the two women had lost touch years ago,
after learning about Madeleine's presentation, they got together to talk
about developing the playgroup project into a larger community initiative to care for children, AIDS orphans, and their caregivers.

Madeleine had been looking for township land on which to develop
her vision of a community center for AIDS care, and she was excited by
the prospect of joining an existing community-based group with access
to vacant land. Madeleine and the Playgroup Mothers formed a trust
with a board, a partnership between the Playgroup Mothers and
Madeleine's NGO, and bought from the City of Cape Town the large
piece of land on which Beatrice had started her original playgroup.
Madeleine became the project's fund-raiser, building a network of
donors, NGOs, and government service providers who would invest in
the project. The trust's vision for the project was innovative, expansive,

and fraught from the start. The group began with planning meetings, lasting hours at a time, in Beatrice's shack. They fought with local authorities, who for a variety of reasons, threw up barriers at various points, one of which was provoked by the implication that Nyanga has an AIDS problem. Madeleine recalls one argument with a local politician who told them, "We haven't got an AIDS problem here in Nyanga. Take your project somewhere they've got AIDS." Madeleine countered, "Now I know we have over 27.8 percent prevalence in Nyanga, which is worse than anywhere, because I've got the Department of Health stats. You want to say to him, 'You silly man.' But you can't. But [the Hope Project] is not just for AIDS; it's for all these other things: capacity building, economic empowerment."

Once the project's founders obtained the necessary permission, their first objective was to develop the land by building a structure to house the day care center (this was the part of the project I followed most closely), and facilitate fund-raising for the other envisioned components of the project.[7] Madeleine and the Playgroup Mothers were determined to build the entire facility using local unemployed men and women, all of whom required intensive on-the-job training due to the severe skills shortage in the area. Thus phase one of the project was to complete the first building on site and begin training local men and women in construction skills. Simultaneously, a vegetable garden was planted and a playground was set up adjacent to the building. Once the building was complete, the project enrolled a hundred children in the preschool and accepted many others into an after-school program. Through Madeleine's fund-raising and connections, the project inherited nineteen AIDS counselors funded by the Department of Health from an NGO that folded. These counselors work in local clinics, refer women to the project's programs, and facilitate income-generating beading and smocking projects for HIV-positive people. The Playgroup Mothers received training as counselors, and some were accepted for paid employment with Madeleine's NGO. The project is building a kitchen and dining room to provide income as well as nutritional support for those receiving assistance from the project's programs.

The project's success is particularly remarkable given its rocky development. The large cast of participants came to the project from radically different backgrounds that cut across class and race lines, and the dramas that erupted throughout the project's development are like a map of post-apartheid racial tensions and mistrust. The Playgroup Mothers and the builders came from Nyanga, but the construction supervisors were brought in initially from a skills training project in a coloured township because of the lack of local skilled construction workers. Some of the staff and counselors come from neighboring African townships, and the fund-raisers and some members of the board come from wealthy white southern suburbs. This remarkable ensemble of contributors shared strong individual commitments to the goals of the project but at times found the challenges of community building within the project overwhelming as various constituencies fought over control, money, and project ownership. The threat of violence, a fact of life in this part of Nyanga, compounded the challenges; many of the outsiders affiliated with the project, including Madeleine, have been attacked, robbed, or carjacked at gunpoint on their way to or from the project site.

The coloured construction supervisor brought in to oversee the first phase of construction looks back on his year with the project with a mixture of understanding, bewilderment, and resentment. He had joined the project with a contractor's zeal to complete the structure in time for a planned donor visit, but he was unprepared for the calamitous sociocultural challenges provoked by the project's vision of building cross-race and cross-class alliances. Madeleine recalls that he, like herself, "didn't have the slightest idea what it was going to involve. But he rolled up his sleeves and got going. We were very naive, had no idea of how difficult it was going to be. He sweated blood over it." For his part, the supervisor felt that he arrived at the project with an incomplete briefing of the board's expectations and the enormous challenges he would face bringing coloured building supervisors to an African township project.

Suspicion and mistrust blossomed immediately between the Afrikaans-speaking coloured building supervisors and the local Xhosa-speaking people hired by the Playgroup Mothers to be trained in construction. The supervisors were suspicious of the workers' conversations, which they could not understand, and the workers were suspicious of the supervisors, whom they viewed, as the construction supervisor came to realize, as "other people from another community, and from another culture—coloureds coming in and taking money from their community." The local builders, supported by the mothers, accused the coloured building supervisors of cultural insensitivity and accused the white board members and the coloured supervisors of underpaying them. Angry at misunderstandings and perceived injustices, the workers periodically halted work to demand lengthy sessions to air grievances, which shocked the supervisors because it threatened the project's ability to meet the deadline for the donors' visit. The coloured supervisors felt variously frightened, attacked, unwelcome, and appalled by the regularity of work stoppages and by the expectation of full democratic process for every decision, leading them to periodically quit, telling their supervisor, "We can't work with these people!"

The construction supervisor came to realize that construction was only a part of his responsibility on site; an equally significant requirement was human development and cultural mediation. He spent countless hours working through issues with his on-site building supervisors and the team of local African workers, helping them learn to talk through misunderstandings, overcome their suspicions, and still make progress on the building. Thinking back over his involvement with the project, he says:

> Maybe some of us realize now how vast the gulf is between some of our racial groups. We don't expect it to be after '94 and the war and the experiences we've had in our country. . . . I think some had the experience often in these communities of people like ourselves from another community, whether it be coloured or white, as a contractor coming in and literally taking most of the money because of expertise and the services that we provide, so most of the money goes out. . . . I think again it's because of how the community was maybe negatively exploited almost by individuals or companies, and this memory stays with them, so they are therefore suspicious or naturally not very open to help the trustworthy, trusting, open relationship, which is what some of us came for, that this is an opportunity for us to get to know our black brothers, to build relationships. But in some of our hearts, maybe, and memories, there's too many stumbling blocks of the past or our past experiences. And I think that, be it the trust, be it some other community leaders, be it people like [Madeleine], that work—maybe myself as well, that work with communities—one of the lessons we should take is to be aware of that, that this is in people's minds. So that before you start a project involving different groups or different individuals that might represent negative experiences in the past, you need to literally first clear the way, prepare people's hearts and minds to be sure that people don't carry that baggage of hurts of the past, exploitation, suspicion, and those type of things, because it will definitely affect whatever projects you are involved in.

The construction workers did meet their deadline, and the donors who visited the site pledged a large sum to support the next phase of the project. The construction supervisor was proud that despite all the conflict on site, not a single builder quit, "and [I told them] that is something that we can be proud of, as a group of individuals from different sections within Nyanga, different backgrounds, never knowing each other, some of them, and ourselves as coming from another, not only community, but different race, or cultural group."[8] His replacement, a trainer with the Department of Labor who was also from a coloured community, ensured that he built into every day an opportunity to discuss interpersonal issues and grievances, as well as time for relaxation and fun, such as competitive bricklaying challenges.

A major source of strain within the project was over control of resources and vision. The Playgroup Mothers who founded the project twenty years earlier feared losing control to powerful outsiders and were critically aware of their intermediary role between outside participants and the local community. If their neighbors refused to support the project, the mothers knew they might end up watching their hard work destroyed by disgruntled community members, as had happened with another project just a few blocks away. Furthermore, some of the most powerful founding mothers felt their vision had been hijacked by the growing focus on HIV and AIDS. They grew suspicious that outsiders were gaining financially through their involvement with the project and became protective of community members who sought employment with the project. They expressed their grievances in the form of public attacks against the outsiders they wished to keep in line, including the construction supervisor, Madeleine, the architect, some board members, and some of the caregivers from outside the community.

The white trust members, the architect, the fund-raisers, and the building supervisors felt traumatized by the fierce accusations leveled against them by the mothers and builders, who were angry about low compensation or project plans with which they disagreed. The construction supervisor—a man who, motivated by his deep religious faith, devotes his life to community building work in a number of townships—described one meeting where the mothers ferociously accused him of cultural insensitivity because they felt the workers were being underpaid:

> [The mothers told me] I have no heart, lack sensitivity, and I'm . . . a couple of other things were said. The accusations were so strong, and from key people, that I could not dissuade the meeting to otherwise. People started believing this, that this is what I was doing. Six to eight months is not enough time for sound trusting relationships to develop to the extent that it could take that type of battering. [Although the issue was resolved after everyone discussed the project finances and realized the compensation was at the maximum possible level], I think the damage was done to our relationship, and I was tested I think—my level of compassion and commitment to the people involved in the project was tested severely.

The construction supervisor's involvement with the project came to an unfortunate conclusion when he was robbed at gunpoint one day as he arrived in Nyanga to distribute the workers' wages. This terrible event had a reconciliatory conclusion, however, as Beatrice, who had so force-fully attacked the construction supervisor in the meeting, was the first to get to him after his assault. She expressed such genuine concern, holding his hand while help arrived, that he was able to forgive her harshness toward him.

Despite the dozens upon dozens of hours of preparatory meetings during the first year of the project's creation, Madeleine bore the brunt of ongoing attacks on her motivation and involvement from three of the founding Playgroup Mothers, who accused her of collecting more than one salary for her work on behalf of the project and of deviously making decisions about fund-raising without consulting them. She thought that their expectation that she should discuss every single decision with them was unrealistic, given the complexity of the project, the number of components involved, and the need to make day-to-day decisions without having to take the time for hours of group discussion about every detail: "It's a day's *indaba* [conference] each time you sit down with them to discuss anything. For them that's the norm. . . . It's quite an attractive way to work. [But] you can't build buildings and raise funds and design programs with it all being processed at the level and the pace that they would like it." Struggling with the conflicts with the powerful older Playgroup Mothers and occasionally feeling near the end of her ability to continue with the project, Madeleine began seeing a therapist to work through her experiences with the mothers. She knows enough about the "incredibly damaged childhood" backgrounds of one of the founding Playgroup Mothers to place their treatment of her in context:

> The thing is, Catherine, the damage in some of these people's childhoods is so *unbelievable* that it's miraculous that they can walk on two feet, let alone make the contribution they have in the playgroup. [Learning their life stories] was like scales falling from my eyes, because I'd slightly idealized them as this wonderful community of strong women. [As an example she lists some of the many abuses suffered by Beatrice during her younger years.] Oh!, on and on and on. . . . You know, it's these sort of stories that have helped me understand where the lack of trust is coming from.

Madeleine understands what it has meant "to set up the project with fifty unemployed, very poor, a lot of them AIDS-affected men and women on site in an area that has become brutalized by poverty. The power that they can wield is through threats—death threats or threats of violence or sometimes even a way of talking which is quite violent." When the architect decided to quit after being summoned by the mothers to a vitriolic meeting about their unhappiness with some aspects of his plans, Madeleine pleaded with him to continue. Acknowledging his rage at the way he was treated, Madeleine told him, "I agree with you, I agree with you. Your instincts are right, but try and understand what we're trying do, why they are like that, that because of that damage we are trying to winch the community out of that."

In our discussions about her enthusiastic and passionate fund-raising for the project, Madeleine's painful struggle with the personal verbal attacks she suffers from some of the older founding mothers is a recurring theme. She understands that the mothers fear losing control of the project, are suspicious about the distribution of the resources she brings in and outsider involvement in the project, and resent the amount of funding oriented specifically toward HIV-positive people. Some of the founding mothers are hostile to the caregivers and counselors from other (African township) communities, despite the fact that they were inherited by the project and are funded by another NGO or the government: "It's very hard for people who've been living in such grinding poverty for so long, and suddenly there are funds coming in. It's hard for them not to feel it should actually be channeled to them. Why aren't they benefiting from this? Although many of the [Hope Project] mothers have been able to get paid employment through this development. . . . But even so, they would like everybody to have salaries, and then perhaps we can throw a few bits to the outsiders."

At the same time, younger Playgroup Mothers look with respect at the determination of the founding mothers. A younger Playgroup Mother and project employee whom Madeleine describes as a bridge between the project and the founding Playgroup Mothers tells me of her admiration for Beatrice's strength and courageousness, describing how inspirational she is for the younger women in the area. Along with some of the founding mothers, she also shares with me her concern that the project has come to focus too much on HIV and AIDS. Madeleine is frustrated with this complaint, believing that the project's orientation was discussed at great length during the planning process:

> But some things don't seem to have registered, because I was absolutely clear from the very start that the center would be for children affected by AIDS and their caregivers. You know, even now, they're saying, "Why can't this building just be our preschool? We don't want to have anything to do with AIDS." And I said, "I got the money to build something for children affected by AIDS. I'm not saying that all the children here have to be infected or even affected. I'm just saying that children who are affected must be given priority." But they don't even want to regard that. They just want

total control over that thing. And I'm saying, "That's not possible. That would be fraudulent. The money has been given for a center for AIDS-affected children."

I just think that their ears were somehow closed. They just wanted to get a building and land and facilities. And the idea of the partnership was that they would bring to the project community liaison and security. And we would bring the funding and first-world schools. They have not brought community liaison. We had to go out and do that, because of conflicts in the community between the mothers . . . and those community members. And then security, we had to provide and pay for. And our night watchman and one of our builders were the ones who were stealing the timber, it turned out!

So whatever they were supposed to bring to the partnership didn't really register for them. They've brought twenty years of working in the community without pay with preschool children, and somehow I feel that the preschool is an acknowledgment of that. Here you are, you did all of that for so long and so well; now you can do it in a beautiful place with a lovely playground. But there must be a committee which gives AIDS-affected children priority. That's all that we ask from them. Otherwise, it's theirs. They can run it as they want. I just got [a large contribution] to fund food for the children in the preschool. I think [another project donor] is going to get salaries for the preschool mothers. So they've *got,* but it doesn't seem to have bandaged up their wounds. . . . If they could feel powerful, they would be more gracious.

Since the hostile responses from a few of the founding mothers to Madeleine's fund-raising efforts so obviously distress and hurt her, and since her involvement in the project exposes her to a risk of violence (such as when she was held up or when shootouts occur on the street outside the project), I ask how she manages to balance their treatment of her with the broader successes of the project. She answers by pointing to anthropology:

What one needs in that sort of situation is all the anthropological detachment one can muster. Yes, detachment. It is the ability to stand back so that one's feelings aren't too hooked in, so that you can say, "what is happening here? Let's just slow this down; let's play it over again and see what's going on." One needs to bring social analysis to the situation. Frank Chikane once said at a conference I went to: "Nowadays we have to use the tools of suspicion that we have been given by Marx and Freud." And I think that is so true. So what I do when things get really difficult or complicated is to try and bring into play a sort of social analysis (Marx's tool of suspicion), asking myself what is going on here, what are the social pressures, the class struggle, what's happening with power in the situation. And the other thing to ask is what are the psychological pressures (Freud's tool of suspicion). Where's this person coming from? . . . All that kind of thing. What damage is there in the situation?

In our last interview Madeleine summarizes her feelings: "And I have to say that it's awkward [with the three Founding Mothers who are antagonistic toward her], but it doesn't destroy my commitment to the project. It's one of the things in the situation, like being held up at gunpoint. It wasn't nice, but one must recover, and like one of those wobbly men, one comes back to standing, honestly."

. . . . .

The Hope Project's successes are obvious to anyone who visits the beautiful facility and grasps the interconnecting programs that support poor and HIV-affected people from the area. Despite major interpersonal challenges, the project's founders found ways to work together across race and class divides to bring substantial benefits to the community in health, education, skills development, income-generation projects, and jobs for many local people. Several of the contractors who were brought in from coloured communities to provide skills training remarked to me in our interviews that when they joined the project they could not imagine it would actually work. The trainer, a man who has vast experience working in township projects throughout the city, asked me in amazement if I'd ever encountered another project like the Hope Project in my studies. He doesn't think there's another community-based building project like it in all of Cape Town.

But the challenges have been enormous. The huge learning curve for everyone involved has meant cost overruns because of the focus on using the building construction as a job-training program and because of the periodical need to stop work for lengthy discussions among project participants. Although the expectation that every single decision would be fully vetted by all founding project participants was viewed as unreasonable and exhausting by some trust members (provoking the resignation of the first trust chairperson), the lengthy discussions that punctuated the project's growth probably have been critical in overcoming the fragility of trust and the easy collapse into destructive stereotypes among project stakeholders. Conflict over the distribution of future resources coming into the project and over the extent to which the project targets HIV-positive people will undoubtedly continue because of the extraordinary poverty of the area and the constant threat of intercommunity jealousy. The ability of all participants to recognize that these challenges are unavoidable in such a project—and are a testament to why they need to keep at it rather than giving up—is extraordinary and, I think, unusual.

The trainer asked me to describe the changes I've witnessed over my various visits to the project site, because he finds it difficult to see the progress his builders have made from his vantage point of being on site every day. "I have to remind myself that things are progressing," he tells me. He pauses and then asks, "Don't you become despondent? How do you keep from becoming despondent?" I sit there looking at his kind, earnest face, thinking, but that's what I'm here to learn from you. The refusal to give up—to become despondent—is rooted in faith, several project participants tell me: for some, their belief that this kind of work is a manifestation of their religious faith and for others, their faith in the ultimate project goals.

THE CIRCLE OF COURAGE

When the principal of Isilimela High School suggested that LEAP tutorials should begin in grade ten rather than grade twelve, she had a particular group of students in mind. Her grade-ten science class that year contained a number of very determined and focused young men who took their studies seriously and had a tendency to volunteer for every extracurricular activity made available to them. Frank, Siyabonga, Ayzo, Kaydo, and eventually Frank's cousin Michael were among the students who joined the LEAP program for grades ten through twelve, adding LEAP to their list of after-school commitments. They had already volunteered to work in the library, to join a program called the Responsible Action and Leadership Initiative (RALI), to participate in other youth leadership organizations such as Educo, programs for street kids, and community development initiatives in their home communities. Although they attended school in Langa, they lived all over metropolitan Cape Town (Philippi, Delft, Guguletu, and Khayelitsha).

Frank played a cornerstone role, bringing together his group from high school in Langa with friends he met when he moved to his grandmother's house in Khayelitsha, including Warra, Anele, and Chris. His former high school principal remarks that even though Frank was among the students with the greatest financial worries, "he was like a ball, you know; the more you hit him, the more he bounces. I admire that boy. I admire him. That boy, he was focused. He knew what he wanted. . . . And he was very influential with the other students, especially the other students in his class, to guide them. . . . Frank and them, I don't think we will ever get students like them again."

The principal's comment reveals her view that this group was notably different from their peers. The young men were remarkable in several ways. They were determined to succeed academically, and they worked hard (and largely unsuccessfully) to force recalcitrant teachers to do their job. They assumed leadership roles at school, counseling other students who brought them personal problems and earning the moniker "The Big Four" (as well as "Pat's boys," in acknowledgment of their close relationship with the school principal, Pat). The principal and other teachers mention their resiliently optimistic attitude, even in the face of extraordinarily challenging financial and family circumstances. In particular, their willingness to volunteer for programs run by people from outside the community differentiated them from other students, who were unwilling to participate in programs where they would be expected to speak English and interact with white people. In one conversation, I asked why only young men were participating in the community-oriented programs students learned about in their high schools. Anele answered: "This is one of the challenges. It's not easy to go out there and volunteer. It's not easy to go out there and say, 'I'm doing something for the benefit of the community.' They didn't instill this thing from the school, to go out there and do this kind of work."

Anele suggested that girls lack self-confidence, and Frank agrees: "They lack self-confidence. You'll find out, nine times out of ten, they're so concerned about their image. Nobody wants to look like a fool. No one wants to volunteer because it makes you look like an idiot in public. So if you ask them to go do something, they won't. . . . Anything that would make them gain the skill and help them understand better, they won't do it. We need to build confidence in these girls. They won't participate in the program because they have no confidence in themselves."

Anele continues: "They're feeling ashamed of being black. . . . I talked to another guy, and he told me it's a fear of exposing yourself because you're black, to whites."

Frank adds: "I remember in some of the projects there are coloured girls. They are looking for knowledge and they're learning, unlike our sisters. They don't do that. When you bring them all together in one place, they feel so stupid, because they can't understand what people are saying. . . . They feel, 'I don't belong here,' you know. They don't feel smart. . . . They say, 'That program is not for us. It's for coloureds and whites.' So they drop it, and they miss it. That's the problem with our sisters in townships."

Using his cousin Michael as an example, Frank concludes: "When Mike speaks, he is slow. When he's speaking, he's thinking. And the girls, they'd be like, 'why is Mike speaking?' If he stands to speak, they're like,

Some members of the Circle of Courage at "the Palace," Khayelitsha, 2004. Photo by the author.

'why doesn't Mike sit down!' I understand where that comes from. She's afraid Mike will make a fool of himself."

The group's willingness to take social risks by exposing themselves to public scrutiny in contexts where they have to speak English and interact with white and coloured people suggests a level of self-confidence but also depends on the mutual support they give one another. During their final three years of high school, the young men began meeting weekly to talk through their experiences of the previous week. Their meetings became discussion sessions in which they offered one another moral support and shared their experiences, sometimes even crying together about their personal struggles. While many of their conversations are earnestly serious, they also approached their challenges with rollicking humor, teasing and laughing at one another's personal misfortunes and even tragedies in order to minimize their impact. After following their progress for three years of high school, I asked if they would be interested in a set of focus group discussions to talk about their experiences as high school students looking for opportunities in their communities as well as their hopes for the future. In particular, I mentioned my interest in recording their strategies for being successful. Frank corrected me: "We are succeeding. We are

Inside "the Palace," Khayelitsha, 2004. Photo by the author.

not successful." Characteristically, they were eager to participate, and so we met weekly over several months in 2003–2004 either at my apartment or at their meeting place in Khayelitsha, a cardboard and corrugated tin shack they called "the Palace."

The young men described their motivation for joining the various programs as part of their journey to understand their communities. Since so few of their teachers actually used classroom time to teach, they spent a lot of time in the back of the classroom during grade ten talking about the issues in their lives and wondering why such things were ignored in their school curriculum, like poverty, crime, and AIDS. "We're out there looking for knowledge," Frank explained. "We're thinking about the same kind of stuff. We're all out there looking for answers to our questions. That makes us see things differently, because we want knowledge about why this is, is there a reason for this."

Kaydo agreed: "It's about us observing and analyzing things that are happening outside."

Understanding and overcoming poverty was high on the group members' list, since all of them came from very poor backgrounds and most lived in squatter camps. In one of our conversations, Anele explained that part of his motivation for doing community development work grew from his frustrated ambitions to study beyond high school.

Anele: I've been raised in very poor family. Most of the things I want to do, I can't access them—

Frank: I see the anger in your eyes sometimes, and I wonder where it comes from—

Anele: —being poor. That is the biggest, biggest challenge.

Frank: I also grew up like that, you know. It makes you think, "My god, this situation . . ." I see the rage in your eyes, like burning energy.

Anele: [Very quietly] I've got lots of things in my mind, and lots of things in my heart.

Group members also realized the failures in their school provided them with at best a compromised education. Apart from the skilled teaching of their principal and one or two others, their years of high school were an exercise in frustrated hopes and ambitions. Confirming my experience during my school visits, they talk for hours about teachers who disappeared for weeks or months at a time, of teachers who spent classroom time napping, complaining, or abusing their students, of science classes without a laboratory, auto mechanics classes without tools, a car, or a workshop. They know that the lack of practical, hands-on training will make them "unskilled labor" when they leave school, a phrase they find demeaning. But they also discuss the poor quality of teaching skills, arguing that having access to laboratory or workshop facilities would make no difference if their schools lacked trained, competent teachers. They clearly have a very low regard for the abilities of their teachers:

Frank: It was a nightmare!

Siyabonga: They were dragging themselves into the job!

Frank: We came to a stage where we were just thinking of dropping out of school because we could just see that we were failing. There was no way we could do the matric. But we hung on, and I'm so proud of us. We just held on. Held on. There was no way of quitting school. We were so down, like going down the drain. We focused so much on matric, and so much on after matric, "after matric," but we knew there was no way we were going to pass matric.

C. B.: Because the teachers weren't showing up, they weren't prepared?

Frank: They were not caring. All you get, they all complained about the school, about the department not paying them very well, and they have to be at school each and every period, which is quite not nice, and sometimes they get their money late in the month, so they complained about a lot of things.

Siyabonga: We didn't know if it's true or not.

Frank: Yeah, we didn't know. We just paid our fees and we believed, this is school, we could come to school and get an education. But we're not getting it. And by the time we understand what is happening, we see the guy is not showing up. Comes back maybe the next week after, saying, "No, I was sick."

Siyabonga: There was one guy who left and didn't come back until July. Remember that guy?

The stories spill out for the next hour as everyone starts talking at once about their disappointments with their education.

Kaydo also speaks about the consequences of having no guidance counselors to oversee a student's curricular trajectory. His grandmother works as a domestic for a family in Seapoint who own a jewelry store and have a son close to Kaydo's age. The son is now the manager of the jewelry store, because he received proper advice about what subjects to study in school, whereas Kaydo had no guidance:

Kaydo: So that kid, I'm twenty and he's nineteen or eighteen, but he's a manager or something like that. I went to school for twelve years, and now after all that I'm here now [volunteering] and he's a manager. And I think that his father or someone in the family said, "OK, you're going to work at the jewelry shop, so you should study these subjects." And then he studied that.

Frank: From the beginning.

Kaydo: Yes. From the beginning. And you will find that most white people do that in South Africa. You will find that we go to school together, but a few years out of school, they are working, driving their own cars, in their own houses. They are doing their own thing. But us, you will find we go to school for twelve years, then you must stay in tertiary for four years, and even then, after four years, we stay at home doing nothing. You see what I mean.[9]

The young men looked to the programs they joined to provide the guidance and skills training they felt were missing from their high school. The organizations offered workshops in a variety of areas, such as community building and leadership training, helping the participants to develop a language for talking about their concerns and for active engagement in social change. Although some of their teachers and fellow students respected them for their determination and dedication to self and

community improvement, the group felt their attempts at talking with
their classmates about their experiences in the workshops were often met
with ridicule. One of our group conversations turned to this topic.

Frank: They gave us a lot of crap in high school. [Mimicking his class-
mates] "You guys like white people!" We try to say to the class
what we see and what we think, what we've learned from the
workshops we've been to about why people are so unhappy out
there. [Our classmates would respond,] "What, do you think
you're Jesus or something? There's nothing you can do about it.
That's how life is!" What we've learned is that whatever it is that
you are doing in life, you are responsible for it, for your life. That's
one thing we've learned from all we've been through. . . . When
you say, "I can't do anything about this," that's when you become
a failure. [He imitates others who would mock them, saying] "Oh,
you think you can fix it? Then go ahead and try." That's what we
get from other people. They'll be like, "Oh, you guys are crazy. All
these projects! They won't help you."

Ayzo: "White people's things." All these people say, "Oh, you guys are
white, you guys have white people's minds, doing these things."

Kaydo: They also tell us we are faking. "You're a faker."

Ayzo: Yeah. They called us fakers.

Siyabonga: For them it didn't sound so well that we started throwing ourselves around like that. When this opportunity comes up, we do it,
we take it. Basically, when it comes to white people, there is still at
the back of the mind that we have to struggle against the whites.
To them, it wasn't so good that we got ourselves so involved with
the white people.

C. B.: Like selling out?

Siyabonga: You might say so. But in their context, they still wanted you to take a
back seat, observe, and we didn't do so much of that. We just threw
ourselves in to see what was in there for us. To them it didn't seem
like we were attending to our parents' struggles, like the way we
were so positive. They couldn't understand our interracial levels. . . .
So that is where the faking thing came in. It's easy to analyze. People
don't just say you are faking this. They say you are faking this because they think that you are not following your background, you
don't understand your background. It seems as if you are putting
yourself in a level that you are not in. They are thinking that way.

The others agree with Siyabonga's analysis and pick up the argument
about the significance of the past. "Forget about the past," Michael says.
"I'm interested in the future."

"You have to know your past," Siyabonga adds. "But if you are dwelling on your past, you are never going to get to the future, because everything is going to be your past." They all respectfully acknowledge that people gave their lives in the struggle against apartheid but argue that defining their contemporary situation through the lens of the struggle would hinder their opportunities.

Kaydo explains: "If I'm trying to understand what happened then, and not being attentive to what is going on right now, how am I going to survive? How am I going to look for work? . . . So I think I first must look around me and see where I am coming from now, and then I can understand what happened then, so I can move forward."

Frank interjects:

> For me, the struggle would be a great memory if we had fought and won the freedom. And then everyone would be free. But, nobody's free. None of us is free. That makes me so mad. It's like, we won the freedom, but certain people are enjoying the freedom, and it makes me so mad about the struggle. People fought and did their absolute best, and I'm so proud of them. But now, the freedom that was captured doesn't even serve the people who fought for freedom. That's why I'm saying the struggle was good, but it doesn't inspire me.

What inspires these young men to join programs and volunteer for community projects is their optimism about the future and a refusal to join their peers in the shebeens, an outlook they carefully nurture in one another. Kaydo mentions his enthusiasm about "an improving South Africa" and acknowledges Frank's frequent admonition that "It's all right to be optimistic. When you see your brother, and he's dying out there. It's a hard life out there. But for us it's a privilege because we wake up every day and we're together. You wake up every day and find that your friend is waking up also, and so it does inspire me. Seeing that you all know me, and we're moving together."

Frank embraces with pride what he calls the authenticity of being from the townships, knowing that is the group's context and reality. The objective is to turn this reality into something positive. Frank says, "I mean we're all soldiers. Boys in townships become a soldier, automatically. It just makes you a soldier. You fight for your life, fight for what you know is right. Do what you think is positive. If there's anything you can change, go and change it. If there's something I don't like in the country, I know what I must do, just go and change it. Some people who fought for our freedom couldn't do what they wanted to. That's why the struggle doesn't inspire me. 'Cause it failed." The others joke that their optimism comes from simply surviving Saturday nights, when gunfire is a regular feature of nightlife where they live.

The group members are acutely aware that many of their peers have chosen lives defined by violence. Even though they have chosen a different path, violence and crime are an ever-present reality in their lives and personal histories. One day Bonisile, the university student from Langa, and I met Frank and Kaydo downtown and couldn't help but notice Frank's damaged face. He recounted a horror story of being badly assaulted by the police in Khayelitsha and the ensuing cover-up when he tried to report it. Frank laughed as he recounted the awful story, but Kaydo and Bonisile listened in stony silence. They talked angrily about the amount of police brutality and corruption in their communities, where Frank's experience is far from abnormal and contributes, they argued, to the general feeling of lawlessness that pervades township life. Bonisile commented that township thugs like to think they're different because they're more willing to use violence and commit illegal acts, but they're wrong. "We are the township. The township is in us," he says about himself and other men like him. "Any one of us could do that if we decided to. I could kill someone." He describes a situation in which he would use lethal force against an attacker. "As my friend says, better he's dead and we visit you in jail than attend your funeral." Their argument is that thuggery is a choice, and it would take very little for a young man in their communities to choose a life of gangsterism and robbery. It is also very easy, they emphasize, to make a decision that could ruin one's life, because the opportunities for such a mistake surround them in abundance.

Obviously, most township residents are not thugs or gangsters, but Frank and Kaydo and the others in their circle acknowledge the constant possibility of such a lifestyle in their communities. They see their life paths—to pursue education and community work—as having been a conscious choice rather than an obvious life path. Each member of the circle describes a childhood marked by violence. Each was raised with corporal punishment in the home and in school, each participated in sometimes quite brutal physical assaults in their younger years, which led to punishments by family members, teachers, and the police, and each has been the victim of robbery and assault. Several became involved with more serious offenses as young teenagers—using and selling drugs, stealing, and knife fighting—and several failed at least one year of school because of their engagement in criminal activity. One was shot several times in an altercation and spent a week in hospital recuperating. Most have lost childhood friends to an early death on the street.

Each group member had a childhood characterized by residential instability, moving between the homes of family and friends. Most came to Cape Town as youngsters from Johannesburg, Durban, or the Eastern Cape, moving between the homes of different relatives. Frank, for example, lived with his maternal grandmother in the Eastern Cape until her death, then came to find his mother in Cape Town before moving in with his paternal grandmother. When that living arrangement didn't work out, he began moving among houses of relatives and friends in different townships. Ayzo also spent his childhood in the Eastern Cape, living with a grandmother until her death, then moved in with his other grandmother until being expelled from school for naughtiness. As a young teenager he came to Cape Town, where he moves between the houses of his mother and other relatives. Warra was born in Cape Town, and although he knows his mother, he has never lived with her. His grandmother took care of him until her death, when he moved in with his aunt's family and then into another friend's home. All talk of their lack of male role models. Several have never met their father, and the only member of the circle who lives with his father tells of a childhood defined by his attempts to defend his mother against his father's alcoholic rages.

Group members' optimism, their enthusiasm for community projects and self-knowledge, and their willingness to dismiss the taunts of their classmates about associating with white people clearly depend on their bonds of mutual support. They acknowledge the support of a few teachers who encouraged their participation in workshops and programs, and they recognize the importance of the exacting discipline of some of their mothers and grandmothers. But mostly they speak of recognizing a mutual desire to make the most of their education and to reject gangsterism. Ayzo explained: "We came up with the same minds; we wanted to do something straight, not do robbing, like not be gangsters. So it's the way we can support each other like that, because if you ever can see us, we don't like something like this. If you can prove that, you can be my friend. All of us, we just combine to do something straight and not do something outside, like gangsterism. So we take a set of steps like joining RALI that can teach us something, something good."

Frank continues: "I look at Kaydo and think . . . we've got a good warrior. Somehow, we've got a gift. We have so much to offer the world. Same with him [pointing to Ayzo], same with all of us. That common thing that brought us here, knowing that we have something that makes us be connected." They talk about their peers who have left high school and are doing nothing, spending time at shebeens and on street corners, and they know the challenges ahead.

The weekly meetings during high school have dwindled since high school ended. High school did not end well for most in the group; only half passed their matric exams. Those who failed suffered a crisis of self-confidence, and most who repeated their matric year failed a second time. Although the principal was terribly disappointed, some of their former teachers blamed their involvement in the programs for their failure, suggesting that their attempts at self-improvement had been pointless after all.

But this is not true. Although the group has split apart over the last year because of work schedules and the long distances between their homes, and most have not found stable employment, they are continuing to succeed. Many members of the circle are still pursuing volunteer and community-oriented work. Warra and Kaydo work in environmental education for nonprofit organizations, and Anele continues volunteering at a community nonprofit while beginning tertiary studies. Siyabonga and Chris are attending technical tertiary schools. Frank, Ayzo, and Michael work in hourly waged jobs. Several have made the transition to manhood. As young African men from very poor families with unstable living situations who are determined to follow a life path of community development and personal integrity, they are South Africa's brightest hope for the future.

. . . . .

The successes of the Circle of Courage are hard to identify, since the participants' primary goal was mutual support to get through high school and avoid the poor life choices of their peers. During high school, they were successful role models and school leaders who distinguished themselves by choosing to take advantage of every opportunity that came through their school. Some did graduate from high school, and all are still pursuing a life path they view as moral.

Nevertheless, all their workshops, programs, and circle support meetings could not overcome the realities of their poor school preparation and their poverty. Several failed their matric exam, to their shock, and those who passed found the job market virtually closed to them. They are some of the most articulate, smart, thoughtful, honest, and motivated people I encountered during my years of research in Cape Town, and yet they struggle to find jobs. South Africa's greatest challenge is to ensure that people like them have opportunities to succeed.

CHAPTER 9

Some Lessons

Ayzo: If there are no whites, we will suffer. But if there are no blacks, they will suffer more. We can suffer better than them because we've got that skill.

C. B.: So you're saying that black people in this country can manage better without help from white people than white people can manage without help from black people. . . . What about partnerships? Because everything you're talking about [in the discussion up until this point] is, do we work under a black person, or do we need a white person, or the skills from a white person? What about the possibility of working in a partnership where each of you brings skills, money, etc. together to a business venture?

Michael: The thing that is going to make a partnership is that both of us contribute. We each have something independent to make our business. I have school training. Our things [skills] are different, but our goal is the same—

C. B.: To make money—

Michael: Yeah. You have some skills that I don't have, and you put your skills on the table, and I put mine, and we decide which way to go with it. But the thing is, the white people, they want to be on top.

C. B.: So there's always that danger, that the white person—

Michael: will want to take over. Yeah.

Circle of courage discussion, December 2003

.   .   .   .   .

242

On balance, though, white South Africa will be called upon to make greater adjustments to black needs than the other way around. We are all familiar with the global sanctity of the white body. . . . This leads me to think that if South African whiteness is a beneficiary of the protectiveness assured by international whiteness, it has an opportunity to write a new chapter in world history. It will have to come out from under the umbrella and repudiate it. Putting itself at risk, it will have to declare that it is home now, sharing in the vulnerability of other compatriot bodies. (Njabulo Ndebele)[1]

WHO IS IN CHARGE?

For those white people who are interested in addressing their lingering guilt or acknowledging the unjust legacies of the past through engaged action, a difficult lesson to learn is how not to be in charge. Suspending assumptions about the normal order of things, especially the normal hierarchy of status, offers one of transformation's greatest personal and interpersonal challenges. Old patterns in which white people do the talking and black people listen, in which white people make the decisions that black people carry out, in which white people evaluate progress and outcomes and black people are praised or reprimanded are dying hard. One woman reflected that white people are accustomed to being in charge, to knowing the answers, and become very uncomfortable when this is no longer the case and they are no longer sure what they bring to the relationship or the setting if they are not in charge. One dimension of transformation is learning how to interact in the absence of the assumption of white superiority. But while learning how to have faith in one another's intentions, skills, knowledge, and abilities is one of the great opportunities in post-apartheid South Africa, developing trust and abandoning condescending and patronizing attitudes, even for the most well-meaning white people, is difficult. I witnessed incident after incident of white condescension toward people of color who were potential partners in community work. A woman who devotes extraordinary amounts of time to a township health care project continually interrupts her black colleagues in meetings to help clarify their points for them. She is utterly committed to this project but cannot see how in her enthusiasm she bulldozes right over her colleagues' comments. In a meeting about a preschool project, the white partner speaks quickly and forcefully to the partner of color, barking short, businesslike questions while leaving the coloured partner hardly any time to respond. The white partner thinks he is being efficient and enthusiastic, but his behavior signals impatience rather than engagement. In a private conversation with me, an Anglophone white politician with widely recognized struggle credentials vents his annoyance at his colleagues who speak Xhosa in the government dining room and his anger at feeling excluded when a funeral service he attended in a Xhosa-speaking township for a former comrade was conducted in Xhosa. He can't understand why they wouldn't speak English out of deference to him and other white non-Xhosa speakers who are present at these gatherings. It has never occurred to him to learn Xhosa.

Disputing such assumptions of leadership and hierarchy can be challenging for people of color assuming new roles in projects long run by white people. One young coloured woman, Sharon, who a few years ago took on the directorship of a well-known organization serving the needs of homeless women and children, recounted to me her first confrontation as director. An important older white donor came to talk with Sharon about Sharon's decision to fire an employee favored by the white former leadership. "I'll never forget it," Sharon says. "She came into my office, wearing her red power suit, and shook her finger in my face, berating and lecturing me. Then she went to leave! I gathered my strength and told her I'd like a chance to talk also, to tell my truth." Sharon says the woman was stunned: "Me speaking back wasn't part of the script." After her initial surprise, the donor sat and listened while Sharon described the reasons for the dismissal. They parted courteously and the donor relationship continues to this day. Sharon recalls this moment as life transforming, because she broke the normal pattern of white lectures and coloured silence, where, in her words, "you don't speak back, you accept the lecture, even if you don't agree." Learning to "speak her truth" led Sharon to introduce a number of changes to the organization's hierarchy, such as making major meetings more inclusive of staff and homeless clients in an effort to break down the parent-child dynamic that previously characterized the relationship between donors on the one hand and staff and clients on the other.

Learning to talk about disagreements with people across race and class lines has hampered the progress of the Hope Project. Some of the founding mothers, who see their initiative from twenty years ago becoming something much different, turn to accusations and personal attacks against their white partners when they feel in danger of losing control. Yet other participants of color tell me they do not feel they have the right to speak to the white fund-raisers about aspects of the project that distress them, such as the compensation paid to laborers. The compensation is very low because the laborers receive training and a certificate asserting their skills, and some of the coloured supervisors wonder if the white board members understand the difficulty of living on so little money. But they do not voice their concerns because they understand the white board members are volunteers, doing the best they can, and the project employees do not feel it's their "place" to question decisions. Developing a common understanding about how to work through disagreements in a way that reflects mutual respect and trust is one of South Africa's significant challenges. For this reason, the Hope Project's exhausting practice of regular pauses to work through differences was also probably the key to its success. The fact that all the project participants stuck with it, returning to project indabas and meetings time and again, is a real testament.

John Gilmour movingly describes his personal journey as a white educator trying to forge bonds with African students in the 1990s as part of the Langa Educational Assistance Programme (LEAP) in Pinelands:

> Understanding what one's own journey is and understanding my own mission in terms of those needs has been the big battle, because initially I started out with the—I'll judge it now as a fairly colonial—view of myself as rescuer or myself as savior [laughing]. . . . I was taking ten people to school in a car that was a four-seater, and I was giving my money away and desperately trying to get everyone to donate everything they had to solve the situation immediately. So, growing from that point—and it was well intentioned and a very necessary part of the journey—to the realization that I'm imposing solutions by doing that. I'm actually assessing solutions and am in fact disempowering people, and it took some very honest students to tell me that. And obviously the trust had grown enough. I was open as a human being to allow that trust to grow, and that possibly is my strength, but they were also bold enough, given that trust, to just confront me and say, "Why are you doing this? What is it that you are really doing? What is this desire to see everyone here as needing you to rescue them?" And I had no answer for that. Complicated psychological causes, no doubt, but then as we started to work at making the Pinelands High School situation a real one, starting from a point of no experience at working in a multicultural way to the goal of becoming an open society, we started to experience victories, we started to experience that kind of openness in young people talking and young people saying, "That's not what we want; this is what we want, this is how we feel. Ask us and we'll tell you!" It's so pathetic, that one has to be taught like that, but that was the journey.

Breaking through white condescension or white assumptions of leadership (or rescue) is one component of the larger transformative project of dismantling stereotypes and judgments about other racial groups so nurtured by apartheid ideology. If the forward steps result from optimism and hope, the backward steps easily fall on familiar stereotypes: "I knew they were like that! We tried, but they'll never change!" The frailty of trust is unsurprising given apartheid's historical baggage. Emile and André of Black Noise joke about efforts to get people together across the racial divide in the spirit of reconciliation, only sometimes, they say, "one of us is pretending." A schoolchild disappointed by unmet promises of partnerships tells a reporter, "Don't come to me with a smile if you don't mean it." A young businessman in Langa who runs a sports tour company and works with a wide range of people in the tour and sports professions comments on how often he hears white people he thinks he knows betray themselves with racist assumptions or comments: " 'I'm not a racist, but . . .' and there's always a *but.*"

The stereotypical assumptions about what each partner brings to the project can be boldly summarized: white people are condescending, want to be in charge, don't listen, are stingy, and often don't mean what they say. Black people are lazy, irresponsible, untrustworthy, and lack initiative. These ugly stereotypes are ready and waiting in the wings, comfortably and quickly trotted out to explain a project's breakdown. The huge optimism characteristic of a new project's birth untempered by a full awareness of historical baggage and unspoken assumptions can produce heartbreak, antagonism, and retreat. It is easier to blame "the other" for ingratitude, sulkiness, lack of response, whatever, than to search one's own soul and confront terribly uncomfortable truths. The early years of LEAP, the efforts at Gardenview Baptist Church, and the problems at the Hope Project all provide examples of the easy retreat into caricatures when efforts are made to reach out but expectations of gratitude are not met.

Sharon, the director of the organization that assists homeless women and their children, suggests that one way across these old patterns is through intimacy. At her organization's annual meeting, she set the chairs so close together that everyone was forced to rub arms with those adjacent, and the people entering and leaving the hall had to brush against those seated in the last row. She chuckles at this strategy, acknowledging that she wanted to compel the different participants—board members, donors, staff, and homeless women living at the shelter—to come into physical contact. Another woman who volunteers substantial time to a preschool project in a squatter settlement near her gated community offers her strong views about what volunteerism must mean in South Africa. Partnering, she insists, "does not mean donating. It means intimacy, involvement, engagement, and working together to develop creative solutions." Intimacy, as Johanna and the parents whose children she counseled experienced at Heatherton Primary School, means building close relationships.

John Gilmour learned this lesson through one of the first Langa students to study at Pinelands. After several years of working together as teacher/mentor/counselor and student, John's closest student from Langa phoned and asked John to come to his home in Langa one Sunday at noon. Amused, John asked what was up. Eric, very serious, replied, "Please, just come. Be here then." After John arrived at Eric's house, Eric showed up with a small child, a little girl. He brought her into the room and left immediately, leaving John sitting there with the child. John, bewildered, sat down to play with the child. After a while Eric returned, and studying John's face, revealed the child was his daughter. At that moment, John—flabbergasted, ashamed, and hurt that Eric felt he couldn't tell him until now—realized the true imbalances in their relationship, in which John had acted as mentor and advice giver, preaching safe sex and condoms to Eric like a father and a minister. How could Eric reveal his sexuality by acknowledging his paternity to John? Eric had not revealed his paternity because he was uncertain about the consequences: "This was really big," Eric recounted to me. "I didn't lie to him, but I didn't tell him the most important thing."

This moment began a rebalancing of the relationship. Eric increasingly adopted the role of adviser to John on his approach to opening opportunities to township learners, reigning in John's sometimes unguarded enthusiasm. Sometimes those who are given access to opportunities abuse their position and should be cut off, Eric feels. "That's the one thing John has learned very slowly: you have to sometimes be hard and tough. That is his weak point, even today. He always wants to find solutions, but you can't always change people's characters." Because Eric feels he understands now how to build quality relationships based on mutual trust and reciprocity, he's wary of peers who seek out relationships with white people to "see what they can get." "It's hard for whites to see when they're being used. When they realize, it can be very destructive. It's not the way to go." John made the transition from mentor and rescuer to partner and colleague.

Gloria Anzaldúa writes about the work of building intimacy by bridging social worlds: "Bridging is the work of opening the gate to the stranger within and without. To step across the threshold is to be stripped of the illusion of safety because it moves us into unfamiliar territory and does not grant safe passage. To bridge is to attempt community, and for that we must risk being open to personal, political, and spiritual intimacy, to risk being wounded."[2] Understanding that intimacy is the goal, rather than rescue or charity, allows potential partners a way to envision their work together. It hinders the romanticization of the poor (as particularly noble or heroic or brave). The self-image of "rescuer" easily disintegrates when those one seeks to help disagree with one's approach or goals and one assumes such disagreement signals ingratitude.

Emphasizing intimacy rather than simply donating might offer a way around another common stereotype that infects project dynamics: the fear of dependency. An example from one of Zerilda Park's partnerships is instructive. I received an invitation to attend a formal dinner meeting of the civic club that was supporting Zerilda Park's projects. My invitation was in recognition of my association with the school and with Raymond, the school's project coordinator, who had recently been inducted as a club member. The meeting that evening was chaired by the club's district governor, who in the post-cocktail, pre-dinner meeting reviewed the club's charitable undertakings for the year: conducting a toys-for-tots collection program, funding a group of four men and women with physical disabilities to visit Cape Town as part of a global tour to raise awareness of the needs of the physically challenged; and sponsoring a city foot race.

As the last order of business, the district governor asked for an update on the partnership begun by the club with Zerilda Park, and he expressed concern about "creating a dependency situation." He wanted to be sure the school was not becoming dependent, asking for handouts and waiting for things to be done for it, and he recounted that the club's mission must be to teach the school about self-improvement and doing things for itself. I was stunned that this was his emphasis and primary concern; he did not express any such concerns or advice about any of the other projects. Raymond had not yet arrived at the meeting and so could not speak on the school's behalf. Another club member shared some minor concerns about the club's involvement with the school, after which the district governor, recognizing my association with the school, called on me to ask my opinion of the potential for creating an unmanageable dependency situation. Caught unprepared by the sudden concern about dependency, I managed to remark that the school had built all its community-oriented projects long before its association with the service club, so I was a bit in the dark about why the school might now become dependent. I mentioned the principal's visionary energy in creating and driving the projects, for which he and Raymond had received a national Impumelelo Award a year before the partnership began with the service club. At the mention of the principal's name, the governor immediately backed off, realizing that another branch of the club had the previous year presented the school principal with an award in honor of his community work.

Raymond did not arrive at the meeting until we were seated for dinner and saying grace, so I recounted the discussion to him later as we walked to our cars. Visibly angry, he explained that he was late to the meeting because he had been assisting a woman in Lavender Hill who had been badly beaten by her husband and was unable to feed her family that evening. "I'm glad I was late, because instead of sitting there listening to concerns about my dependency, I'm out there 'sowing the seeds of love,'" a reference to the district governor's definition over dinner of the club's mission. "I'm doing things in the community and not sitting around over a fancy dinner and talking about it."

The service club has made substantial contributions to the school's projects, and several club members make the effort to attend school ceremonies and public events. The club members are genuinely committed to helping to improve the infrastructure of the school, and several are involved in other community-oriented ventures elsewhere in Cape Town as well. In conversations with me about their service undertakings, they stress the need they feel to participate in the new South Africa and to contribute to resolving the inequalities left over from apartheid. Despite their best intentions and clear commitment, however, school staff and teachers describe to me how they feel condescended to and marginalized during club functions held on behalf of the school and at school ceremonies attended by invited members of the civic club. One teacher recalled an event—her first at the service club—when she was accompanying the students who were to perform for the event; she was ignored by the club members, who treated her as though she were invisible, part of the support staff "whom one didn't chat with." Another very involved teacher recalled that at that event, club members asked, "Are you the principal? Deputy principal? Oh, only a teacher?" and then seemed mildly confused about his status and how they were to talk to him. Remarking on other ways they feel belittled in their interactions with well-meaning club members, one teacher wonders if Zerilda Park teachers should learn better how to take the initiative at introducing themselves and starting conversations. Another teacher describes his discomfort at feeling like he is viewed as a charity recipient rather than a full partner. "I want to see a partnership, not just them giving money and thinking we're a charity case. They must tell us what they want from us. What do we bring to this relationship?"

. . . . .

We as normal people can do more than politicians for real reconciliation. Real reconciliation is not: "*Ag* shame, *sies tog,* come over to my house so that I can show you my collection of African art." It is more than that. It is honesty and a deep, real understanding of first ourselves, then the other (I hate to put it this way) and respecting our discoveries from a position of love. (Sandile Dikeni)[3]

.   .   .   .   .

In their 2003 article in *Business Day,* Stephen van der Westhuizen and Johann Kritzinger argue that despite ten years of democracy, those who feel their experiences of humiliation, disrespect, and discrimination have not been heard will continue to feel frustration and resentment in the workplace.[4] Democracy and legislation to address past injustice "will not normalise our society nor bridge the racial divide until the emotional facet of what it felt like to be discriminated against and treated with disrespect and hatred is heard and acknowledged."

Obviously intimacy does not come easily, as Gardenview's experience demonstrates. The path to intimacy is a long and circuitous one, dependent all partners believing that the goal is worth it. Most important, it requires those entering into a partnership to expose themselves in novel ways, to listen, and to be acutely aware of their respective subject positions, namely, the historical baggage they carry with them. Transformative projects at the grassroots level depend utterly on the ability of project participants to develop trust and faith in one another, to speak openly yet show mutual respect, and to discuss decisions in an open and democratic forum. Democracy can be very painful and long-winded. But when people are trying to form partnerships and become intimate across old divides, there is no alternative. Indabas, workshops, and staff support retreats were critical to the success of LEAP and the Hope Project and the efforts of the Circle of Courage students. Balancing the sense of urgency with the need for dialogue, the immediacy of community needs with the importance of laying a firm base for the development of a mutually shared vision of transformation, is the trick. This is, in fact, the way democracy is built from the ground up.

CONTRADICTIONS

Explaining to me how she manages living between her home in Newlands and her work in Nyanga, Madeleine says: "Do you know the idea of reconciling opposites? It was a sort of alchemical idea initially, but Jung and all his followers have built on it a lot. It's a way that if you want to come to individuation, to adulthood, you have to try and hold the tension between two opposites always, which makes individuational adulthood not a release from tension or suffering, but acceptance of the fact that you're in that tension. It's helpful for me in South Africa where we have a polarized society."

.   .   .   .   .

Johanna recounted to me a troubling moment at Heatherton Primary School when one day the principal vented his frustrations with the neighborhood to her. "Agh! These coloured people!" she quoted him as saying. "I know I'm coloured too—but these people, they're so lazy! They don't want to work or make any kind of effort. I'm fed up!" Johanna was dumbstruck, and although she has her share of frustrations with poor teaching and irresponsible parenting, she felt the need to frame a coherent response. She wanted to tell him: "Don't you know how much effort went into making these people passive? Don't you know how they came to live here, what has been done to them, the sense of hopelessness that pervades this place? And what about your advantages? You're a professional, comfortable, middle class, a pastor and a school principal. They don't have what you have." The irony is obvious: the professional coloured man venting to the white volunteer woman about the uselessness of the population they are both working together to serve—she out of a sense that it is her responsibility to attend to the injustices of the past, and he as a professional and out of a sense of compassionate responsibility to the community of his birth. Johanna could not voice her response aloud to the principal—she isn't yet sure it's her place to respond—so she tried to process the irony as she recounted the incident to me. How can community leaders address the decades of oppression that have produced dependence and submission in some impoverished coloured neighborhoods? Johanna mentioned the claim by some of the mothers at the school that apartheid didn't affect them. She doesn't know how to respond to their profound lack of historical awareness of the impact on their lives of apartheid racism, forced removals, constraint, and paternalism.

Transformative initiatives, by definition, are fraught with contradictions, because their goal is changing the status quo. They are working against a social order that defines the social identities and power relations of the project participants, and the normal human tendency is toward stability rather than transformation, even if the status quo is damaging. Breaking through old patterns of dependency, for example, is hard for people conditioned to blame themselves and their communities for their own poverty. The young men in the Circle of Courage refused to define themselves by their poverty and by the low self-esteem and lack of self-confidence they felt in many of their peers. But most of their peers and teachers did not support their efforts at personal development, mocking them for imagining that participation in "white people's organizations" would benefit them. Zerilda Park's achievements are sometimes mocked by neighboring schools, whose staff members snipe that Zerilda Park mistakenly "thinks it's a Model C school." These are challenges that can only be met by visionary community members who act as mentors and leaders, creating a new language of self-identity and self-confidence people in the community find compelling and desirable. Al Witten spoke such a language to his staff, students, and parents, using the force of his optimism and insistence on improvement to inspire other members of his community. Beatrice was such a force for the Hope Playgroup Mothers, although other project participants often find her interventions more harmful than helpful. Nevertheless, they recognize that the Hope Project would not have been possible without her determined energy and participation. Pat Qokweni, the principal at Isilimela, offered support and encouragement to the Circle of Courage members at her school, ensuring they recognized that she believed in them and their potential. Emile of Black Noise galvanizes young people on the Cape Flats to embrace an African identity, become self-reliant, and support positive community initiatives. Finding ways to manage if not reconcile opposing sentiments and forces—being in charge versus listening; charity versus partnership; dependency versus initiative; pessimism versus optimism; the status quo versus change; community jealousy versus community support; democratic versus authoritarian decision making—is critical to a project's success because they contain the power to destroy a project's efforts.

.   .   .   .   .

Antiracism scholars Vron Ware and Les Back write: "Each situation, each place of protest, each example of DIY (do it yourself) culture has the potential to unite people on the basis of hope, anger, determination, empathy, and a desire for change. Participants may be divided on other matters outside the one at hand, but the political conversations, disagreements, and insights that can happen are important elements of the process of politicization, which can lead to new subjectivities, new identifications, and an increased sense of acting politically."[5]

LIVING IN THE GAP

A common theme among those engaged in the work of transformation is the narrowing of their social world and the feeling that they live a liminal life suspended between different worlds. Fozia, the white Afrikaner woman who converted to Islam when she married a Muslim man, says she lives an "in-between life" with the new family she has created with her husband. Madeleine, living in Newlands and working in Khayelitsha and Nyanga, calls her lifestyle "living in the gap." The Circle of Courage members formed their group as a support mechanism against challenges that they were "selling out" and turning into coconuts because of their friendly associations with white people and involvement in multiracial organizations. As Bonisile, the anthropology and psychology university student, pursues graduate work at a predominately white university, he finds it increasingly difficult to maintain meaningful relationships with his childhood friends still living in Langa. Yet at the university he feels like "an experiment . . . the black guy they brought in to show they can do it." "Everywhere I go," he says about the university community, "I feel like I have an extra coating of black that I wear around." Bonisile resolves his contradiction by returning to live in Langa, where he was raised, to work with township students. "If I'm going to feel out of place, let me feel out of place there," he tells me. "I have nothing more to prove at the university."

This feeling of in-betweenness, while ontologically stressful, also offers exciting possibilities for people willing to negotiate living in the gap. The presence of a support structure or a mentor seems to be critical to the success of those choosing to live in a culturally liminal space. For the young men in the Circle of Courage, finding mentors and support organizations they could join was critical to their ability to fashion optimistic, hopeful identities for themselves as community workers who had turned away from an alternative trajectory of crime, substance abuse, and violence. Making and finding safe spaces to work out their issues of adolescence was perhaps the most important aspect of their trajectories. I spoke with dozens of young people in African townships who are deeply troubled by questions about the role of tradition and history in their identities. While initiation rituals are uniformly practiced by those who follow Xhosa culture, other rituals of marriage and gender relations are undergoing serious revision and negotiation in the context of urban life. A network of trusted friends with whom one can work out a satisfying path to manhood and womanhood offers a promising model. The required life skills course at LEAP provides exactly such a safe space and is recognized by school authorities as one of the most important of the school's innovations in ensuring students' success.

One Sunday I attended a barbecue at John Gilmour's house with his family and friends, many of whom are also educators. John had just resigned from his post at Abbott's and had turned down a prestigious job offer to develop his plan for a new LEAP school. Two of the men at the party were also moving on to new jobs, as headmasters of private schools outside of Cape Town. Over the course of the afternoon everyone talked about the new direction these two men were taking with their upcoming moves, but no one asked John about his plans. His circle's utter lack of interest in his career change helped me see what an extraordinary choice John had made, especially in the context of what his peers are doing as they move up the ladder.

I asked John about his friends' silence, and he concurred that there is a reluctance to acknowledge what he is doing. His friends will ask him if his financial situation is okay and if everything is okay with the family. They want to hear he is fine and things are going well. But they don't ask about the things that to him seem really exciting, like what educational approaches he plans to take in his new school or how he plans to tackle the issues and challenges of starting a new school for African-language learners partnered with Bishops. He acknowledges that they would avidly ask such questions if he was starting a new private, alternative, expensive school like Cedar House or Reddam. But to the contrary, John feels his friends almost pity him. During his year of planning and fund-raising for his new school, the headmaster at the school where he occasionally counseled students would ask in passing, "How's it going, everything on track? You'll always have a job here if things don't work out." He never expressed the slightest interest in John's vision.

The problem with living in the gap is that it can be a very lonely place. Raymond, the project coordinator at Zerilda Park who devotes his life to community work, sometimes disconsolately talked of his work as "shoveling sand"; his progress was often invisible to him. Johanna suffered bouts of disabling depression, where she felt overwhelmed by the challenges at Heatherton and unsupported by her own community in the work she had chosen. Madeleine sees a therapist to work through her low points. Madeleine, Sharon (the director of the organization that assists homeless women), Emile (of Black Noise), and John all talk with me over the years about their efforts to nurture their staff through the frustrations of transformative work, in which it is often difficult to see progress. The work of transformation can be socially isolating, the setbacks are overwhelming, and public recognition is rare. They talk about the one child, the one dancer, the one mother successfully helped by their organizations' efforts, holding that success dear and as evidence that their hard work is worth it.

Anthropologists talk about the tension between individual experience and awareness and broader patterns of discourse and interaction. What is it that makes one person a transformer, another a reluctant adherent to the status quo, and another a racist retrograde? What is it that allows one person to cognize and challenge a perverse social order and another to accept it as legitimate or unchangeable? Grappling with this question of individual choice versus social context over tea one day, anthropologist Susan Levine and I reviewed the tools anthropology makes available to us for understanding such situations. We concluded that the best anthropologists can do is look for patterns. But sometimes becoming transformative is a matter of chance or unpredictable peculiarities of circumstance. Anthropology often wants life histories to be microcosms of the whole—to tell the story of many through the narrative of one. But one person's story is often just that, and we should avoid the impulse to generalize one person's story to everyone. To do so is to minimize the effort, faith, and energy it takes to be a transformer and to suggest that everyone has this choice or ability. In fact, probably most people do not have the courage and guts to sustain the setbacks, disappointments, and uncomfortable self-scrutiny that are required to actively work for social change. Thus it is all the more important to recognize and acknowledge those who do and to look for ways to provide support for their work. Veret Amit and Nigel Rappaport write: "Individuals are more than their membership of and participation in cultural collectivities. For it is individuals who make and maintain cultural worlds—remake them continuously through their creative cognitions—and it is individuals in interaction who make and maintain communities."[6] A particular strength of anthropology is its ability to track and document the creative undertakings of individuals and the ways such individuals find one another and reinforce one another's efforts and imaginings. Documenting such efforts allows us to glimpse future possibilities and to develop cognitive maps for nurturing and developing transformative work. One of the most important lessons I have learned from this research is the importance of mentors and networks of support for those engaged in the hard work of changing the status quo.

Recognizing that Americans "go beyond their private lives only under special circumstances, such as a threat to their values or household economy," anthropologist Catherine Lutz and her colleagues undertook a study in North Carolina to address the question of what motivates Americans to political participation and engagement. Her analysis identifies the important function of role models, people who "model leadership and inspire perseverance, re-energizing others with the attitude that they can get things done. They also inspire some by their insistence on the value of having a vision of what change is needed, a vision that can reveal a path out of the problematic present."[7] Such role models, the vanguard of grass-roots transformation, however, often struggle with feelings of uncertainty and feel that they are working in isolation against criticism and aversion. Lutz records these feelings in her study, where she found the most strik-ing barrier to political engagement was fear: fear of crime if political ac-tivities required participants to be on the street or to go door to door; fear of "alienating neighbors by disagreeing with them"; and fear "of retalia-tion, either economic or physical violence, should one try to change the status quo through political activity."[8] Previous chapters have docu-mented the fact that South Africans share these same fears. The trans-formers I profile have overcome such fears to plunge into their work, but their references to "living in the gap," living an "in-between life," having their work ignored by their friends, "shoveling sand," depression, and ex-haustion reveal the ongoing toll of their work. It is true that dramatic structural change will not occur through a few small-scale interventions, but the transformers I have profiled here know that transformation will never occur without their efforts. Their success is that their lowest lows can't compete with their emphatic optimism and their faith that their end goal is worth the struggle.

. . . . .

It is Christmas day, 2003. John Gilmour and Eric Dilima have organized their annual Christmas festivities in Langa. John has brought a group of friends, acquaintances, and students to spend the day in Langa; Eric, Bonisile, and several other men from Langa dress up as Santa Clauses and walk the streets distributing candy to children. Volunteers have do-nated the candy, the use of a cotton candy machine for a street party on Harlem Street, and many dozens of food hampers for a neighborhood project that feeds and cares for the poorest of the community. At the con-tainer that houses the project, a large group gathers in the front yard as the food packets are being distributed to the assembled families. As al-ways in situations like this, the high emotions surrounding food distri-bution are compounded by the presence of a large group of outsiders, and the blackening sky suggests a huge thunderstorm is imminent. Everyone begins grabbing for umbrellas and pushing through the crowd to find a protected spot. As I dash inside the container, I notice John has remained standing in the yard as thick dark clouds are approaching from all sides and everyone else is running for cover. He is staring upward, pointing at one solitary little sunny patch of blue sky, saying, "See? It's clearing up!" Although we were about to be engulfed in a downpour, it did indeed pass quickly to become a sunny, beautiful day.

MAKING CHANGE

What do all the examples I have profiled here add up to? What difference do these projects and networks of care make in transforming Cape Town, overcoming racism, and combating poverty? I believe they make a world of difference. First, these kinds of projects and networks implicate people in the process of building democracy. By bringing people together into spaces where they must learn to work together toward a common goal, Capetonians who participate in these kinds of initiatives are learning the art of democracy and are taking personal responsibility for South Africa's future. As Emile YX? told me about his devotion to his work, "Someone's got to be paying attention when the bubble bursts"— that is, when the poor become frustrated by the slow pace of transformation. Anthropologist Anna Tsing talks about the concept of friction in this kind of work, suggesting that it doesn't matter whether everyone agrees about how to achieve a goal, or even what the goal should be.[9] The friction that occurs among those working for social change may in fact actually be the point of the encounter—that people are talking and engaging, even arguing and struggling to make themselves understood and to understand one another.

Clearly, grassroots projects and local-level, small-scale, neighborhood-based initiatives are not transformative in a revolutionary way. The political revolution already happened, bringing to power a new government and a new political order, which is supposed to be enabling changes throughout the political, economic, and social systems. But the work of transformers leads to subtle and sometimes momentous shifting of power relations within small, local networks of human interaction. Anthropologist David Graeber notes the potential effectiveness of local-level networks in eventually producing structural change by building a new society "within the shell of the old," but using democratic methods.[10]

What the projects described here accomplish, along with the thousands of others like them, is to construct networks of care and human connection. The importance of such networks and what they signify in South Africa should not be underestimated or trivialized. Such networks, argues Helen Epstein in her new book on efforts to combat HIV and

AIDS in Africa, are essential. Epstein shows how ground-level, intimate work by small Ugandan-based NGOs that cropped up throughout the country as the AIDS epidemic exploded became the decisive factor in Uganda's successful efforts to combat the epidemic.[11] While not the only factor, the work of people within their neighborhoods, while largely ignored outside their communities and certainly outside of Uganda, was a major part of Uganda's "invisible cure" that resulted in plummeting rates of HIV infection at a time when the epidemic was skyrocketing elsewhere on the continent. Epstein argues that the highly localized networks of care that knit together neighbors and brought people together in the most intimate spaces of daily life to support one another through the ravages of the disease created a social structure that enabled people to confront the reality of AIDS and change their behavior to better protect themselves against the disease.

The lesson from Uganda about how such small-scale, localized initiatives became part of Africa's solitary success story in the fight against AIDS demonstrates the critical importance of local networks of support, interpersonal trust, and mutual responsibility. These are aspects of social life that are hard to introduce from above by wealthy NGOs and government programs. They have to be built from the ground up, and they have to be recognized for their transformative power in changing minds, behavior, and the feelings people have about their mutual humanity and connectedness.

Notes

INTRODUCTION

Epigraph: Pieter-Dirk Uys, *Elections and Erections* (Cape Town: Zebra Press, 2002), 78.

1. "Chasing the Rainbow: A Survey of South Africa," *Economist*, 8 April 2006, 4.

2. Adam Ashforth, *Witchcraft, Violence, and Democracy in South Africa* (Chicago: University of Chicago Press, 2005), 90. See also Jeremy Seekings and Nicoli Nattrass, *Class, Race, and Inequality in South Africa* (New Haven, CT: Yale University Press, 2005).

3. The Gini coefficient is a ratio that can vary from zero, which indicates perfect equality, to one, which indicates perfect inequality. It is derived from a mathematical formula that measures the inequality of income distribution.

The State of the Nation: South Africa, 2004–2005, ed. John Daniel, Roger Southall, and Jessica Lutchman (Cape Town: Human Sciences Research Council, 2005), favorably discusses the government's early twenty-first-century turn (at least as a "working hypothesis" [xxxi]) toward a more interventionist approach to the economy. The chapter by Benjamin Roberts ("Empty Stomachs, Empty Pockets: Poverty and Inequality in Post-apartheid South Africa," [479–510]) provides a critical review of poverty indices for the first post-apartheid decade.

4. Much of this historical overview is drawn from Leonard Thompson, *A History of South Africa* (New Haven, CT: Yale University Press, 2001).

5. Afrikaner trekkers migrating to the northeast of the cape colony claimed land abandoned by Africans fleeing warfare within the Zulu and other African polities, calling their new home the Natal Republic and extending citizenship only to Afrikaner trekkers. When the British speedily took over the republic, many of the trekkers continued their journey toward the west, founding the Orange Free

State and the Transvaal. British colonial policy in Natal set several important precedents. During the final decades of the nineteenth century, the British imported thousands of Indian indentured laborers to work in Natal sugar plantations, developed the policy of indirect rule to control Africans through controlling their chiefs (which was extended to other African colonies as a form of colonial control), created a system of reserves for Africans (the precursors of apartheid-era Homelands), and provoked the birth of Gandhi's political movement of passive resistance (which he later took to India).

6. Thompson, *History,* 164.

7. Ibid., 214.

8. See Jeremy Seekings, *A History of the United Democratic Front in South Africa, 1983–1991* (Cape Town: David Philip; Oxford: James Currey; Athens: Ohio University Press, 2000).

9. See Richard Wilson's book on popular responses to the TRC: *The Politics of Truth and Reconciliation in South Africa: Legitimizing the Post-Apartheid State* (New York: Cambridge University Press, 2001).

10. Francis Wilson, "Addressing Poverty and Inequality," in *After the TRC: Reflections on Truth and Reconciliation in Cape Town,* ed. Wilmot James and Linda van der Vyver (Athens: Ohio University Press, 2001), 177–184.

11. Seekings and Nattrass, *Class, Race, and Inequality.*

12. Allister Sparks, *Beyond the Miracle: Inside the New South Africa* (Johannesburg: Jonathan Ball Publishers, 2003), 193. The following offer critical assessments of ANC economic policy during the first decade of democracy: Seekings and Nattrass, *Class, Race, and Inequality;* Francis Wilson, "Globalization: A View from the South," in *Beyond Racism,* ed. Charles Hamilton, Lynn Huntley, Neville Alexander, Antonio Sérgio, Alfredo Guimarães, and Wilmot James (Boulder, CO, and London: Lynne Reinner, 2001), 323–350; Zine Magubane, "Globalization and the South African Transformation: The Impact of Social Policy," *Africa Today* 49, no. 4 (2002): 89–110.

The literature on inequality in South Africa is vast. In addition to those already cited, a selection of relevant recent studies includes Fantu Cheru, "Overcoming Apartheid's Legacy: The Ascendancy of Neoliberalism in South Africa's Anti-Poverty Strategy," *Third World Quarterly* 22, no. 4 (2001): 505–527; Wilmot James and Jeffrey Lever, "The Second Republic: Race, Inequality, and Democracy in South Africa," in Hamilton et al., *Beyond Racism;* Hein Marais, *South Africa: Limits to Change: The Political Economy of Transition* (London: Zed Books; Cape Town: University of Cape Town Press, 2001); Nicoli Nattrass and Jeremy Seekings, " 'Two Nations'? Race and Economic Inequality in South Africa Today," *Daedalus* 130, no. 1 (Winter 2001): 45–70; Nicoli Nattrass, "Gambling on Investment: Competing Economic Strategies in South Africa," in *Between Unity and Diversity: Essays on Nation Building in Post-Apartheid South Africa,* ed. Gitanjali Maharaj (Cape Town: David Philip, 1999); Sampie Terreblanche, *A History of Inequality in South Africa, 1652–2002* (Pietermaritzburg: University of Natal Press, 2002).

13. Michael K. Brown, Martin Carnoy, Elliott Currie, Troy Duster, David B. Oppenheimer, Marjorie M. Shultz, and David Wellman, *White-Washing Race: The Myth of a Color-Blind Society* (Berkeley: University of California Press, 2003), 3.

14. Theresa Oakley-Smith, "Ten Years On, We're Still in Denial," *Star,* 14 May 2003, http://www.thestar.co.za/index.php?fArticleId=145225.

15. Thabisi Hoeane, "Closing the Race Debate No Way to Resolve Tensions," Institute for Justice and Reconciliation, 7 November 2004, http://www.ijr.org.za/publications/archive/media-articles-and-programmes/closedeb/?searchterm=hoeane (accessed 16 June 2007).

16. City of Cape Town, Census 2001, http://www.capetown.gov.za/census-Info/Census2001-new/Cape%20Town/Cape%20Town.htm (accessed 16 June 2007).

17. Sarah Nuttall writes: "The city form—and the city lives to which it gives rise—is the most conducive space to the remaking of culture and identity, because it is the place of most difference—where difference, that is the juxtaposition of culture works to revise and reread the orthodox, any stable notion of who is who. But is it? Aren't cities also the places of the most effective surveillance in which people—as in apartheid's spatial geography—are confined, segregated, monitored and rendered violently invisible to others not in their 'group'? . . . It is precisely within a culture of surveillance, or difference, and its legacy, that highly charged border crossings are likely to occur, that people will find ways of walking, unsurveyed—forms of agency that help to create a new culture of the city. The city even where it is a space of segmentation or regimentation, is also a space of creolisation." Sarah Nuttall, "City Forms and Writing the 'Now' in South Africa," *Journal of Southern African Studies* 30, no. 4 (2004), 731–748. Nuttall suggests that identifying the ways in which people "walk forward, unsurveyed," the ways in which people move across historically and violently structured racisms, "may be the only way to write South Africa out of a past and into a future" (748).

18. Cited in Nuttall, "City Forms."

19. Ibid.

20. From Uys's "Symbols of Sex and State" performance, Baxter Theater, 30 May 2001.

21. See, for example, Ashforth, *Witchcraft.*

22. City of Cape Town, Census 2001.

23. The report also shows that for every one hundred people in Cape Town, fifty-six are not economically active (children, the elderly, etc.). Of the remaining forty-four, eight are unemployed, twenty-eight work in the informal sector, and eight have formal employment (Ashley Smith, "Shocking Divide in City's Rich and Poor," *Cape Times,* 14 June 2002, 1, 4).

24. Statement of Deputy President Thabo Mbeki at the opening of the debate in the National Assembly, "Reconciliation and Nation Building," National Assembly, Cape Town, Republic of South Africa Department of Foreign Affairs, 29 May 1998. Available at www.dfa.gov.za/docs/speeches/1998/mbeko529.htm (accessed 16 June 2007).

25. Sparks, *Beyond the Miracle.*

26. Cited in Christopher Colvin, "Introduction: Contingency and Creativity: South Africa after Apartheid," *Anthropology and Humanism* 28, no. 1 (2003): 3–7.

27. Ibid., 4.

28. Sandile Dikeni, *Soul Fire: Writing the Transition* (Pietermaritzburg: University of Natal Press, 2002), 117.

29. Todd Gitlin, "Varieties of Patriotic Experience," in *The Fight Is for Democracy: Winning the War of Ideas in America and the World,* ed. George Packer (New York: Harper Collins, 2003), 126.

CHAPTER 1. SEDUCTION

1. Some anthropologists in the first half of the twentieth century clearly saw public education as part of their disciplinary mission—for example, Franz Boas on race and intelligence and Margaret Mead on adolescent sexuality and gender roles.

2. After writing this chapter I came across an essay by Cris Shore that makes a similar observation. Remarking on questions about whether anthropologists "can ever really 'know' other people's subjectivities," Shore notes that some anthropologists argue "that all we can ever really write about with authority and accuracy is ourselves." Cris Shore, "Fictions of Fieldwork: Depicting the 'Self' in Ethnographic Writing," in *Being There: Fieldwork in Anthropology,* ed. C. W. Watson (London: Pluto Press, 1999), 29. Also, see the interesting discussions about the anthropologist's narration of self in ethnographies about others in Renato Rosaldo, "Subjectivity in Social Analysis," in *Culture and Truth* (Boston: Beacon Press, 1993); and Henrietta Moore, "Master Narratives," in *A Passion for Difference* (Cambridge: Polity Press, 1994).

3. This meeting took place a decade after white government schools were opened to all races, and the preceding decade had offered ample opportunity for such schools to engage in conversations about how to manage curricular and demographic transformation. This particular school prided itself on having taken a leading role in pioneering the new curriculum. Nevertheless, it was remarkable that a decade into transformation, every member of the teaching faculty except one was white (even the Xhosa teacher for the upper grades was white, and the school authorities recognized his command of Xhosa was inadequate), and the discourse had shifted to holding on to standards and traditions. While my hope for an acknowledgment of the efforts to embrace an ongoing agenda of transformation may have been naive, the insistence on stability and tradition reflected a meaningful and typical stance held by many such schools.

4. This explains why there are so few ethnographies of groups like right-wing militias and racial hate groups. Gusterson is one of the few who broke that tradition, doing fieldwork at the Lawrence Livermore National Laboratory among the physicists who built the nuclear bombs that Gusterson, as a young peace activist, had protested against. His decision to move to Livermore, California, and write a book, *Nuclear Rites: A Weapons Laboratory at the End of the Cold War* (Berkeley: University of California Press, 1998), was motivated by his desire to understand how people who built weapons of mass destruction could possibly justify to themselves what they did for a living. Similarly, in their book *Out of Whiteness* (Cambridge: Cambridge University Press, 2001), Vron Ware and Les Back reflect on the tensions they experience in working to dismantle white supremacy while doing fieldwork with people who champion white racism.

5. See, for example, the reviews of anthropology in South Africa prior to 1994: R. J. Gordon and A. D. Spiegel, "Southern Africa Revisited," *Annual Review of*

Anthropology 22 (1993): 83–105; and Adam Kuper, *Among the Anthropologists: History and Context in Anthropology* (London: The Athlone Press, 1999).

6. See Fiona Ross's work on women's testimony before the TRC, *Bearing Witness: Women and the Truth and Reconciliation Commission in South Africa* (London: Pluto Press, 2003); and on an informal settlement's conversion to formal housing, *Houses without Doors: Diffusing Domesticity in Die Bos* (Pretoria: Human Sciences Research Council, 1995); Susan Levine's work as part of the STEPS documentary film project on HIV/AIDS in southern Africa (STEPS for the Future Impact Study, 2003) and her work on child labor on South African wine farms, "Bittersweet Harvest: Children, Work, and the Global March against Child Labour in the Post-Apartheid State," *Critique of Anthropology* 19, no. 2 (1999): 139–155; and Sally Frankental's work on the South African Jewish experience, "A Frontier Experience: Israeli Jews Encounter Diaspora in Cape Town, South Africa," in *Jewries at the Frontier*, ed. Sander L. Gilman and Milton Shain (Chicago: University of Illinois Press, 1999), 155–184.

7. Cris Shore, "Introduction: The Quality of Being There," in Watson, *Being There*, 27.

8. Studying a community to which one belongs and with which one is already intimately familiar presents a somewhat different set of challenges. For a review of anthropological reflections on doing anthropology at home, see Mariza G. S. Peirano, "When Anthropology Is at Home: The Different Contexts of a Single Discipline," *Annual Review of Anthropology* 27 (1998): 105–128. Other interesting reflections on being an anthropologist at home include Lila Abu-Lughod, "Writing against Culture," in *Recapturing Anthropology*, ed. Richard Fox (Santa Fe, NM: School of American Research Press, 1991); Kath Weston, "The Virtual Anthropologist," in *Anthropological Locations*, ed. Akhil Gupta and James Ferguson (Berkeley: University of California Press, 1997); and Micaela di Leonardo, *Exotics at Home* (Chicago: University of Chicago Press, 1998).

9. Signithia Fordham, *Blacked Out: Dilemmas of Race, Identity, and Success at Capital High* (Chicago: University of Chicago Press, 1996).

10. Clifford Geertz, "Deep Hanging Out," *New York Review of Books*, 22 October 1998, 69–72.

11. Adam Ashforth's superb *Witchcraft, Violence, and Democracy in South Africa* (Chicago: University of Chicago Press, 2005) offers a deeply sensitive, insightful account of Sowetans' experiences of spiritual insecurity provoked by post-apartheid transformation.

12. David Graeber, *Fragments of an Anarchist Anthropology* (Chicago: Prickly Paradigm Press, 2004), 12.

13. Carolyn Nordstrom, "Theory That Laughs and Cries" (presented at the American Anthropological Association meetings, Philadelphia, Pennsylvania, 4 December 1998); Ruth Behar, *The Vulnerable Observer: Anthropology That Breaks Your Heart* (Boston: Beacon Press, 1996).

CHAPTER 2. LEGACIES

1. Quoted from Mamphela Ramphele's "Response" to Neville Alexander, "Prospects for a Nonracial Future in South Africa," in *Beyond Racism*, ed.

Charles Hamilton, Lynn Huntley, Neville Alexander, Antonio Sérgio, Alfredo Guimarães, and Wilmot James (Boulder, CO, and London: Lynne Reinner Publishers, 2001), 505.

2. I listened to many conversations around dinner tables about District Six's significance for people who had attended high school in District Six and who had relatives displaced from District Six. District Six's history has received a lot of public attention because of its visibility, because of the fine efforts of the District Six Museum, and because it remained mostly uninhabited following its demolition. Most township tours begin at District Six, using it as the foundational story for understanding the creation of townships on the Cape Flats. But the conversations I heard were much more ambivalent about the foundational importance of District Six. One man who had been very involved with school protests in Athlone in the 1970s pointed this out to me: "We never even thought about District Six. It wasn't part of our experience. It's only now because they organized the museum and all the programs that we're thinking about it. But for us [his generation, living in Athlone], the struggle wasn't about that. It was racism, passes, education, equality, dehumanization. We knew District Six was being torn down, but it wasn't that important at the time." As for others of his generation who were protesting in their communities, the destruction of District Six was but one relatively minor component of the broader struggles against apartheid.

3. John Western, *Outcast Cape Town* (Berkeley: University of California Press, 1996). See also Vivian Bickford-Smith, *Ethnic Pride and Racial Prejudice in Victorian Cape Town: Group Identity and Social Practice, 1875–1902* (Cambridge: Cambridge University Press, 1995).

4. Grant Saff, *Changing Cape Town: Urban Dynamics, Policy, and Planning During the Political Transition in South Africa* (Lanham, MD: University Press of America, 1998), 86.

5. The Coloured Labor Preference Policy was implemented in the 1950s to protect the economic and social interests of the Western Cape's coloured population against the influx of Africans. In addition to mandating that employers could hire Africans only if the Department of Labor certified that coloured workers were not available for the job, the policy also set African labor quotas and attempted to implement controls on African property ownership. Richard Humphries, "Administrative Politics and the Coloured Labor Preference Policy during the 1960s," in *Class, Caste and Color: A Social and Economic History of the South African Western Cape,* ed. Wilmot G. James and Mary Simons (New Brunswick, NJ: Transaction Publishers, 1992).

6. G. P. Cook, "Cape Town," in *Homes Apart: South Africa's Segregated Cities,* ed. Anthony Lemon (Bloomington: Indiana University Press; Cape Town: David Phillip, 1991), 26–42. On the history of settlement in Crossroads, see also Western, *Outside Cape Town;* J. Cole, *Crossroads* (Johannesburg: Ravan Press, 1987); and Pamela Reynolds (with W. B. Eerdmans), *Childhood in Crossroads: Cognition and Society in South Africa* (Cape Town: David Philip, 1989).

7. Cook, "Cape Town." Cape Town's African population mushroomed with the repeal of the pass laws in 1986. A. Gilbert, A. Mabin, M. McCarthy, and V. Watson, "Low-Income Rental Housing: Are South Africa's Cities Different?" *Environment and Urbanization* 9, no. 1 (1997): 133–147.

8. Saff, *Changing Cape Town*.

9. Ibid.

10. Noting the lack of research on the urban rental market in South Africa, Gilbert et al. ("Low-Income Rental Housing") report that a 1993 survey of African townships in six major South African cities showed a majority of the population were renters, many renting backyard shacks or the space in which they had constructed a shack from their own materials. Gilbert et al.'s research in Guguletu suggests the rental market in backyard space developed more out of compassion than profit seeking on the part of landlords, who require very low rents: about twenty-one rand per month for space for a shack built by tenants (whose average per capita income was about R232 per month). The researchers attribute the poor quality of the backyard shacks to a number of factors, including poverty, split families, the reality of very low yields from property investment in black areas, and apartheid state policy, which "destroyed any possibility of self help consolidation" (p. 143) because of ongoing forced removals, discouragement of any black entrepreneurial activity, laws against black property ownership, and destruction of building and construction expertise through emphasis on ensuring that the black workforce remain unskilled.

11. Ivan Turok, "Persistent Polarisation Post-Apartheid? Progress towards Urban Integration in Cape Town," *Urban Studies* 38, no. 13 (2000): 2349–2377. The quotation is from p. 2371.

12. Unfortunately, the post-apartheid government has not been able to meet its promises for new housing for those packed into informal settlements. Although minimal services (communal water taps, bucket latrines, electricity) have been brought to many squatter communities, subsidized and low-income housing construction remains woefully inadequate. In 2004, the City of Cape Town acknowledged a housing backlog of 245,000 households, growing at an alarming rate of 16,000 new households a year. City of Cape Town's 2004 Draft Integrated Development Plan, http://www.capetown.gov.za/idp/IDP.pdf (accessed 18 June 2004). The report numbers Cape Town's informal settlements at seventy-one, housing 325,000 people.

13. The 1980s saw a very modest softening of racial zoning in Cape Town. Some black families purchased homes in white neighborhoods, using whites as nominees—a risky undertaking that depended on substantial trust and goodwill. Gray areas began emerging, and in 1988 new legislation allowed local authorities to zone nonracial residential areas. Landsdowne and the Wynberg/Ottery border were declared a free settlement zone in 1990, and the first nonracial civic association was created in the gray area of Rondebosch East. These areas were characterized by mixed white/coloured residents. When laws against black property ownership were repealed in the 1980s, few Africans could afford to buy township residences, much less move into more expensive neighborhoods. See Anthony Lemon, "The Apartheid City," and G. P. Cook, "Cape Town," in Lemon, *Homes Apart*. Some township residents have received title to the homes they occupy, but many continue to struggle to pay for now-privatized services, such as water, electricity, and telephone.

14. Sean Jacobs and Ron Krabill, "Mediating Manenberg in the Post-Apartheid Public Sphere: Media, Democracy, and Citizenship in South Africa,"

in *The Limits to Liberation after Apartheid: Citizenship, Governance, and Culture*, ed. Steven L. Robins (Oxford: James Currey; Athens: Ohio University Press; and Cape Town: David Philips, 2005), 161.

15. Clifford Shearing and Jennifer Wood, "Nodal Governance, Denizenship, and Communal Space: Changing the Westphalian Ideal," in Robins, *Limits to Liberation*, 97–112.

16. The phrase "traditional gatekeepers" is from Turok, "Persistent Polarisation," 2367.

17. Quotations are from the City of Cape Town's 2004 Draft Integrated Development Plan, 35, 49, http://www.capetown.gov.za/idp/IDP.pdf (accessed 18 June 2004). The plans to develop a safe node in Khayelitsha, home to half of Cape Town's unemployed residents according to city officials, are a hopeful indication, as is the development of the Klipfontein corridor, which includes a rapid bus line. A few studies of localized development initiatives in impoverished communities demonstrate the enormous tensions and communication difficulties among various role players in small-scale projects. See, for example, Steven Robins, "At the Limits of Spatial Governmentality: A Message from the Tip of Africa," *Third World Quarterly* 23, no. 4 (2002): 665–689; S. Oldfield, "Local State Restructuring and Urban Transformation in Post-apartheid Cape Town," *GeoJournal* 57 (2002): 39–47.

18. Turok, "Persistent Polarisation," 2373.

19. Although Salomie's home language is Afrikaans, she spoke in English during our interviews.

20. The South African Communist Party and the Congress of South African Trade Unions launched a campaign against redlining, but a bill to forbid redlining practices in the country's banking and financial institutions was pulled from consideration and is under further study.

21. Siyabonga's home language is Zulu. Our interviews were all in English.

22. Michael K. Brown, Martin Carnoy, Elliott Currie, Troy Duster, David B. Oppenheimer, Marjorie M. Shultz, and David Wellman, *White-Washing Race: The Myth of a Color-Blind Society* (Berkeley: University of California Press, 2003), 227, 228.

23. Jeremy Seekings, "Review Essay: Are South Africa's Cities Changing? Indications from the Mid-1990s," *International Journal of Urban and Regional Research* 27, no. 1 (2003): 197–202.

24. See *Sunday Times*, 28 April 2002, sundaytimes.co.za/2002/04/28/news/news13.asp (accessed 15 September 2004).

25. *Sunday Times*, 23 April 2000, sundaytimes.co.za/2000/04/23/news/cape/nct11/htm (accessed 15 September 2004).

26. These composite quotes are drawn from conversations I had with many white property owners and real estate agents in Rondebosch, Claremont, Newlands, and Constantia.

27. This land claims case has been resolved. Some of the claimants accepted compensation, and others have been granted rights to unoccupied land in the area from where they were evicted. The announcement can be viewed at http://www.capetown.gov.za/press/Newpress.asp?itemcode=1776 (accessed 16 June 2007).

28. "Claremont Is a Powder Keg!" *Southern Suburbs Tattler,* 11 July 2002; also 18 July 2002.

29. Saff, *Changing Cape Town.*

30. The District Six Museum has been indefatigable in its efforts to encourage public discussion and awareness about the impact of forced removals.

31. Ramphele, "Response," 506; quoted in Allister Sparks, *Beyond the Miracle: Inside the New South Africa* (Johannesburg: Jonathan Ball Publishers, 2003), 21.

32. Quoted in Sparks, *Beyond the Miracle,* 21.

33. Jane Hofmeyr, "The Emerging School Landscape in Post-Apartheid South Africa," (speech presented for the Independent Schools Association of South Africa, 30 March 2000), cited in Alan Morris, "A Decade of Post-Apartheid: Is the City in South Africa Being Remade?" *Safundi* 5, nos. 1–2 (2004).

34. Mamphele Ramphele, *Steering by the Stars: Being Young in South Africa* (Cape Town: Tafelberg, 2002), 92.

35. John Gilmour, personal communication, 16 June 2004.

36. Morris, "A Decade of Post-Apartheid," 6.

37. Of course, the "American dream" that anyone who is motivated and works hard can climb the ladder to economic success is as much a myth in the United States, as demonstrated in many studies. For example, Michael K. Brown et al., *White-Washing Race;* Karen Brodkin, *How Jews Became White Folks and What That Says about Race in America* (New Brunswick, NJ: Rutgers University Press, 1999); Kath Weston, "Class Politics and Scavenger Anthropology in Dinesh D'Souza's *Virtue of Prosperity,*" in *Why America's Top Pundits Are Wrong: Anthropologists Talk Back,* ed. Catherine Besteman and Hugh Gusterson (Berkeley: University of California Press, 2004), 154–179.

CHAPTER 3. IGNORANCE IS NOT BLISS

1. Some of the specific points raised by parents focused on their discomfort with standard white cultural practices at the schools—for example, the emphasis on selling tickets to downtown performances rather than food as fund-raisers, the constant complaints about falling standards and changing values, and the habitual talk about rugby at parents' functions.

2. Thanks to Fiona Ross for highlighting the significance of this label. These are particularly loaded accusations in South Africa's context of violence against those accused of being informants or "sellouts" and of historical tensions in families torn apart when family members were assigned different racial classifications.

3. Quoted in Bram Peeters, "The Lighter Side of Life in SA," *Cape Argus,* 3 October 2002, 13.

4. I attended several comedy venues, both professional and informal, in which the performer played with stereotypes and identity crossing: white men imitating Indian merchants having an argument about sex while tending their vegetable stalls, a coloured comedian role-playing the responses of the family of a coloured bride and the family of her white groom at the wedding reception, and

so on. On a few occasions, I asked members of the audience if they thought such performances might carry racist undertones. While most audience members I spoke with felt the performances were humorous commentaries on stereotyping, one woman, commenting on the skit of the Indian shopkeepers, acknowledged that while the performance might be "prejudicial," the audience laughter reflected the liberation of simply being able to watch and engage in such role-playing.

5. Hip-hop presents an interesting study of integration, because although the founders of hip-hop in Cape Town came from coloured communities, during the past decade, white youth have been drawn into hip-hop. Hip-hop venues are thus integrated, but the earlier founders maintain a critical commentary on white domination and racism and are critical of those perceived as selling out.

6. Formed by middle-class white women during apartheid, the Black Sash offered legal and other assistance to people charged with anti-apartheid crimes and attempted to shame the government by holding silent public protests while wearing black sashes as a symbol of mourning.

7. In its manual *Learning to Live Together,* the Institute for Justice and Reconciliation discusses how fears about crime and physical security reinforce racial prejudice, stereotypes, and segregation in South Africa. Fanie du Toit, ed., *Learning to Live Together: Practices of Social Reconciliation* (Rondebosch: Institute for Justice and Reconciliation, 2003).

8. I thought things would get a bit more interesting when the host of our meeting asked a student working in the next room to join the meeting for a moment. In the late 1990s this student had left an impoverished township home for nine months to travel to the United States on an independently organized visit. The student explained that returning to school in Cape Town was difficult after the time abroad because his schooling was disrupted, but that he managed to adapt to being home thanks to the support of his friends, teachers, and mentors. Ignoring the student's comments about his ability to adapt to being home, the man instead focused on how study abroad programs mustn't disrupt a student's schooling.

9. Another example: One day while browsing in a downtown art gallery I came across a stunning pastel, so I inquired about the artist. The white gallery owner responded vaguely that the artist was "from the township. He's been shot. It's been very hard." She mentioned that he lacked formal training and was just "emerging" as an artist.

"Which township is he from?" I asked.

"Oh, he moves around quite a bit among them. I really don't know. You know, we don't know the townships, you see, because of the system here for all those years. We never went there. Now we don't go there because of the danger. I'm not really even sure of what they're all called." Thinking perhaps she didn't want to reveal his location to ensure a commission for herself, I asked about another (white) artist whose work was on display, and she happily responded with information about him, where I could locate him, where else I could see his work. A few months later I came across another drawing by the first artist in the PanAfrican Market, and again I inquired about him.

"Oh, he's a good friend of mine!" responded the stall's owner. "He lives in Langa. Two years ago he exhibited at [another gallery across from the first gallery] and won first prize in their competition, which was a trip to exhibit in Germany." This information stunned me, because I couldn't believe that the white gallery owner wouldn't know about this artist's local and international profile.

Although it is perhaps unfair to guess, two possibilities strike me as explanations for the discrepancy in responses between the two gallery owners. One is that the former gallery owner was marketing the artist (to me, an American) as a "struggling township artist with no formal training who had been shot," a line that undoubtedly works with tourists and other consumers of art for whom such a description provides a kind of native authenticity. But I also wonder if she really did not know much about the artist and had a difficult time seeing beyond the "struggling untrained township artist" category herself. Could it be that not even the potential economic benefits of more aggressively and professionally marketing this "emerging" young artist could enable her to overcome her dismissive categorization of him as a township artist who had been shot?

10. One tour guide of color chuckled as he told me that his white South African clients will often feel comfortable challenging his description of life in District Six or contributing their own memories of District Six as a slum, but "they don't say a word in the townships."

11. Other than the few reconciliation nongovernmental organizations, schools, and media/arts venues that attempt to facilitate border-crossing, work environments and places of worship offer structured arenas with strong possibilities for ideological transformation and integration. Commenting on the extent to which white South Africans remain in denial about apartheid realities a decade after the advent of democracy, columnist Theresa Oakley-Smith suggests the workplace is the ideal arena to begin "addressing difference within a broader framework of history," because work is where most South Africans first "have the opportunity for same status contact with people of other races." Oakley-Smith argues that companies would benefit from such dialogue because "those workplaces where employees feel understood by and understand their colleagues are likely to be places where morale and motivation are high, places characterised by mutual respect where productivity and profitability are also high." Theresa Oakley-Smith, "Ten Years On, We're Still in Denial," Star, 14 May 2003, http://www.thestar.co.za/index.php?fArticleId=145225.

12. Allister Sparks, Beyond the Miracle: Inside the New South Africa (Johannesburg: Jonathan Ball Publishers, 2003), 96. The TRC held media hearings in September 1997, thus inviting public reflection on the ethical possibilities available to the media in a context of authoritarian domination and official misinformation. The Institute for Justice and Reconciliation's Second Reconciliation Barometer Survey reports that almost three-quarters of the survey's respondents would like the media to play "a more proactive role in furthering public dialogue" on things like nation-building and transformation, although significantly more blacks, coloureds, and Indians than whites made this assertion. Karin Lombard, "Opportunities and Obstacles: The State of Reconciliation: Report of the Second Round of the SA Reconciliation Barometer Survey (Rondebosch: Institute for Justice and Reconciliation, May 2004).

13. Among other things, the Institute for Justice and Reconciliation conducts biannual surveys of about 3,500 South Africans on racial attitudes and regularly

publishes commentaries and analyses on racial reconciliation. The institute's very useful publications, several of which I cite in this book, can be accessed on its website at http://www.ijr.org.za.

14. Undine Kayser, "Imagined Communities, Divided Realities—Engaging the Apartheid Past through 'Healing of Memories' in post-TRC South Africa" (PhD diss., University of Cape Town, 2005). Thanks also to Fiona Ross for emphasizing the importance of the imagination.

15. See Beverly Daniel Tatum, *"Why Are All the Black Kids Sitting Together in the Cafeteria?" and Other Conversations about Race* (New York: Basic Books, 1997), which explores efforts at integration in U.S. schools.

16. Personal communication from the counselor, June 2004.

17. Sandile Dikeni, *Soul Fire: Writing the Transition* (Pietermaritzburg: University of Natal Press, 2002), 221.

18. Linda Chisholm, "The State of Schools," in *State of the Nation: South Africa, 2004–2005,* ed. John Daniel, Roger Southall, and Jessica Lutchman (Cape Town: Human Sciences Research Council, 2005), 220–221.

19. I am grateful to Anne for allowing me to write about the art she shared with me.

20. None of the township schools with which I had contact offered art instruction or art programs. All of the formerly white schools where I interviewed offered robust art programs. The private art school Frank Joubert does offer an outreach program to township teachers and children, but because the need is so great and resources slim, participating township teachers and children receive only a few hours of art instruction over the course of a year.

21. Craig Fraser, *Shack Chic: Innovation in the Shack-Lands of South Africa* (Cape Town: Quivertree Publications, 2002). Thanks to Susan Levine for making this connection.

CHAPTER 4. FIELDWORK DISCOMFORTS

1. In these situations, I generally tried to find a middle road that allowed me to stick to my principles while also recognizing and adhering to local cultural mores. I generally did not talk to men alone, I usually sat and ate with the women at feasts after a short visit with the men's group, I sometimes prepared coffee for the demanding neighbor and sometimes adopted local women's humor to send him packing. I also used humor and feigned exaggerated jealousy in response to suggestions of a second wife, and I kept my mouth closed and listened to the government official's speeches. But my responses deferred to locally recognized appropriate gender roles: my husband also confronted the neighbor and told him to stop demanding coffee, and he was the one who intervened in cases of domestic abuse. My experiences in Somalia and in South Africa are not comparable, however: defending my principles as a woman in a patriarchal context bore little resemblance to being white in a context of historical white domination.

2. Anthropologists are moving away from this expectation, as evidenced by the superb ethnographies written by anthropologists who did not live in the communities about which they have written.

3. Gay Seidman, "Is South Africa Different? Sociological Comparisons and Theoretical Contributions from the Land of Apartheid," *Annual Review of Sociology,* 1999: 433–434.

4. Ran Greenstein, "Identity, Race, History: South Africa and the Pan-African Context," in *Comparative Perspectives on South Africa,* ed. Ran Greenstein (London: Macmillan, 1998), 12.

5. 24 July 2002.

6. MK stands for Umkhonto We Sizwe ("Spear of the Nation"), founded following the Sharpeville massacre in 1960 as the military wing of the African National Congress.

7. See chapter 2, note 37.

8. Douglas Massey and Nancy Denton, *American Apartheid: Segregation and the Making of the Underclass* (Cambridge, MA: Harvard University Press, 1993), 63; cited in Michael K. Brown, Martin Carnoy, Elliott Currie, Troy Duster, David B. Oppenheimer, Marjorie M. Shultz, and David Wellman, *WhiteWashing Race: The Myth of a Color-Blind Society* (Berkeley: University of California Press, 2003), 42. See also Gary Younge, "A Promise Not Kept," *Guardian* (Manchester), 15 May 2004.

9. By all accounts Cape Town has a high crime rate, despite the government's recent efforts to direct more resources into policing. At the conclusion of 2003, the Institute for Security Studies reported that the Western Cape had the highest rate of murder, property crimes, assault, and common robbery in the country. Ted Leggett, "What's Up in the Cape? Crime Rates in Western and Northern Cape Provinces," *Crime Quarterly* 7 (2004), http://www.iss.co.za/pubs/CrimeQ/No.7/Leggett1.htm (accessed 16 June 2007). Leggett suggests the Western Cape's high crime rate may be linked to its high level of reported possession of illegal firearms, high levels of substance abuse, and the particular socioeconomic circumstances of the coloured Cape Flats population. Crime disproportionately affects coloured Capetonians, followed by Africans and then whites.

A number of informative studies trace the history of crime and gang activity in Cape Town, including the recent corporatization of gang activity and links between urban gangs and international syndicates. Don Pinnock, *The Brotherhoods: Street Gangs and State Control in Cape Town* (Cape Town: David Philip, 1984); Don Pinnock, *Ganging as Rites of Passage* (Cape Town: David Philips, 1995); Gary Kynock, "From the Ninevites to the Hard Livings Gang: Township Gangsters and Urban Violence in Twentieth-Century South Africa," *African Studies* 58, no. 1 (1999): 55–85; Steffen Jensen, "Of Drug Dealers and Street Gangs: Power, Mobility, and Violence on the Cape Flats" *Focaa* 36 (2000): 105–116. See also Jonny Steinberg, ed., *Crime Wave: The South African Underworld and Its Foes* (Johannesburg: Witwatersrand University Press, 2001); Mark Shaw and Peter Gastrow, "Stealing the Show? Crime and Its Impact in Post-Apartheid South Africa," *Daedalus* 130, no. 1 (2001): 235–258; and the quarterly reports by the Institute for Security Studies in its publication *South African Crime Quarterly.*

10. Philippe Bourgois writes of his rage at the violence perpetrated by the crack dealers he studied and at the self-destructive behaviors of his crack-addicted neighbors in Spanish Harlem. His moving accounts of field research describe how

he navigated between anger at those he studied and empathetic analysis of the structures of systemic racism and exclusion that saturate his interlocutors' lives. Philippe Bourgois, "Confronting Anthropology, Education, and Inner-City Apartheid," *American Anthropologist* 98, no. 2 (1996): 249–258.

11. The recent genocidal murders of millions of minority and indigenous peoples in Rwanda, Sudan, Somalia, and Guatemala demonstrate the appalling result of violent racism and subjugation. See Philip Gourevitch, *We Wish to Inform You That Tomorrow We Will Be Killed with Our Families* (New York: Farrar, Straus and Giroux, 1998); Alison des Forges, *"Leave None to Tell the Story": Genocide in Rwanda* (Paris: Human Rights Watch/International Federation of Human Rights, 1999); Beatriz Manz, *Paradise in Ashes: A Guatemalan Journey of Courage, Terror, and Hope* (Berkeley: University of California Press, 2004); Catherine Besteman, *Unraveling Somalia: Race, Violence, and the Legacy of Slavery* (Philadelphia: University of Pennsylvania Press, 1999).

CHAPTER 5. STILL WAITING

The title of this chapter refers to Vincent Crapanzano's book *Waiting: The Whites of South Africa* (New York: Random House, 1985).

1. Karin Lombard, "Can White South Africans Rise to the Challenges of Economic Compromise?" *Cape Times,* 2 April 2003.

2. Meredith and Susan are of English background. Johanna and Ilze are of Afrikaner background. Although my research does not include the northern suburbs and thus does not capture the views of Afrikaner residents in those neighborhoods, my interviews and conversations did include about a dozen unrelated people from Afrikaner backgrounds whose decision to settle in the southern suburbs reflects their discomfort with stereotypical Afrikaner worldviews. For example, one man moved to Cape Town from another city about five years ago but has not even informed his family members in the northern suburbs of his relocation because he can no longer tolerate their racism. In the quotations that follow, I usually indicate whether the speaker is of Afrikaner background, although I wish to avoid the suggestion that Afrikaner and English attitudes about race and status are predictably distinct.

3. The English southern suburbs provided a major base of support for the opposition party in Parliament during the apartheid years. Opposition to the National Party, however, did not translate into support for the ANC or other anti-apartheid activist or political groups. After 1994, the southern suburbs remained the major base of support for the post-apartheid opposition party, the Democratic Alliance.

4. See Mahmood Mamdani, *Citizen and Subject: Contemporary Africa and the Legacy of Late Colonialism* (Princeton, NJ: Princeton University Press, 1996); Vivian Bickford-Smith, *Ethnic Pride and Racial Prejudice in Victorian Cape Town: Group Identity and Social Practice, 1875–1902* (Cambridge: Cambridge University Press, 1995); Paul Maylam, *South Africa's Racial Past: The History and Historiography of Racism, Segregation, and Apartheid* (Aldershot, UK: Ashgate, 2001).

5. Anthony Marx, *Making Race and Nation: A Comparison of the United States, South Africa, and Brazil* (Cambridge: Cambridge University Press, 1998). Courtney Jung similarly argues that by the 1980s, the National Party government had overcome the Afrikaner-English divide that characterized politics in the 1940s through the 1960s by emphasizing how much whites collectively had to lose if apartheid ended. Courtney Jung, *When I Was Black: South African Political Identities in Transition* (New Haven, CT: Yale University Press, 2000). Other sources on the consolidation of "white" as a political and cultural category include Hermann Giliomee, *The Afrikaners* (London: Hurst and Co., 2003); S. Marks and S. Trapido, eds., *The Politics of Race, Class, and Nationalism in Twentieth Century South Africa* (London: Longman, 1987); Robert Ross, *Status and Respectability in the Cape Colony, 1750–1870* (Cambridge: Cambridge University Press, 1999); George M. Fredrickson, *White Supremacy: A Comparative Study in American and South African History* (New York: Oxford University Press, 1981); Deborah Posel, *The Making of Apartheid, 1948–1961* (Oxford: Oxford University Press, 1997); Saul Dubow, "Colonial Nationalism, the Milner Kindergarten and the Rise of 'South Africanism,' 1902–1910," *History Workshop Journal* 43 (1997).

6. I heard several stories from white people that attest to the tensions inherent to this construction. One woman, for example, spoke of her resentment about her English in-laws' condescension toward her because of her Mediterranean ancestry (a condescension, she noted, that extended to Afrikaners as well). On another occasion, I witnessed an interesting exchange at a local nature preserve, when one of the white visitors asked another white visitor about her background. She responded that she was from Durban. The questioner persisted, asking for further details, suggesting there was something "interesting" about her face. She replied that she had been educated at Stellenbosch and then moved to Cape Town, where she had educated her children at southern suburbs boys' schools. He continued to persist until she finally told him that her ancestry was Lebanese. "I thought so," he concluded, finally satisfied.

7. Anthony Marx, "Apartheid's End: South Africa's Transition from Racial Domination," *Ethnic and Racial Studies* 20, no. 3 (1997): 474–496; the quotation is on p. 489. Mohamed Adhikari notes that coloureds who had assimilationist aspirations and fully bought in to liberal values of success based on individual merit "were shocked at the generous peace granted to the vanquished Boers and the continued disfranchisement of blacks in the former Boer republics." Mohamed Adhikari, "Coloured Identity and the Politics of Coloured Education: The Origin of the Teachers' League of South Africa,." *International Journal of African Historical Studies* 27, no. 1 (1994): 113.

8. A 2004 opinion piece in the *Mail and Guardian* notes "an ongoing belief among white South Africans that whiteness is beyond scrutiny" (5 April 2004). Some thoughtful research is appearing on whiteness in South Africa, promising a growing attention to constructions of whiteness and white privilege. See, for example, Melissa Steyn, *"Whiteness Just Isn't What It Used to Be": White Identity in a Changing South Africa* (Albany, NY: SUNY Press, 2001); Gerhard Schutte, *What Racists Believe: Race Relations in South Africa and the United States* (Thousand Oaks, CA: Sage, 1995); Deborah Posel, "Whiteness and Power

in the South African Civil Service: Paradoxes of the Apartheid State," *Journal of Southern African Studies* 25, no. 1 (1999): 99–119. On post-apartheid Afrikaner identity, see June Goodwin and Ben Schiff, *Heart of Whiteness: Afrikaners Face Black Rule in the New South Africa* (New York: Scribner, 1995); Antjie Krog, *County of My Skull* (Johannesburg: Random House, 1998); Mads Vesergaard, "Who's Got the Map? The Negotiation of Afrikaner Identities in Post-Apartheid South Africa," *Daedalus* 130, no. 1 (2001): 19–44. Artists have been much more precocious than academics in interrogating whiteness.

9. A few white people I spoke with mentioned how, through the Truth and Reconciliation Commission (TRC), they learned for the first time of the abuses conducted in their name by their government. While revelatory for some, most white people I spoke with felt the TRC had been useful but that it was allowed to go "too far" and had become damaging to reconciliation. "There have got to be limits" and "it's time to move on" characterized responses to questions about the importance of the TRC in their lives.

10. Robert Ross notes an early concern with such standards in his research on status and respectability in nineteenth-century Cape Town: "According to Sir Langham Dale, the Superintendent-General of Education in the Colony, the high quality schooling provided for instance by the South African College School in Cape Town was designed 'to keep the children of the higher and middle classes up to the standard of their peers in Europe,' thus ensuring their 'unquestionable superiority and supremacy in this land.'" Ross, *Status and Respectability,* 92; embedded quotation from Sir Langham Dale, "The Cape and Its People," in *The Cape and Its People,* ed. R. Noble (Cape Town: J. C. Juta, 1989), cited in Edna Bradlow, "Children and Childhood at the Cape in the 19th Century," *Kleio* 20 (1988): 14.

11. Sandile Dikeni, *Soul Fire: Writing the Transition* (Pietermaritzburg: University of Natal Press, 2002), 72.

12. In recent years the campaign slogan for the Democratic Alliance party has been "Take Back Your City," which many read as anti-African and directed at white and coloured voters who fear that Cape Town is being taken over.

13. The Institute for Justice and Reconciliation's 2003–2004 South African Reconciliation Barometer indicates that only 16 percent of whites interviewed nationally say they would approve of mixed marriages within their family. Karin Lombard, "Schools Offer Best Hope for Integration," *Sunday Independent,* 7 November 2004.

14. Allister Sparks, *Beyond the Miracle: Inside the New South Africa* (Johannesburg: Jonathan Ball Publishers, 2003), 6–7.

15. Later, she likened "the underprivileged blacks" to a dog that has been abused: "You put out your hand and it will bite you. It needs to learn that you are friendly."

16. Letter to the editor, *Cape Argus,* 3 August 2002, 14. Note the reference to "your government."

17. Bryan Rostron, "Heart of Whiteness," *Mail and Guardian,* 22 December–4 January 2001, 30.

18. My interlocutors are confusing retrenchment because of the contraction of the economy with job loss because of employment equity initiatives. Although

it is against the law to fire a white person in the name of employment equity, whites find it much easier to blame white retrenchment on black employment initiatives than on the local economic effects of globalization. See, for example, P. A. K. Le Roux, "Affirmative Action and the Individual Employee," *Contemporary Labour Law* 9, no. 4 (1999): 31–38. I am grateful to the labor lawyer Jose Jorge for advice and information about the effects of South Africa's new labor laws.

19. Karin Lombard, "Why Do SA Whites Fear the Future?" *Cape Times,* 7 July 2004.

20. June 2001.

21. The occupation of white-owned farms by war veterans in Zimbabwe was dominating the news in South Africa. President Mbeki refused to bow to pressure from white South Africans and from the opposition party to publicly denounce Mugabe's handling of the situation and his increasingly authoritarian practices, opting instead for diplomacy and negotiation. Challenging Mbeki's stance, the Democratic Alliance made the plight of white farmers in Zimbabwe a central issue. Commenting on the DA's obsession with Zimbabwe, a white acquaintance reported that Trevor Manuel observed in a private meeting that more people are killed in Manenberg (an apartheid-created Cape Flats community now characterized by poverty and gang violence) every month than all the white farmers killed in Zimbabwe.

22. I am grateful to John Gilmour for arranging this visit to Parliament, courtesy of Sue van der Merwe, now deputy minister of foreign affairs.

23. The Home for All Campaign was started as a mechanism for white people to overcome their guilt about apartheid in a contributive, practical way. The campaign offered an opportunity for white people to sign a statement apologizing for their complicity in apartheid and acknowledging that apartheid unfairly benefited them, and it created a forum in which white people could offer their skills to those desiring training and assistance. A few years after its creation it was renamed the Home to All Campaign.

24. The May 2004 report of South Africa's Alcohol and Drug Abuse Research Group confirms this perception: "There has been a large increase in treatment demand for heroin as a primary drug of abuse in Cape Town" (p. 1). The report also notes a substantial increase in heroin use by females, by lower socioeconomic populations, and in the proportion of heroin patients who are coloured. South African Community Epidemiology Network on Drug Use (SACENDU), *Update,* 20 May 2004 (Cape Town: Alcohol and Drub Abuse Research Group, Medical Research Council), http://www.sahealthinfo.org/admodule/sacendumay2004.pdf (accessed 24 May 2004).

25. Dikeni, *Soul Fire,* 65.

26. For example, I heard a rumor about one company that avoided having to hire people of color by instead laying off white employees to meet the desired affirmative action ratio. A South African rugby official told me that under the early affirmative action language that supported the hiring of people from "previously disadvantaged groups," South African rugby clubs avoided having to recruit men of color by defining working-class white men as "previously disadvantaged."

27. Ivan Booth, *Reasons to Stay,* (Cape Town: Interactive Africa, 2002); Brett Bowes and Steuart Pennington, eds., *South Africa: The Good News* (n.p.: Bowes and Steuart, 2002); and Bowes and Steuart, *South Africa: More Good News* (n.p.: Bowes and Steuart, 2003); "The Boomerang Brigade," *Fairlady,* 14 March 2001, 41–42; the Proudly South African campaign Web site is http://www.proudlysa.co.za/; the Positively South African Web site is http://www.positivelysa.co.za/index03.asp. Christopher Colvin offers a similar list of publicity materials that promote a positive image of South Africa. Colvin, "Introduction: Contingency and Creativity: South Africa after Apartheid," *Anthropology and Humanism* 28, no. 1 (2003): 3–7.

28. Mondli Makhanya, "Whites Must Come on Board," *Sunday Times,* 5 September 2004.

29. Thabisi Hoeane, "Closing the Race Debate No Way to Resolve Tensions," *Sunday Independent,* 7 November 2004.

30. The quotation is taken from my notes of Uys's show at the Baxter Theatre on 30 May 2001.

31. The trauma suffered by white commandos who committed atrocities on behalf of the apartheid government is discussed in nonfiction: see the chapter on Paul Erasmus in David Goodman, *Fault Lines: Journeys into the New South Africa,* (Berkeley: University of California Press, 1999). In fiction, see Mark Behr, *The Smell of Apples* (London: Abacus Press, 1996). For news articles about support groups for white veterans, see, for example, Lynda Gilfillan, "War Vets Doing It for Themselves," *Mail and Guardian,* 16–22 May 2001.

32. 24 May 2001.

33. Similarly, economist Sampie Terreblanche writes: "Many whites (especially younger people) are inclined to say that they themselves did nothing wrong, and can therefore not be blamed for the effects of white domination and apartheid. However, they clearly do not understand the systemic character of colonialism, segregation, and apartheid, and their collective responsibility for what has happened. Those who are not prepared to acknowledge the evils of white domination and accept responsibility for apartheid's residues, are usually adamant that the large-scale 'benefits' (broadly defined) that accumulated in their hands and in those of their parents and grandparents during the extended period of colonialism belong to them and them alone. But what these whites fail to realize is that these 'benefits' are 'contaminated,' because they were largely accumulated by means of systemic exploitation. It is rather hypocritical of whites to claim these benefits with greedy self-righteousness but decline any responsibility (directly or indirectly) for the evil of colonialism and its ugly consequences." Sampie Terreblanche, *A History of Inequality in South Africa, 1652–2002* (Scottsville, South Africa: University of Natal Press, 2002), 5. Terreblanche argues that ANC policies and the process of the Truth and Reconciliation Commission have allowed white people to continue to believe in the myth that they owe nothing to the poor.

34. 12 August 2002.

35. From *Hottentot,* the name given to the local Khoikhoi population by Dutch settlers. The term is derogatory.

36. Fanie du Toit, "Proud to Be White, Free to Be African," *Cape Argus,* 9 July 2001.

37. Lisa mentioned that there is an unforgivability of blackness too, although she wouldn't presume to define it. "But in terms of history, it is there."

CHAPTER 6. DODGING BULLETS

The chapter title alludes to the "one settler, one bullet" slogan adopted by the Pan-Africanist Congress as an anti-white expression of black solidarity.

1. Noel Ignatiev, "The Point Is Not to Interpret Whiteness but to Abolish it," presented at the conference "The Making and Unmaking of Whiteness," University of California, Berkeley, 11–13 April 1997.

2. Michael K. Brown, Martin Carnoy, Elliott Currie, Troy Duster, David B. Oppenheimer, Marjorie M. Shultz, and David Wellman, *White-Washing Race: The Myth of a Color-Blind Society* (Berkeley: University of California Press, 2003).

3. Vron Ware and Les Back, *Out of Whiteness: Color, Politics, and Culture* (Chicago: University of Chicago Press, 2002), 7, 8.

4. Richard Dyer, *White* (London: Routledge, 1997), 4.

5. George Lipsitz and Peggy Macintosh were among the earliest writers to gain widespread recognition for listing specific cultural and material benefits of whiteness. Ruth Frankenberg is often cited as one of earliest writers on white invisibility. George Lipsitz, *The Possessive Investment in Whiteness: How White People Profit from Identity Politics* (Philadelphia: Temple University Press, 1998); Peggy Macintosh, "White Privilege and Male Privilege: A Personal Account of Coming to See Correspondences through Work in Women's Studies" (Wellesley College Center for Research on Women Working Paper 189, 1988); Ruth Frankenberg, *White Women, Race Matters: The Social Construction of Whiteness* (Minneapolis: University of Minnesota Press, 1993).

6. Melissa Steyn, "White Identity in Context: A Personal Narrative," in *Whiteness: The Communication of Social Identity*, ed. Thomas Nakayama and Judith Martin (Thousand Oaks, CA: Sage, 1999), 265.

7. Gayatri Spivak, *The Post-Colonial Critic: Interviews, Strategies, Dialogues* (New York: Routledge, 1990); quoted in bell hooks, *Black Looks: Race and Representation* (Boston: South End Press, 1992), 177.

8. Philippe Bourgois, "Confronting Anthropology, Education, and Inner-City Apartheid," *American Anthropologist* 98, no. 2 (1996): 249–258.

9. Brett Williams, "Poverty among African Americans in the Urban United States," *Human Organization* 51, no. 2 (1992): 164–174.

10. Reflecting on the impact of her work in Langa's hostels as an engaged researcher, the anthropologist Mamphela Ramphele writes about the symbolic importance of taking an interest in the lives of those treated dismissively and inhumanely by their government and their employers. She also notes that her questions on coping mechanisms provided an opportunity for her interlocutors to critically reflect on their circumstances and to evaluate their actions, a philosophical undertaking sometimes overlooked when people are struggling to make ends meet. Mamphela Ramphele, *A Bed Called Home: Life in the Migrant Labor Hostels of Cape Town* (Cape Town: David Philip; Athens, OH: Ohio University Press; Edinburgh: Edinburgh University Press, 1993).

11. See, for example, Lila Abu-Lughod, *Veiled Sentiments: Honor and Poetry in a Bedouin Society* (Berkeley: University of California Press, 2000); and Ernestine McHugh, *Love and Honor in the Himalayas: Coming to Know Another Culture* (Philadelphia: University of Pennsylvania Press, 2001).

12. See, for example, Jean Briggs, *Never in Anger: Portrait of an Eskimo Family* (Cambridge, MA: Harvard University Press, 1970); and Paul Stoller, *In Sorcery's Shadow: A Memoir of Apprenticeship among the Songhay of Niger* (Chicago: University of Chicago Press, 1989).

13. Nancy Scheper-Hughes, *Death without Weeping: The Violence of Everyday Life in Brazil* (Berkeley: University of California Press, 1992).

14. Bryan Rostron, "Heart of Whiteness," *Mail and Guardian,* 22 December–4 January 2001, 30.

15. Respectively, violence peaked post-Soweto 1976, during the 1986 state of emergency, and in 1992, as the peace talks were under way; the state's use of torture escalated during 1984–88; African males between thirteen and twenty-four tended to be the most frequent victims of violence; the Inkatha Freedom Party perpetrated the most killings; and the South African police perpetrated the most torture. Richard Wilson, *The Politics of Truth and Reconciliation in South Africa: Legitimizing the Post-Apartheid State* (Cambridge: Cambridge University Press, 2001), 58.

16. Given the problematic tendency in anthropology to make individuals into collective constructs, Vered Amit and Nigel Rappaport observe that "an anthropological appreciation might be reached of sociocultural milieux as encompassing and composed of individual difference, indeed, in a significant way constituted by it: by self-conscious individuals making an ongoing diversity of meaningful worlds through which they continue to move." Amit and Rappaport, *The Trouble with Community: Anthropological Reflections on Movement, Identity, and Collectivity* (London: Pluto Press, 2002), 138.

17. Nancy Scheper-Hughes, "In a Divided Nation within a Divided World, Never Has an Anthropology Degree Been as Valuable or as Needed" (commencement address to graduating anthropology students, University of California, Berkeley, 3 June 2005), http://www.berkeley.edu/news/media/releases/2005/06/03_hughes.shtml (accessed 17 June 2007).

CHAPTER 7. IDENTITY ISSUES

Epigraph: Mamphela Ramphele, "Response" to Neville Alexander, "Prospects for a Nonracial Future in South Africa," in *Beyond Racism,* ed. Charles Hamilton, Lynn Huntley, Neville Alexander, Antonio Sérgio, Alfredo Guimarães, and Wilmot James (Boulder, CO, and London: Lynne Reinner Publishers, 2001), 506.

1. Nick Shepherd and Kathryn Mathers, "Who's Watching *Big Brother?* Reality Television and Cultural Power in South Africa," *Africa e Mediterraneo* 38 (2002): 67–69.

2. A 2005 news article promoting the community-building and transformative goals of the 2005 Cape Town Festival observed that visitors to Cape Town from elsewhere in Africa always ask, "Where are the black people?" Iain Harris

quotes festival director Yusuf Ganief: "Cape Town is far behind the rest of the country in terms of transformation. And arts and culture is surely the key to unlocking transformation in Cape Town. It's the one commodity that can interact with every sphere of life and bring them together." Iain Harris, "Party for Change," *Mail and Guardian*, 11 March 2005.

3. As we will see, a very different dynamic operates outside such white-dominated settings, where acting white has a negative currency.

4. Elaine Salo's research on young people's media consumption in Manenberg addresses this point. See Salo, "Negotiating Gender and Personhood in the New South Africa: Adolescent Women and Gangsters in Manenberg Township on the Cape Flats," in *Limits to Liberation after Apartheid: Citizenship, Governance, and Culture*, ed. Steven L. Robins (Oxford: James Currey; Athens: Ohio University Press; Cape Town: David Philip, 2005), 173–184.

5. 28 December 2003.

6. 2 May 2001.

7. See Cheryl Hendricks, "The Burdens of the Past and Challenges of the Present: Coloured Identity and the 'Rainbow Nation,' " in *Ethnicity and Democracy in Africa*, ed. Bruce Berman, Dickson Eyoh, and Will Kymlicka (Oxford: James Currey, 2004), 113–128; Robert Ross, *Status and Respectability in the Cape Colony, 1750–1870: A Tragedy of Manners* (Cambridge: Cambridge University Press, 1999); Vivian Bickford-Smith, *Ethnic Pride and Racial Prejudice in Victorian Cape Town: Group Identity and Social Practice, 1875–1902*, (Cambridge: Cambridge University Press, 1995); Denis-Constant Martin, "The Burden of the Name: Classifications and Constructions of Identity: The Case of the 'Coloureds' in Cape Town (South Africa)," *African Philosophy* 13, no. 2 (2000): 99–124.

8. Bickford-Smith, *Ethnic Pride*, 39. Hendricks agrees, noting that by 1948, "coloured identity was already an embedded identity." Hendricks, "Burdens of the Past," 117. Denis-Constant Martin writes of a pre-1948 coloured working-class culture that was celebrated by Cape Town's political and intellectual elites. Denis-Constant Martin, "What's in the Name, 'Coloured'?" in *Social Identities in the New South Africa: After Apartheid*, vol. 1, ed. Abebe Zegeye (Roggebaai, South Africa: Kwela Books, 2001), 249–267.

9. See Martin, "What's in the Name?". Shamil Jeppie cites a 1925 speech by D. F. Malan at the first Cape Malay Association meeting, where he elaborated on the shared histories of whites and Malays, noting their equal and shared civilized status and jointly created language. Jeppie, "Re-Classification: Coloured, Malay, Muslim," in *Coloured by History, Shaped by Place: New Perspectives on Coloured Identities in Cape Town*, ed. Zimitri Erasmus (Cape Town: Kwela Books, 2001), 80–96.

10. Bickford-Smith, *Ethnic Pride*, 186.

11. Mohamed Adhikari, "Coloured Identity and the Politics of Coloured Education: The Origin of the Teachers' League of South Africa," *International Journal of African Historical Studies* 27, no. 1 (1994): 101–126; quotation from page 106.

12. Martin, "What's in the Name?" 253.

13. John Western, *Outcast Cape Town* (Berkeley: University of California Press, 1996).

14. Some well-known portraits of the tensions and traumas of negotiating the color line in the United States include Nella Larsen's novellas, *Quicksand* (1928) and *Passing* (1929); Nella Larsen, *"Quicksand" and "Passing,"* ed. Deborah E. McDowell (New Brunswick, NJ: Rutgers University Press, 1986); and the essays in the section "Children Passing in the Streets: The Roots of Our Radicalism," in *This Bridge Called My Back: Writings by Radical Women of Color,* 3rd ed., ed. Cherríe L Moraga and Gloria E. Anzaldúa (Berkeley, CA: Third Woman Press, 2001).

15. Sean Field, "Fragile Identities: Memory, Emotion, and Coloured Residents of Windermere," in Erasmus, *Coloured by History,* 107.

16. The fluorescence of Black Consciousness in the 1970s offered a strong and effective challenge to white cultural supremacy in the context of the anti-apartheid struggle. However, Black Consciousness ideology had a much greater impact among coloured elites and intellectuals than among the coloured working class.

17. Don Pinnock, "Ideology and Urban Planning: Blueprints of a Garrison City," in James and Simons, *Class, Caste and Color,* 168. See also Western, *Outcast Cape Town;* and Charmaine McEachern, "Mapping the Memories: Politics, Place, and Identity in the District Six Museum, Cape Town," in *Social Identities in the New South Africa: After Apartheid,* vol. 1, ed. Abebe Zegege (Roggebaai, South Africa: Kumela Books, 2001).

18. Vivian Bickford-Smith, Elizabeth van Heynbingen, and Nigel Worden, *Cape Town in the Twentieth Century: An Illustrated Social History* (Cape Town: David Philip, 1999); Colin Bundy, " 'Action, Comrades, Action!' The Politics of Youth—Student Resistance in the Western Cape, 1985," in James and Simons, *Class, Caste and Color,* 206–217. Frank Chikane writes, "The passivity of parents was seen by their offspring as resulting from experience in the 1960s of the oppression of the system. The 1960 declaration of the State of Emergency, the banning of the African National Congress and the Pan African Congress, detentions, torture, and long-term imprisonment all contributed to this state of affairs. In short, because of the repressive nature of the apartheid regime in the early sixties, the children saw the black masses as almost completely silenced and made to live in fear for almost two decades." Chikane, "Children in Turmoil: The Effects of Unrest on Township Children," in *Growing Up in a Divided Society: The Contexts of Childhood in South Africa,* ed. Sandra Burman and Pamela Reynolds, (Johannesburg: Ravan Press, 1986), 340.

19. Jeremy Seekings, *A History of the United Democratic Front in South Africa, 1983–1991* (Cape Town: David Philip; Oxford: James Currey; and Athens: Ohio University Press, 2000); see also Humphries, "Administrative Politics," 169–179. Hendricks also mentions that while coloured intellectuals were drawn to Black Consciousness ideology, the majority of coloureds were rather drawn to the potential benefits of the Coloured Labor Preference Policy. Hendricks, "Burdens of the Past."

20. Bundy, " 'Action, Comrades, Action!' " 210.

21. See also Hendricks, "Burdens of the Past," on this point.

22. Some commentators suggest that coloured voters are exercising their

right to make the new National Party responsive to them, as the majority. See William Finnegan, *Crossing the Line: A Year in the Land of Apartheid* (New York: Persea Books, 1994); and Nancy Scheper-Hughes, "Mixed Feelings: The Recovery of Spoiled Identities in the New South Africa," (presented at the Conference on Identity: Personal, Cultural, National, Chinese University of Hong Kong, National Humanities Center, 2–4 June 1994), http://www.nhc.rtp.nc.us/publications/hongkong/scheper.htm.

23. Erasmus, *Coloured by History*, 24.

24. Hendricks notes, "Coloured identity, as an internally culturally fragmented and racialized identity, has always been perceived as lacking cultural validity and the very existence of the group, *qua group*, has been challenged." Hendricks, "Burdens of the Past," 125.

25. Erasmus, *Coloured by History*, 16.

26. Deborah A. Miranda and Analousie Keating, "Footnoting Heresy: Email Dialogues," in *This Bridge We Call Home: Radical Visions for Transformation*, 3rd ed., ed. Gloria E. Anzaldúa and Analouise Keating (Berkeley, CA: Third Woman Press, 2001), 207.

27. "La Conciencia de la Mestiza: Towards a New Consciousness," in *Making Face, Making Soul: Haciendo Caras: Creative and Critical Perspectives by Feminists of Color*, ed. Gloria Anzaldúa (San Francisco: Ann Lute Books, 1990), 379.

28. Shannon Jackson writes: "The civilizing mission of urban planners and administrators has taken hold amongst generations of Coloureds who embrace, on many levels, the European/Western model of nuclear family, private home, and respectable lifestyle. But organized resistance has also occurred, particularly by labor unions establishing affiliation with communists and Black nationalists. . . . The tensions between the two positions, accommodation on the one hand, resistance on the other, continue to shape the terms and symbols of identification being involved in the effort to reinscribe this territory. These tensions also set up ambivalent relationships to both white and black African identity/culture where some claim 'we are black and not so-called or even separately defined Coloured' while others or the same individuals under different circumstances will claim 'we are a separate group, Coloured, and proud of it.'"

The process of reclaiming District Six offers an opportunity to transcend this division, Jackson notes, because it can allow for memories of fluidity, hybridity, and social cohesion without also requiring ethnic coherence. Jackson makes the point that it is Coloureds, not Africans, Indians, or whites, who are claiming the urban center of Cape Town as emblematic of their history (and thus, in the process, making Cape Town's history the history of coloured experience).

29. Hendricks, "Burdens of the Past," 125.

30. Rosemary Lombard, (Honors thesis, Department of Anthropology, University of Cape Town, 2001).

31. Emile's philosophy is detailed in his book manuscript, *My Hip Hop Is African and Proud*, and on his Web site, www.blacknoise.co.za. Cape Town's other well-known hip-hop groups, Prophets of Da City and Brassie Vannie Kopp, explore race, culture, and identity in their work as well, although not with the same systematic focus and community orientation. Cape Town's hip-hop scene

has been analyzed by researchers such as Sandra Kloppers, Adam Haupt, Rosemary Lombard, and Lee Watkins.

32. Special permits were issued to a limited number of black students who applied to study subjects at the University of Cape Town that were not offered at coloured universities, such as drama.

33. Similarly, McEachern notes that for former District Sixers, "imagining a South African identity for themselves *is* radical," as is embracing an identity as a Capetonian. Charmaine McEachern, "Mapping the Memories: Politics, Place, and Identity in the District Six Museum, Cape Town," 242.

34. Erasmus, *Coloured by History*, 25.

CHAPTER 8. TRANSFORMERS

1. For each case study I followed a similar set of ethnographic practices. I spent time at each project site and interviewed a variety of individuals involved in each project, many numerous times, over several years. When I was away from South Africa, I continued following the progress of each project by e-mail and hosted representatives from most of the projects here in the United States.

2. Isilimela has recently built a school hall and beautified its grounds.

3. According to John, "It only really became very clear in my mind towards the end of the year 2001, the extent of the educational inequality, when I had contact with somebody from COSAT, a college in Khayelitsha, who had documented the history of the Khayelitsha schools. Of fifteen secondary schools in Khayelitsha in the year 2001, only forty-three learners from a matric group of nine thousand attempted maths higher grade, in other words, mathematics as a requirement for university entrance. Forty-three out of nine thousand. And the pass rate in those fifteen schools overall was something like 35 percent in that year, but for maths it was minuscule. Only six people in the whole of the Western Cape—I'm talking about African language speakers—managed to get above 60 percent for maths and science, in the whole of the Western Cape." With this information, John approached the corporation that owned his school with a proposal to develop a support program based within his school, but he was ignored.

4. "Zerilda Park Projects: Towards a Better Tomorrow," photocopied document, n.d.

5. In 2001, Zerilda Park had to turn away four hundred children and had a waiting list at the preschool of one hundred names.

6. Kader Asmal and Wilmont James, "Education and Democracy in South Africa Today," *Daedalus* 130 (2001): 185–204.

7. The structure would contain the day care center, which would continue to be managed by the Project Mothers, as well as a lunch and aftercare program for siblings and HIV-affected children from the community, envisioned in the project proposal as "a place of mothering and care for the children, so that, after their mothers' deaths, they can return for the same reassurance and support that they received earlier—but now from other caregivers. It is intended to be a home away from home—without being a residential institution. It is intended that anyone

who is a caregiver to an orphaned child or to a family of orphaned children will find support and resources at the Centre for themselves."

8. One builder left the project before its completion, which disappointed the construction supervisor until he learned the circumstances. The man's wife and daughter had been attacked and brutally raped by a neighbor, and the man quit coming to work in order to care for and protect them. The family knew the assailant, but they were too frightened of possible consequences to report him to the police. The construction supervisor was deeply distressed about the situation, which gave him further insight into the challenges people live with in the community.

9. John Gilmour confirms this point. Reviewing the high school transcripts of students applying to attend the LEAP schools clearly demonstrated to him the lack of course selection, career, and post-secondary guidance in township schools. He is heartened by the government's announced intention to increase the vocational offerings from 10 percent of the curriculum to over 30 percent.

CHAPTER 9. SOME LESSONS

1. "'Iph' Indlela? Finding Our Way into the Future: The First Steve Biko Memorial Lecture," *Social Dynamics* 26, no. 1 (Winter 2000): 43–55, excerpts published in the *Cape Times,* 28 November 2000.

2. Gloria Anzaldúa, preface to *This Bridge We Call Home: Radical Visions for Transformation,* 3rd ed., ed. Gloria E. Anzaldúa and Analouise Keating (Berkeley, CA: Third Woman Press, 2001), 3.

3. Sandile Dikeni, *Soul Fire: Writing the Transition* (Pietermaritzburg: University of Natal Press, 2002), 70.

4. "Firms must heed emotional dynamics," Business Day 29 May 2003.

5. Vron Ware and Les Back, *Out of Whiteness* (Cambridge: Cambridge University Press, 2001), 12.

6. Veret Amit and Nigel Rappaport, *The Trouble with Community: Anthropological Reflections on Movement, Identity, and Collectivity* (London: Pluto Press, 2002), 139–140.

7. Catherine Lutz, "Roadblocks and Gateways to Political Action: Hope, Fear, and Political Autobiography," presented at "Local Democracy . . . An Uncertain Future? A Public Workshop," University of North Carolina, Chapel Hill, 2–3 March 2001, http://www.unc.edu/depts/anthro/talks/democworkshop.htm (page 6, accessed 10/5/2004). The material from this paper is included in an excellent new book: Dorothy Holland, Donald M. Nonini, Catherine Lutz, Lesley Bartlett, Marla Frederick-McGlathery, Thaddeus C. Guldbrandsen, and Enrique G. Murillo, Jr., *Local Democracy Under Siege: Activism, Public Interests, and Private Politics* (New York: New York University Press, 2007).

8. Ibid., 9.

9. Anna Tsing, *Friction: An Ethnography of Global Connection* (Princeton, NJ: Princeton University Press, 2004).

10. David Graeber, *Fragments of an Anarchist Anthropology* (Chicago: Prickly Paradigm Press, 2004), 7.

11. Helen Epstein, *The Invisible Cure: Africa, the West, and the Fight Against Aids* (New York: Farrar, Strauss, and Giroux, 2007).

Index

Abbotts (private school), 193, 253–54
activism, 191–92. *See also* Circle of
  Courage; Gardenview Baptist Church;
  Heatherton Primary School; Hope
  Project; Langa Educational Assistance
  Programme; Zerilda Park Primary
  School
Adhikari, Mohamed, 169, 273n7
adoptions, cross-race, 121–22
Adrian, 78, 106, 115, 158
aesthetics: African, hip-hop and, 182–84;
  African, local support for, 132; Euro-
  American, African originality subverted to, 129, 164–65, 166–68; Euro-
  American, cultural dominance of,
  146–47; of the impoverished, appropriation of, 95–98; transformative
  nature of, 278–79n2
affirmative action programs: as "anti-
  white" initiative, 131; corporate avoid-
  ance of, 132, 275n26; need for, at Gardenview Baptist Church, 218; as
  promoting incompetence, 19, 118;
  unskilled/uneducated blacks not helped
  by, 11; white fears of, 118, 122,
  124–27, 129; white retrenchment
  blamed on, 275n18
African identity, 252, 253
African National Congress (ANC): banning of, 280n18; challenges facing, 9;
  coloured mistrust of, 176–77; electoral
  victory of (1994), 1, 9; Freedom Charter of, 7; government terrorism against,
  31; leadership of, as corrupt, 30;
  National Party local electoral victories
  and, 15; neoliberal economic policies
  adopted by, 2, 10–11; secret white negotiations with, 8; white/coloured op-

position to, in Cape Town, 12, 111;
  white opposition to apartheid and, 135
African originality: local support for,
  132; subversion of, 129, 164–65,
  166–68, 172–73
African Political Organization, 169
African Renaissance, 129
Africans: apartheid-era immigration restrictions, 47–48; attending coloured
  schools, 91–92; during colonial period,
  259–60n5; Coloured Labor Preference
  Policy and, 264n5; coloured mistrust
  of, 173–74, 224–26; coloured racism
  against, 177–78; fears of being taken
  over by, 274n12; forced relocation of,
  6, 169; impact of crime on, 271n9;
  labor quotas, 264n5; percentage of, in
  Cape Town, 13; poverty among, 18;
  transformative agendas among, 192;
  unemployment rate among, 11; white
  stereotypes of, 169, 195
Afrikaaner Weerstandsbewegung, 87
Afrikaans language, 5
Afrikaners, 5; English vs., 113–14,
  259–60n5, 273n5; mixed marriages of,
  140–43
AIDS. *See* HIV/AIDS
AIDS counselors, 222, 223
AIDS orphans, 152, 221, 222–23,
  228–29, 282–83n7. *See also* Hope
  Project
Alexander, Neville, 153–54
alternative lifestyles, 143
American Apartheid (Massey and
  Denton), 104
"American dream," 267n37
Amit, Vered, 255, 278n16
amnesty, 9–10

CALIFORNIA SERIES IN PUBLIC ANTHROPOLOGY

The California Series in Public Anthropology emphasizes the anthropologist's role as an engaged intellectual. It continues anthropology's commitment to being an ethnographic witness, to describing, in human terms, how life is lived beyond the borders of many readers' experiences. But it also adds a commitment, through ethnography, to reframing the terms of public debate—transforming received, accepted understandings of social issues with new insights, new framings.

Series Editor: Robert Borofsky (Hawaii Pacific University)

Contributing Editors: Philippe Bourgois (University of Pennsylvania), Paul Farmer (Partners in Health), Alex Hinton (Rutgers University), Carolyn Nordstrom (University of Notre Dame), and Nancy Scheper-Hughes (UC Berkeley)

University of California Press Editor: Naomi Schneider